Strategic Customer Care

An Evolutionary Approach to Increasing Customer Value and Profitability

STANLEY A. BROWN

WILEY

John Wiley & Sons Canada, Ltd

Toronto • New York • Chichester • Weinheim • Brisbane • Singapore

John Wiley & Sons Canada Limited
22 Worcester Road
Etobicoke, Ontario
M9W 1L1

Canadian Cataloguing in Publication Data
Brown, Stanley A., 1946-
Strategic customer care: an evolutionary approach to increasing customer value and profitability

Includes bibliographical references and index
ISBN 0-471-64342-4

1. Relationship marketing.   2. Customer relations.   I. Title

HF5415.55.B76 1999   658.8   C99-930655-3

Production Credits
Typesetting: Lakshmi Gosyne
Cover Design: Fizzz Design Inc.
Printer: Tri-Graphic Printing

Printed in Canada

10 9 8 7 6 5 4 3 2

C O N T E N T S

Why is it that some organizations—even in industries that are booming—achieve long-term and profitable growth while their competitors fail to perform?

In my experience, it boils down to one key factor: top corporate performers understand who their most valuable customers are and what unique needs they have. These leading organizations relentlessly pursue long-term relationships by offering differentiated service to them based on their unique needs.

Understanding—and living—this precept of Strategic Customer Care is one of the reasons why American Express dominates the corporate card business. It's one of the reasons why you'll find M&M Mars bars near the cash registers in every hypermarket, super store, corner store and retail outlet in the world. It's why British Airways is so popular with business travelers of all nationalities, and why L'Oréal is now the world leader in cosmetics and hair-care products.

In every case, these businesses have achieved long-term success by implementing Strategic Customer Care: They focus on their most valuable customers. British Airways, for example, offers special services for their frequent flying business customers throughout the customer experience, from pre-boarding to in-flight to post boarding. They differentiate themselves from their competitors, as M&M Mars does in its relationship with wholesalers and retailers by establishing a permanent dialogue with them to fully understand their needs and fulfill them on a differentiated basis. They approach customer care with a long-term focus, enabling them to take advantage of the profitable web of relationships that can develop over time. American Express nurtured its relationships so well it expanded into travel and tourism through travel agencies and by co-branding cards with airlines and hotel chains. L'Oréal trains top hair stylists all over the world, and has done so for more than 50 years.

The customer care processes implemented by these organizations target specific customers and add value to their businesses by providing tailored, differentiated service. Not only does this increase the profitability of their customers but it enhances customer loyalty—and increases their own profitability as well.

Continuously executing this circle of cause and effect is key to achieving sustainable and profitable growth. And the secret to ensuring the highest profitability possible is this: maximize the value of your Customer Equity by taking care of your most valued customers, one by one.

To help organizations achieve sustainable and profitable growth, PricewaterhouseCoopers has created a global management consulting service known as *Market and Customer Management (MCM)*. Our goal is to help organizations understand and anticipate the needs of an enterprise's current and potential customers through proper deployment of skilled customer-facing personnel, optimal process and enabling technologies. MCM is one of our fastest growing consulting areas, with more than 1,200 consultants dedicated to market and customer management on a global basis.

PricewaterhouseCoopers is also dedicated to thought leadership—to helping organizations succeed in the face of competitive challenges. This book, *Strategic Customer Care,* provides that leadership.

It is a practical book based on examples, best practices case studies and work carried out for PricewaterhouseCoopers clients. But it is much more than a collection of anecdotes. It provides a route map to help you achieve Strategic Customer Care—and the long-term and profitable growth that results.

Because of its practical and implementation-oriented approach, *Strategic Customer Care* is an important cornerstone for organizations truly seeking success in a highly competitive and rapidly changing marketplace.

DENIS COLLART
GLOBAL LEADER
MARKET AND CUSTOMER MANAGEMENT
PRICEWATERHOUSECOOPERS
PARIS, MARCH 1999

PREFACE

Every organization—big or small, public or private—exists today in an environment that has little semblance to the traditional business environment of yesterday. In today's world, it's a corporate jungle out there—a wild and dense jungle of rapid and continuous change.

As our technology gets better and better and global barriers melt away, we are poised to explode into the twenty-first century with unprecedented force. We will find ourselves in situations ripe with unpredictability, where our measure of success will depend on our ability to adapt. In this new teeming corporate jungle, a supercharged era of commerce and high-tech capabilities, all organizations must ask the same question—will we survive?

My answer is an emphatic "Yes"—if you embrace the key practices/skills outlined in the first part of this book and follow through on the route map (a process to achieve strategic customer care) provided in the later chapters.

What makes this concept of customer care different? It is best practices based, grounded on research collected from three sources: IDEAS 97, the seventh in a series of annual surveys designed to discover the best practices in customer care (refer to Appendix A for a brief description of these seven studies), the PricewaterhouseCoopers Customer Care Best Practices Database, and the day-to-day experiences of our work with clients.

This concept of customer care does not come from academic notions but is based on fact and actual practice. The fundamentals underlying the evolution of customer care (Part I of this book) stem from the best practices of the many corporations with whom we've had the pleasure of working, as well as others who have been generous enough to share their experiences with us.

Your survival will begin with different levels of service, reserving your best for your most valuable customers. But how do you get there? Where do you start? How do you identify your most valuable customers? And once you know who they are, how do you determine the service you'd like to give them—service that keeps them with you for the long haul?

This is where the evolution of customer care comes into play. You won't be able to find the answers to these questions until you've gone through our strategic customer care process (Part II of this book). Through our research we've discovered that in order to reach the goal of differentiated service for your most valuable customers, all companies must evolve through three stages of customer care. I have written this book to share with you the principles underlying the evolution of customer care—a preparation for your own evolutionary process—and then a clear step-by-step route map that will help you to develop ways to take you to where you want to go. That goal is success.

I invite you to take this journey with me. It is an important journey that is rooted in the best practices of organizations that have found the path to survival and success.

In order to survive, today's organizations must embrace evolution wholeheartedly and, as Charles Darwin discovered in the middle of the last century, evolution comes down to a single, all-important concept: the survival of the fittest.

Customers are the lifeblood of every organization. The simple fact is that without our customers we will not survive. This book focuses on helping you and your organization survive the ever changing corporate and commercial environment, equipping you with tools of customer care that will bring you into the twenty-first century, feet set firmly on the path of evolution.

PREPARING FOR THE JOURNEY: WHY CUSTOMER CARE?

In the first part of this book, you will find an in-depth discussion of the fundamental practices and skills underlying the concept of differentiated customer care. Consider this the foundation pillars that will support your customer care process.

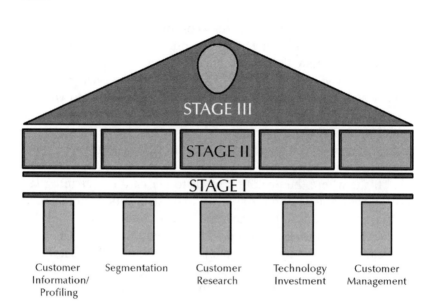

| Customer Information/ Profiling | Segmentation | Customer Research | Technology Investment | Customer Management |

As you evolve through the stages, you must ensure that the pillars grow. If they are underdeveloped or not of equal strength, cracks will appear, and your structure, your customer care process, may fail. As you evolve through each stage of the customer care process, these pillars will become stronger and more developed. The more they grow, the more robust a customer care process they will support.

To be successful, you must progress through these three distinct stages of customer care gradually but with purpose. Wherever your organization stands along this evolutionary process, it must move forward as its customer care focus matures. Again, I cannot overemphasize the importance of understanding these three stages and identifying which stage of the process your company currently is in. Remember that you can't get to where you want to be until you know where you are.

THE THREE STAGES

Stage I is **Customer Acquisition**. Organizations in this stage are focused on attracting new customers almost exclusively and less thought is directed towards keeping the customers they already have. "Command and control" issues (an overemphasis on micro managing, from expenses to frequency of calling on which accounts) dominate management thinking.

In Stage II, organizations are in a **Customer Retention** mode. Having moved beyond the need to acquire customers, companies in this stage recognize that their customers are a scarce commodity that can be retained only through an emphasis on creating a relationship and demonstrating that you care about them and appreciate their business. All customers are valuable, if we can keep them for a lifetime (customer-for-life).

Stage III organizations are in **Strategic Customer Care**. Companies in this stage realize that in order to survive and be profitable they must view customers as assets, and like all assets, some are simply more valuable than others. Stage III companies leverage this information by providing differentiated service to that valuable minority. But because all customers are assets, they set minimum standards of care, but only their best customers deserve the best care.

What does it mean when you have reached Stage III? Stage III organizations have implemented strategic customer care. They provide a level of support that truly meets the customers' needs. The products and services provided are differentiated, proactive, and focused on customer profitability. These needs are reflected in the mantra "Know me...hear me...help me prosper."

Know me: Know who I am when I call, my needs (both long- and short term); understand the industry in which I operate and the challenges I face. Make me feel that you appreciate my business and value our relationship.

Hear me: Listen to my needs and act accordingly; listen when I complain or give you suggestions, and get back to me quickly, to show me that this effort was worthwhile (and remember, all customers have an option: they can still walk away).

Help me prosper: Help me become more profitable. If I become more profitable because of actions that you take with me (and that may come from the products that I buy from you or from suggestions that you provide to me on how I can get better), I will continue to buy from you.

And so the evolutionary process pushes onward, but before you and your organization can embrace the Stage III—the strategic customer care process provided in the second part of this book—you must be able to recognize the stage of evolution at which your company currently stands. When organizations try to move to another stage of the evolutionary process without an accurate understanding of where they're starting from, they will, sooner or later, flounder. That's because, without a clear recognition of your place in the evolutionary process and an understanding of how it works, the path to success becomes strewn with potholes and icy patches.

SOME PITFALLS ALONG THE EVOLUTIONARY PATH

What problems can plague an organization that unwittingly tries to move to the next stage in the process before it's ready?

- **Too much, too soon.** In their eagerness to take advantage of available tools and technologies designed to help them serve their customers better, organizations too often try to use new technology and tools before they've developed the necessary skills required to do so properly.

- **Inadequate customer research.** An organization can be completely dedicated to the customer care process and have access to the most up-to-date technology, but without an extensive database of customer information it simply cannot properly categorize its customers into appropriate groupings. And without proper groupings, it cannot even begin to implement marketing strategies that target the needs of its most profitable customers. Yet, all too often, organizations will fall into this trap—attempting to market to their most profitable customers before they have the necessary information to determine who these customers are and what their needs are.

- **A lack of best practices.** A successful evolution along the stages of the customer care process demands that organizations develop best practices within each stage of their evolution before they can progress to the next stage. Many companies do not recognize the value of this—that these best practices provide the stable and steady foundation on which to build new best practices along the evolutionary path.

THE ROUTE MAP TO SUCCESS

The second part of this book provides you with a route map—one that charts the 12 interrelated steps you will need to take in order to progress towards Stage III—strategic customer care. Remember, this process of customer care is one that every organization *must* embrace in order to survive the immense changes we all face. The route map I've outlined in this book is unique, based not on theory but rather on the best practices of today's successful organizations. It will give you the tools to recognize where you stand in the customer care evolutionary process and how to progress. These best practice organizations recognize the importance of differentiated and strategic customer care and know where they are headed. They have changed their way of thinking from the old tried and true and understand how the evolved organization achieves and maintains profitability.

ARE YOU READY TO MOVE ON?

Are you and your company ready to take the evolutionary plunge? The success of the customer care process requires your wholehearted commitment, which can be given only if you understand the importance of the evolutionary process and can accept all its implications. To go forward, you and your organization must be ready and willing to go beyond traditional customer care practices. You must recognize that these traditional practices are only the first stage in your organization's evolution. You must be willing to accept the concept that customers are assets that do not all have the same value. This means being ready to reserve your best care solely for your best customers.

Through this book, you and your organization can place yourself among the ranks of those successful companies poised to enter the new commercial world of the twenty-first century. The question is, are you ready?

ACKNOWLEDGEMENTS

Books, like houses must be built on a strong foundation. In the case of this book, there are four strong cornerstones that have supported me in my efforts

The first cornerstone is Mike Stoneham, the leader of PricewaterhouseCoopers' Management Consulting Services in Canada. My thanks for his support and encouragement over the years. His leadership and insight have been important to me.

The second cornerstone is my colleagues in the Market and Customer Management practice around the globe, and to my team at the Centre of Excellence in Customer Care, for their insight, assistance, and contributions. Special appreciation goes to Denis Collart, the Global Leader of the Market and Customer Management practice at PricewaterhouseCoopers for his enthusiastic support.

The third cornerstone is my publisher, John Wiley & Sons Canada, Ltd. This is our third book together, and each time the process has been rewarding. Special thanks to Karen Milner, Diane Wood, Beth Bruder, and Elizabeth McCurdy for once again including me in their family and helping me through this process.

The fourth and most substantial cornerstone is my family, in particular my wife Rhonda and children Lowell, Brian, Cynthia, and Neil, for their continued patience and support during those lost weekends and vacations...and who never believe me when I say "this is my last book."

Thanks to all of you and a special wish to the "little princess," Elena Rachelle, and those that follow her—"enjoy life."

STANLEY BROWN
APRIL, 1999

Part One

The Skills Needed Before You Start

THE FIVE FOUNDATION PILLARS THAT DEFINE YOUR CURRENT AND FUTURE STAGE OF EVOLUTION

The first part of this book addresses the fundamental practices and skills that organizations must build upon in order to complete the evolutionary process toward Stage III customer care. Each chapter will explore one of the five key skills. It will then discuss the knowledge that you will need to acquire in order to start the process and move on to examine each individual principle for a more in-depth analysis.

The chapters that make up Part I of the book will provide you with a skill set—in essence, the foundation pillars to allow you to evolve toward Stage III customer care. The principles described in Part I play a very important role in the evolutionary process because until you understand the fundamentals underlying the evolutionary process toward strategic customer care, you will not be able to use the tools and methods described in Part II to your best advantage.

Essentially, then, Part I prepares you for the journey toward Stage III customer care. But consider the analogy described earlier: as you start the process, your pillars are not that well developed, nor is your process of strategic customer care. The need to move on to Stage II grows, and these pillars evolve and strengthen to support a more robust process.

These five pillars represent the following:

1. Customer/information profiling (Chapter 2)—As you evolve through the three stages (described in more detail in Chapter 1), the detail kept on your customer base must change. Chapter 2 provides you with this guidance.

2. Segmentation (Chapter 3)—Your customers fall into natural groupings. Depending on your stage, however, the criteria used to define these groupings/segments must change. Chapter 3 provides the process and rigor to do this.

3. Customer research (Chapter 4)—Not all customers are the same, and therefore the techniques used to uncover the voice-of-the-customer must reflect their relative importance. Also, as you evolve to the next stage, so must your customer research skills. This chapter guides you through this key step.

4. Technology investment (Chapter 5)—It's not the *best* technology but rather the *right* technology for your stage in the evolutionary process. As you progress through to Stage III, so must your technology and your skill in using it. Chapter 5 provides you with these guidelines to ensure that your investment matches your needs.

5. Customer management (Chapter 6)—As you progress through the stages, your treatment of your customer base must change. This chapter provides you with guidance on how you must treat this customer base as you evolve.

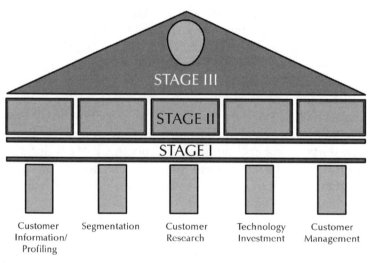

Strategic Customer Care Process

To be strong, and able to evolve to Stage III customer care, each of the five pillars must be built to the same height and fortified, before you can raise the pillar to the next height.

At first glance, you might think that these skills and practices that we call the pillars are traditional concepts that organizations involved in customer care have practiced for quite some time. In a way, this is true, but as we examine these concepts in greater detail, we'll also add the perspective of organizations who have evolved from Stage I to Stage III. Their learnings and best practices will help to ensure that your pillars will be built effectively and efficiently.

To be honest, most organizations don't fall completely within one stage or another. This is not an ideal situation, because if one pillar is more developed than another, stress occurs, and the potential for disaster. Would you build a structure that way? Of course not, but it seems that some organizations choose to build their customer care that way. Would you construct the third floor before you built the second floor? Not likely, yet some organizations do just that by investing in technology that far outreaches their capabilities and needs. Would you make one pillar thinner than all the others? Hardly, that's inefficient, yet some organizations gather too little information on their customers, only to have to build it up at a later date, at greater expense.

In the pages that follow, we will see how to avoid these pitfalls.

Are you prepared to start the evolutionary process and aggressively pursue Stage III customer care? If so, here is a process that will, with certainty, lead to success. All it requires is resolve and commitment on your part.

So, let's start with building the foundation.

The Stages in the Evolution of Customer Care

BUILDING THE FOUNDATION: WHERE ARE YOU, RIGHT NOW?

This book, which has been designed as both a preparatory guide and a route map, will not be of much help to you unless you figure out exactly where you and your organization stand along the customer care evolutionary path. Before you can get to where you want to go, you must first know where you're coming from.

So, if you want to survive in the twenty-first century, and if you're ready to commit to the evolutionary path of customer care and ultimate success, let's take that first step. Let's find out—where along the evolutionary process do you and your organization stand right now?

POSITIONING FOR SUCCESS: SQUARE D

The following provides an example of an organization focused on strategic customer care. As you read through this example, think through the changes in culture and competencies that the organization went through, and the process it now goes through to provide differentiated service to its strategic customers. You will note how the organization defined and selected its most strategic customers, the detail it went through to identify and understand customer needs and requirements, and how it used technology to facilitate the sharing of information and the delivery of strategic customer care.

Square D is a 93-year-old company that manufactures electrical distribution, industrial control and automated products for industrial plants and commercial and residential buildings. In 1991 it merged with France's Groupe Schneider to become a significant international player, and its operations now include over 180 manufacturing facilities and more than 600 sales offices in 130 countries worldwide. Its 1996 global sales totaled $8.3 billion, with North American earnings growing by more than 39 percent over the previous year.

Although it was performing, at least in the United States, at what many would consider an acceptable level—3 to 4 percent growth, mirroring that of the general economy—the organization did not consider this performance to be adequate, particularly in light of the new global challenges it faced. Square D therefore set out on a new path that would lead it to concentrate on a select few strategic customers, create differentiation and align the organization for the mutual success of both the organization and its customers.

Square D achieved its re-engineering with exemplary results. Today it projects an increase in sales of double the rate of growth of the US economy and operating earnings that will reach 12 to 15 percent by the year 2000. The reasons for its success include selecting customers with the most potential, knowledge management, strategic account management, customer involvement and corporate culture.

Selecting Customers with the Most Potential

At the heart of Square D's efforts was a bold step to define certain accounts as "strategic." Rather than base its selection strictly on current revenue, the organization looked at a combination of factors, including potential, ability to purchase across the product offering and, most importantly, the customer's current growth strategy in key growth markets around the world. Fundamentally, however, Square D wanted customers that would have long-term strategic value, but simply choosing the "right" customers without following up with appropriate action will not yield successful change. The company realized that its select customers wanted superior results regardless of where they were doing business, and it decided that it was willing to expend the effort for these special accounts.

Knowledge Management

Square D also realized that its traditional customer information was insufficient to allow it to bring about the changes it wanted. It therefore created its own in-house database that it would make available to every member of the account team no matter where they were. The organization created a database specifically for this purpose, internally funding its development and maintenance.

Square D also reaped another benefit from the database. The company earns numerous patents—about one a week, but customers don't care much about those patents, no matter how prestigious. What they wanted were the latest technical innovations that could be delivered and work for them as soon as possible. To address these needs, Square D had to keep customers up-to-date on what its researchers were doing and at the same time, make sure that its managers remained alert to these client needs. The database provided the answer.

If Square D can use its database tool well, it can save its customers both time and money, and that translates into more business across more countries. In the words of the VP of Strategic Accounts, Rodney Hightower, "With heavy investments necessary, our competitive advantage—and return on investment—must be enhanced by bringing products to market quickly."

Strategic Account Management

Square D also realized that actions speak louder than words. An essential element to the process it was developing was its ability to respond quickly to customers' needs—needs that it realized would be unique to each customer. Once it discovered that its customers valued coordinated worldwide support, fast delivery of high-performance products and solutions to market, and value-added services and support, Square D was able to differentiate itself from low-cost providers of similar products.

Enter Square D's strategic account management team, which is integral to the company's customer care process. The team includes both full-time core team members and part-timers, a full-timer being anyone who spends more than half of his or her time on the account. Because of the team's composition, it is able to deal with all the necessary functions of selling, designing, supplying and servicing strategic customers. And to address any issues related to the proper allocation of staff to the team, Groupe Schneider, in turn, established a global operating committee composed of senior managers from five countries who work to facilitate solutions, share experience and further develop the strategic approach.

Customer Involvement

Square D also realigned its entire organization around its customers and their markets rather than around its products or the regions in which it operates. This focus means that everyone in the organization—from the sales engineer who takes the order, to the assembler who builds the equipment on the shop floor to members of senior management—understands the customer's needs.

At present, the company has less than 50 strategic accounts, the goal being to start with a manageable number and grow from there. In selecting these customers, its goal was to act collaboratively with them for mutual benefit. For that reason, Square D looks for signs of "alliance behavior" in its customers and works with each to nurture the goal of mutual benefit. What are the signs of alliance behavior?

- Trust and a mutual-benefit operating philosophy
- Open lines of communication and information sharing
- Development of joint solutions
- Joint investment in technology development
- Purchases with no competing bids
- Customer participation in the product development process
- Access to competitors' usual business
- Consultation in designing new products or manufacturing processes

However, the bottom line is still to increase customer value, and Square D accomplishes this by going beyond selling to understanding what drives the customers' businesses. To that end, the company invites customers to participate in team meetings and make suggestions. This understanding allows

Square D to meet its customers' needs and ultimately enhance customer value.

Corporate Culture

To make the strategic approach work, Square D realized that a culture change would be necessary. To effect this change, team members were required to go through specialized training. The training program coached the team through the concept of alliance-based behavior, which requires paying as much attention to the customer's supply chain as to Square D's own revenue and margins. Training also focused on other areas such as teamwork, group dynamics and change.

Square D demonstrates what can be accomplished if there is a commitment to differentiation. While all organizations should strive for this, it may be necessary to progress through the stages of customer care gradually and build on its foundation. But that means that an organization must realize in what stage it is in today, and what foundation pillars it must strengthen. The section that follows takes you through that first step, helping you identify your current stage in the evolution of customer care.

THE STAGES OF EVOLUTION

You may have your destination clearly in mind—to hold your place firmly among organizations who rank as the fittest, those that have equipped themselves to forge ahead into the ever changing new century with the certainty and adaptability of the chameleon. But keep in mind that evolution is a process, not a destination. Much as the chameleon developed its ability to adapt to the continuous physical changes in its environment and perfected its visual awareness such that it can see in two directions at one time, so too must your organization evolve toward Stage III of the customer care evolutionary process.

What is the pinnacle of customer care to which most organizations should aspire? The results from the PricewaterhouseCoopers IDEAS 97 provide us with the answer. The survey of 1,500 organizations uncovered an interesting fact. Organizations all seemed to fall within one of three distinct stages or phases of customer care: customer acquisition, customer retention and strategic customer care. We reviewed the research findings and observed the extent to which they had invested and used technology. We also considered the degree of customer care delivered and if it was in any way differentiated to any particular customer group. Lastly, we looked at the "people" factor, the organizations' dedication to training and empowerment.

As we collected examples of best practices in customer care, we discovered another key element to the puzzle. Organizations that identified themselves as having achieved Stage III customer care had learned the skills required for each previous stage of evolution before they took the step into Stage III.

What does this mean for the smart organization? Find out what stage you're at in the evolutionary process, then learn the skills you'll need to evolve to the next stage. And once you've achieved Stage III? Recognize that the process of evolution never stops. Does that mean a Stage IV or even Stage V in the future? Quite possibly, but right now, let's concentrate on getting to Stage III.

Stage I: Customer Acquisition

According to the IDEAS 97 Survey, 35 percent of the respondents fell into the first stage of customer care. In this initial stage, organizations work to develop best practices with the goal of expanding their customer base.

Obviously, as the name implies, the focus of Stage I organizations is on acquisition of customers, but there are other characteristics that distinguish the Stage I organization. For example, companies within Stage I generally compete in the marketplace primarily in terms of price only. They are commodity suppliers, with a singular goal of attracting customers, and hopefully profit, through volume. There are, however, two distinct features of the Stage I organization.

Command and Control Technology

While Stage I organizations will say that they believe it's critical to use technology for the benefit of their customers, more than 80 percent of these companies actually use technological investments to focus on internal "command and control" issues rather than enhancing customer satisfaction. In other words, these organizations employ their technology primarily to monitor and oversee their sales force.

> *TIP*
>
> **Command and Control**: Management uses technology to keep an eye on the front line, which, in many cases is the sales force. The technology typically used are electronic expense reports, contact reports, and sales tracking and contact management software.

Because the Stage I organization's goal is to build a solid customer base, an emphasis on making the sales force more effective is not only reasonable but necessary. However, there is always the strong, and understandable, temptation at this stage to use technology to enhance control of salespeople rather than to focus on increasing effectiveness.

How does a best practices organization use technology when in Stage I? These organizations have automated the process of tracking customer data, so they know their customers better. This knowledge helps them in building that all-important foundation, the solid customer base.

> *Technologies to Improve Sales Force Effectiveness*
>
> Get ready to work toward becoming a Stage I best practices organization. Here are two examples of technologies that will help your organization to increase the effectiveness of your salespeople: 1) networked personal information systems that use a variety of sales force automation tools; and 2) contact management software.
>
> These tools will also give you a hidden benefit. These systems and software also provide your management team with access to customer data which will prove invaluable in developing strategic action plans (additional data will be provided in Part II). By properly employing these technologies, your organization will be well on its way to achieving the goal of the first stage of customer care evolution—the establishment of a solid customer base.

Training

Stage I organizations will generally use generic or common training to enhance the success of their customer acquisition strategies. A typical Stage I organization will approach the training process with a "one size fits all" attitude that simply lumps together training in computer skills, telephone systems, customer focus and corporate culture, without any regard to the trainee's job position and whether or not he or she actually needs the skills being taught in order to do the job.

So, what's wrong with this? Stage I best practice organizations develop far more selective training programs. They tailor training to the needs of both the individual and the job position, and many will even go so far as to establish competency grids for each staff member. The result is a training program that takes into account the established skill sets of individual employees and discovers the employees who are better equipped to deal with customers effectively and profitably.

The Stage I Best Practice Organization

What are the characteristics of the best practice organization in Stage I of the evolutionary process? In general, these best practice organizations:

- Have automated customer data tracking software that gives both their sales force and their management team easier access to invaluable customer-base building information.
- Recognize the importance of optimizing training programs so that the focus remains on training individuals to perform the details of their specific job descriptions more profitably and more efficiently.
- Spend a significant amount of time on best practices bench marking—always striving for improvement.
- Continually analyze their current customer care processes, again with an eye toward improvement.
- Stay focused on the need to conduct customer research.

In other words, the Stage I best practice organization, while still working toward the goal of building the solid customer base, also understands where it is now and where it wants to go.

Stage II: Customer Relationship Management

Approximately 59 percent of IDEAS 97 Survey respondents had moved through the evolutionary process into Stage II, the customer relationship management mode. These organizations had successfully built that all-important base of customers, and their focus was now on keeping them.

Remember the customer data that Stage I organizations were learning to gather? At Stage II of the evolutionary process, organizations begin playing with separating customers into categories using the information collected during Stage I. This, in turn, helps them to better manage—and market to—different customer relationships.

What Is Customer Segmentation?

What is segmentation and what makes it work? Segmentation is the process of dividing customers into groups with similar characteristics, as shown in the box below. Customers grouped together will generally possess similar needs, so, by categorizing customers into like groups, your organization is better able to identify the customer needs associated with each segment. Once you know your customers' needs, it's much easier to determine what services are necessary to enhance delivery of customer care to a wide range of customers. And that is successful customer care: a great number— the *right* number—of customers experiencing a great deal of satisfaction.

TIP

Segmentation Factors

Customer groups can be generated by a variety of factors, including:

- Revenues
- Industry
- Product
- Region

How you choose to divide your customers will depend on what makes sense in any given situation. Remember, as well, that best practice organizations will also segment based on customer needs. (For more on customer segmentation, see Chapter 4.)

Importance of Technology

As in Stage I, technology plays an important part in an organization's progress through Stage II of the evolutionary process. While segmentation can be used to successfully manage customer relationships, the hard fact is that it will only be as successful as the process and technology used to segment the customers themselves.

A state-of-the-art customer information retrieval system is therefore crucial to successful segmentation.

Despite their focus on retaining their customers, however, more than half of the IDEAS 97 Survey respondents who ranked in Stage II admitted that their customer information retrieval systems still needed improvement. In other words, these organizations are not employing state-of-the-art systems—and therefore are not segmenting and serving their customers as effectively as they should be. This makes it even more difficult to retain the customers they worked so hard to acquire in Stage I.

While the results of the IDEAS 97 Survey show that the majority of organizations find themselves in Stage II of the customer care evolutionary process, the survey findings also indicate that many of these Stage II organizations do not know how to move on to Stage III. Those that have done so generally learned from the best

---

Are You Reaping the Benefits of the Internet?

The IDEAS 97 Survey indicated that an astonishingly small number of Stage II organizations are using the Internet in their customer relationship management process.

How can the Internet make a difference? Internet applications allow your customers direct access to the experience and knowledge of your organization in a number of key areas:

- Product configuration (how various components of your product fit together with other products. Product specifications and pricing would also fall into this)
- Electronic catalogues
- Order management (allowing customers to order remotely)
- Customer service (to allow customers to check on order status or inventory availability)

Your Internet presence gives your customers "hands-on" experience by letting them participate in many of the decisions that have an impact on the end product and service they buy from you. When they use the applications on your Web site, your customers gain a sense of immediacy and involvement in your organization. And finally, the Internet can prove invaluable in helping to collect the customer information necessary to maintain the utility of your information database. (For more information about the Internet as a customer care tool, see Chapter 5.)

practices of others and transitioned into Stage III, our pinnacle of evolution.

If Stage II organizations do not focus on completing their evolution through Stage II, they run the risk of getting stuck in a quagmire. By not moving forward, they increase the likelihood of failure—that they will no longer be fit enough to win the battle for survival of the fittest.

TIP

Technology and the Stage II Best Practice Organization

Do you see your organization moving towards best practice status during its evolution through Stage II? Here are some ways the Stage II best practice organization employs technology:

- They use state-of-the-art customer information retrieval systems.
- They integrate sales and customer-service related software systems with inventory, production, accounting and financial systems in order to not only serve their customers better, but also to segment them more effectively.
- They use Internet applications and groupware tools to assist in sales and enhance service.

Stage III: Strategic Customer Care

Only six percent of the organizations surveyed in IDEAS 97 have moved through the evolutionary process to Stage III. These organizations had worked to acquire and retain their customers and are now focused on increasing the value and profitability of their customers through enhanced customer care.

Not All Customers Are Created Equal

Organizations in Stage III of the evolutionary process have broken away from traditional thinking as a result of their recognition that customers are *not* created equal. Some customers are, inevitably, more profitable than others. While every Stage III organization sets a minimum standard of customer care for all, the best care is reserved for the best customers.

Your best customers are not just those who are your most profitable. Stage III organizations recognize that customer relationships that are in essence strategic partnerships allow them to increase their own profits by focusing on enhancing the customer's profits. Some of your best customers may not be your most profitable ones—yet. In choosing your select group of customers, you need to look at a lot more than current profitability. In fact, as we will discuss shortly, there are a number of other factors to consider, among them, the potential to purchase more of the same products, additional (related or unrelated) products and services, and the willingness to establish a strategic relationship with your organization (more on this in Chapter 3). Because Stage III companies understand the profitability of their customers and have developed extensive customer segmentation systems that group their customers according to their value, they are better able to:

- Design marketing strategies that target their most profitable segments
- Train their employees to easily identify the profit potential of customers
- Design pricing structures based on the buying behavior and product/service use of their most profitable customers
- Use clear and concise messages that have the most meaning for customers in the most profitable segments

---

Stage III: How Best Practice Organizations Use Technology

Best practice organizations in Stage III of the evolutionary process use technology primarily to assist them in addressing the needs of their most profitable customers:

- Extensive development of customer segmentation systems allows best practice organizations to easily separate customers by profitability and more.
- Best practice organizations recognize the many advantages of database marketing and employ database marketing systems to aggressively target their most profitable customer segments.
- In their use of database marketing systems, best practice organizations place their emphasis on shared data—data more extensive in nature than the information collected in Stage II for the purposes of market segmentation.
- Their effective use of technology and information tools highlight the best practice organization's understanding of the link between their technology and information investment and the associated returns from their customer base.

The Knowledge Pipeline

Just as it was in the earlier stages, once again, technology is crucial to attaining success in Stage III of the evolutionary process. Stage III organizations use technology not simply to categorize customers into like groups, but also to track performance in a number of dimensions, for example, market swings (identifying either new markets or competitors, or shifts in market sector profitability). This is accomplished through access to a vast array of both customer *and* corporate information. (More on that in Chapter 2.)

A successful database marketing system emphasizes shared data. This very extensive data collection includes, in addition to customer sales and support information:

- Field service information
- Quality assurance information
- Competitive intelligence

The key to using the knowledge pipeline is accessibility. The information contained in the pipeline must be accessible to everyone in the organization. In other words, it must be enterprise-wide. This ensures that all key players in your organization have access to the vital information that is so necessary in making critical marketing decisions for your company's most crucial market: your most profitable customers.

TIP

Knowledge Pipeline: The pipeline is a mechanism to both disseminate information to those most in need of it as well as facilitate the updating of information and best practices from any point within the organization. The ultimate objective of the knowledge pipeline is to have current, reliable information to allow for informed decision making.

Outsourcing of Noncore Competencies

Another characteristic distinguishes the Stage III organization from companies still in the two earlier stages. Stage III organizations more actively outsource their noncore competencies—those activities, such as training, pension administration or even customer service, that do not define its existing or potential competitive advantage. In fact, Stage III best practice organizations commonly outsource noncore activities and processes, including database marketing and customer care, to specialized organizations. Additionally, these companies also recognize the value of forming strategic alliances with other supplier companies in order to provide their customers with a full range of services that they otherwise could not offer.

This does not mean that by labeling something noncore you are acknowledging that they are not "core" to your company's success; rather, it's a recognition that other organizations are better qualified to perform these activities.

WHAT STAGE ARE YOU IN?

Each of these stages of customer care can be equally effective, provided it's the stage that's most appropriate for your organization at that given moment in time. So if you're in Stage I or Stage II of the evolutionary process, don't fret. Remember, once you've taken the first step—identifying the point from where you're starting your journey—the route map provided in the second half of this book can be used to take you to where you want to go.

If you're lucky enough to already be ensconced in Stage III, this is *not* the time to sit back and rest on your laurels. The process of evolution never stops. Even best practice organizations must continually look to improve on their best practices into better ones!

Now that we have talked about the three stages, there are a number of questions worth posing. At what stage are you and your organization? Where exactly does your organization fit within this evolutionary process? The following questionnaire will enable you to place your organization on the evolutionary continuum of customer care, and therefore, determine how to advance from there.

A Self-Assessment

Stage I Organizations

If you answer yes to most of the following questions, chances are your company is a Stage I organization focusing mainly on customer acquisition.

❑ Are you still mainly building your customer base? Stage I organizations are in acquisition mode. New customers are being added daily, weekly, monthly, and the more the better.

❑ Is your primary focus on acquiring customers? Stage I organizations are more concerned about quantity and less concerned about quality.

❑ Have you invested in technology that enhances the effectiveness of your sales force? Stage I organizations invest in technology that is more focused on efficiency and effectiveness.

❑ Does your technology focus on command and control issues, such as monitoring your sales force? Within Stage I organizations, management control is more important than giving your employees the authority to make decisions on their own.

❑ Do your training programs provide your employees with one-size-fits-all training? For Stage I organizations, all employees are provided with the same type of training, regardless of position.

❑ Do your training programs focus primarily on customer service? Stage I organizations are more concerned about customer service training, than product or technical training.

❑ Do you compete primarily on price? Stage I organizations operate in a commodity market environment where pricing is the customer's main motivator to purchase.

Stage II Organizations

If you answer yes to most of the following questions, you're likely in the second stage of the evolutionary process—customer retention.

❑ Have you already established a strong customer base? For Stage II organizations, the customer base is more stable.

❑ Do you keep detailed profiles of the customers you've worked so hard to acquire? Stage II organizations are in the process of building a more detailed database than just names and addresses.

❑ Are you currently focused on segmenting your hard-earned customers into groups, perhaps based on customer needs? Stage II organizations divide customers into groups that have common characteristics.

❑ Do you fall just short of offering your customers differentiated service? Stage II organizations recognize that some customers are more important than others but are less likely than Stage III organizations to offer different levels of service to them.

❑ Are you beginning to use the Internet to help you manage your customer relationships? Stage II organizations are finding new uses for providing information to customers but are not yet able to interact with them over the Web.

Stage III Organizations

Welcome to Stage III if you can answer yes to most of the following questions:

❑ Do you outsource your noncore competencies? Stage III organizations recognize that they may not be the most efficient and effective in all internal operations.

❑ Have you segmented your customers based on profitability? Stage III organizations understand the importance of driving for increased profitability versus increased revenue and how this type of segmentation will affect sales force resourcing.

❑ Can you identify your most strategic customers? For Stage III organizations, this is a fundamental capability and focus.

❑ Have you assessed which segments cost you the most and the return on your investment in those segments? Stage III organizations offer differentiated service and increased sales team dedication to their most strategic customers.

❑ Can you readily identify the needs of your most profitable group of customers? Stage III organizations track and react to those customers offering the greatest long-term benefit to the organization. They are most concerned about obtaining input on concerns, issues and needs and reacting to them.

Running before You Can Walk

Too often organizations try to do too much too soon. While becoming a Stage III best practice organization should, in most cases, be your company's main customer care goal, it's critical that you understand the importance not only of evolving from stage to stage but also evolving *through* each stage. In other words, your organization needs to experience each stage in order to develop the best practices that will provide the foundation upon which you can build for continued growth in each subsequent stage.

How do you know if you're trying to run before you can walk? Has your organization:

- Tried to implement technological applications before you and your people are ready for them?
- Tried to focus on the latest tools and strategies without first making sure that they're appropriate for the needs of your customers?
- Tried to practice the principles of Stage III of the evolutionary process before mastering the principles of Stage I and Stage II?

Trying to run before you can walk can hurt. At best, you run the risk of losing your financial investment in Stage III skills and technology because your organization simply hasn't advanced far enough in the evolutionary process to reap the benefits of these tools. At worst, you run the risk of losing your customers. And remember, your customers are the lifeline of your business.

Where Am I Going, and Why Do I Want to Get There?

Customer Satisfaction Is the Name of the Game

Why is customer satisfaction so important? You've probably heard the golden rule of customer care many times before. It costs five to ten times more to get a new customer than it does to keep an existing one. The question is how do you keep your existing customers? In a nutshell, you do it through a focus on customer care.

Customer-care focused organizations have developed study after study showing the correlation between customer satisfaction and market share and revenues.

IBM[1] recently conducted an empirical research study which showed that the satisfaction level of their customers has a direct impact on the organization's market share.

---

[1] IBM AS/400 Division, Rochester, Mn.

In this study, based on interviews with customers and employees, the organization identified that key drivers for increased market share were productivity, cost of quality and importantly customer satisfaction.

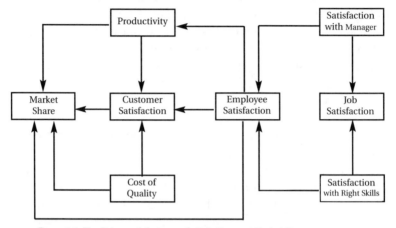

Figure 1.1: The Drivers of Customer Satisfaction and Market Share

They further discovered that the factor that affected customer satisfaction and productivity was primarily *employee* satisfaction. Customer satisfaction also translated into additional revenues—IBM found that a one percentage point increase in customer satisfaction levels generated $257 million in extra revenues over a five-year period. Another study found that customers who ranked themselves as being satisfied to very satisfied—four and five on a five-point scale—represented over 95 percent of all purchases.

- According to a study by Toyota, customer satisfaction is directly correlated to both loyalty and customer-to-customer recommendations.
- Toyota also found that their customers' intention to purchase another product from them is based directly on their levels of satisfaction with respect to both the sale itself and the service received. In fact, even those customers who ranked themselves as being satisfied (a four on a five-point scale) were six times more likely to defect to a competitor than those who rated themselves as being completely satisfied (a five on a five-point scale).
- An August 1992 *Business Week* article reported that "boosting customer retention rate by 2% has the same effect on profits as cutting costs by 10%."

- According to *Fortune* magazine, long-term customers create profits. The article explored a Bain & Co. research study that showed that customers who remain with you over time go through an evolution of sorts that can prove very profitable to your organization.[2]

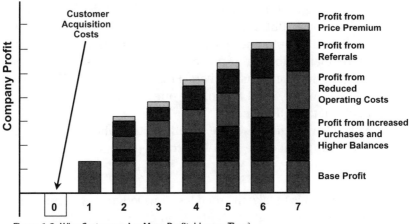

Figure 1.2: Why Customers Are More Profitable over Time[3]

In conjunction with the implementation of best practices in customer care and the development of appropriate products and services, volume of sales to the long-term customer increases while the cost of serving these accounts drops over time. Furthermore, long-term customers tend to eventually become advocates for your products and services, and ultimately you can develop a strategic customer/supplier relationship that enables you to charge a premium price. The net effect? Increased profits through increased revenues and reduced costs.

LESSONS LEARNED

Before you can set off on your journey to achieving strategic customer care, you must find out where you are right now. The evolution of customer care progresses through three stages: Stage I—Customer Acquisition; Stage II—Customer Relationship Management; and Stage III—Strategic Customer Care.

---

[2] "Why Some Customers Are More Equal than Others." *Fortune*, September 1994.

[3] Frederick F. Reichheld and W. Earl Sasser Jr., "Zero Defections: Quality Comes to Services," *Harvard Business Review*, September-October 1990.

It is important to note that every organization must pass through every stage before moving on to the next. It is only in this way that it is able to build the skills and abilities that create the proper foundation which allows it to move onto the next stage in the evolutionary process.

In order to start on this customer care journey, however, you must be committed. The route map outlined in this book is based on best practices. But in order to achieve best practice status, you must follow the route and not deviate from the proven path. And this particular path, while proven, is nevertheless still ground-breaking in its concepts. Robert Frost once said, "Two roads diverged in a wood, and I / I took the one less traveled by /And that has made all the difference."

Not all organizations have the time, the wherewithal or the commitment to take the road less traveled. Which road will you take?

If your decision is to take the road less traveled, then you must start with strengthening your five foundation pillars, the first of which is Customer Profiling, the chapter which follows.

CHAPTER TWO

Who Are Your Customers?

THE NEED FOR CUSTOMER PROFILES

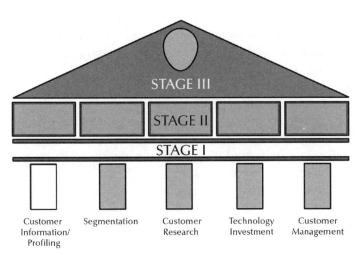

Figure 2.1: The Pillars of Strategic Customer Care—Customer Information/Profiling

Whether you're a Stage I organization actively building a solid customer base, a Stage II company that has turned its focus to superior customer care or a Stage III business that segments and markets to your customers according to profitability, one fact will always hold true for you. Customers are the lifeline of your company. The more you know about them—our first pillar—the more focused you will become.

BUILDING THE FOUNDATION: WHO ARE MY CUSTOMERS AND WHAT ARE THEIR NEEDS?

In order to prepare for your evolutionary journey, you need to turn your focus toward your customers, but depending on the stage of evolution you and your organization are in, you will see your customers in very different ways. Stage I companies are interested mainly in quantity—the more customers, the merrier. In Stage II, organizations begin to worry about actually keeping the customers they worked so hard to acquire in the previous stage. And in Stage III, businesses focus on reaping the benefits of customer segmentation.

The one common denominator in all three stages, however, is the customers themselves. Whether you are interested in their numbers, their loyalty or their profitability, you must have them in order to survive. Knowledge in this area, as with most things, is the key. The first thing that you must examine is what your customers really need from you as a supplier on whom they can rely. Once you have an understanding of your customers' needs, you can move more easily on your journey through the stages.

Prepare for your journey by first exploring:
- What your customers need from you.
- Why you need to build customer profiles, and how you should go about doing it.
- Whether a database of customer information will provide you with the assistance you need.
- What role your customers play in the customer/supplier relationship.

Since not all customers are the same, it is not surprising that their needs will vary individually and over time. It is in Stage III that the evolving organization truly uses this knowledge to power its evolution into the future, turning its focus on the segment of its customer base that proves the most profitable.

The IDEAS 97 research results highlight another important point. Despite the fact that customers vary, they nevertheless all have certain common needs when it comes to their suppliers. These needs fall into the following key categories:

- Business and industry-specific knowledge
- Service orientation
- Long-term focus
- Customer focus

Your customers may not even be aware of their needs in these areas. In many cases it's likely that they haven't really thought about what they need specifically from their suppliers. This holds true particularly for the customer of the Stage I organization, which has a tendency to focus primarily on getting the best price possible for the products or services it needs. Despite this, you will find that even the customer of the Stage I organization will intuitively seek suppliers capable of meeting these needs—whether or not they vocally express their needs to you.

In other words, the underlying needs are there—hidden, perhaps, but seeking to be met all the same. By developing a better understanding of these needs, you can equip your organization to develop stronger customer/supplier relationships.

Business and Industry-Specific Knowledge

Much like your own organization, your customers want the best for their customers and shareholders. If you can provide your customers with specialized, industry-specific knowledge (such as competitors or new market entrants, as well as possibly trends in the marketplace and how that might affect them) that enables them to provide the best to their customers, you will find that you have gone a long way to earning your customers' respect. Particularly during tough economic times or periods of extreme organizational stress and changes, customers appreciate suppliers who are willing to work with them toward finding and implementing the best possible solutions.

As a supplier with superior business and industry-specific knowledge, your goal will be to provide your customers with:
- Practical and insightful advice that's easily implemented and beneficial to both you and your customer.
- A willingness to address the issues your customer faces and work with it as a team.
- Help in expanding the number of solutions available by enlarging your customer's knowledge base.
- Specialized knowledge of your customer's business and the industry in which it operates.

The key is to use your knowledge of the industry to position yourself as your customers' business partner.

Service Orientation

Your service orientation also plays an important role in the development of your customer/supplier relationships. By becoming a supplier that can provide the type of service your customer needs, you will be well on your way to entrenching customer loyalty.

In general, customers seek from their suppliers:

- *Responsive service.* They need to know that you'll be there, whenever and wherever they need you.
- A *proactive relationship.* They want to be involved, particularly when your actions have a direct impact on their performance.
- *Frequent, personal contact.* Even during times when there's no real emergency, give your customers a call to see how things are going. Regular personal contact builds the strongest customer relationships.
- *An interest in their health and prosperity.* They may not need you right at this moment, but both oral and written communication of helpful comments serves to show that you have their health and prosperity in mind.
- A *true partnership.* Without a doubt, your ability to provide your customers with the solutions to their problems serves as the single most important determinant of the successful customer/ supplier relationship.
- A *willingness to involve them in the development of your product/service strategies.* At each stage of the process, demonstrate your respect for them as your business partner. Involve them in strategy formulation and execution and also the assessment of strategic success.

Long-Term Focus

Customers want suppliers who think of them as a customer-for-life. Short-term thinking on your part has the potential of jeopardizing your long-term relationships with your customers. Remember, once you have acquired them, you need to keep them, otherwise all your hard work will go to waste. You must remember that a long-term customer relationship requires you to develop relationships with your customers' people that stretch over generations.

Customer Focus

When you involve your customers in the development of your strategies, you reap an additional benefit: the ability to focus more clearly on meeting their needs. By developing and strengthening your focus on your customers, you will no longer be merely another supplier in a long faceless line of suppliers who are able to produce technically proficient products and services. Instead, your strong customer focus lets you put your heart into your customer relationships. It pushes you to the front of the line.

IN WHICH SUPPLIER CATEGORY DO YOU FALL?

Another important piece of information that should be included in each of your customer profiles is a description of your current supplier status. This relationship will fall into one of five categories;

1. **The Transactional/Competitive Supplier**. In this category, you are a "me-too" supplier. Merely one of many who can meet your customer's needs, your customer is mainly concerned with obtaining the best price and delivery. It shouldn't surprise you that your customer would likely rank its satisfaction level as "moderately satisfied" or "satisfied" and could shift to a competitor without warning.

    This transactional/competitive positioning is sometimes described as a "no home base" position. When you have a "home base" with a customer, you have a customer buying center in which you own a majority share position. Home base positioning can be established not just with a customer but also within the different buying centers in the organization. This can sometimes lead to situations where you have developed a strong relationship with one buying center in a customer's organization—a home base position—while at the same time you may be regarded as simply a commodity supplier—with no home base—by another buying center within the same organization.

TIP

What Is a Customer Buying Center (CBC)?

Large multidivisional customers have numerous buying centers, each of which might well be considered a separate customer. In developing your action plan, you need to identify and under-stand the key buying centers in the customer's organization, both past and future. For each buying center, you must also iden-tify the issues and context facing all the key players. Develop a strategy to position yourself with the main decision makers, cul-tivate all influencers and prepare a defense against those influ-encers who may not be favorably disposed to you and/or your organization.

Ongoing dialogue on a broad set of issues will likely produce clear and mutually agreed upon definitions of areas where you can be helpful, resulting in solution-oriented proposals being accepted and the completion of projects that enhance relation-ships. The result? Repeat business.

---

2. **The Niche Supplier.** If you are a niche supplier, you most likely have one home base within your customer's organization but no opportunities to cross-sell your products or services. While the potential exists to improve your share of the available business, you will be able to accomplish this only with new products and services. And, because there is no depth to the customer relation-ship, even with the development of new products and services you will find it difficult to improve your positioning.

3. **The Diversified Supplier.** If you find yourself in this category, you're on the right track. Your customer sees you as a value-added supplier, although not yet a strategic partner. While, like the niche supplier, you likely hold a single home base, your customer values your judgment, giving you the opportunity to move beyond this single home base positioning.

4. **Major Provider.** Although your relationship with your customer cannot be described as a strategic partnership, you are well on your way. Your customer sees you as a valued supplier and respects your input. You most likely have at least two home base positions, and the potential exists for further cross-selling.

5. **Strategic Partner.** This is the pinnacle of customer/supplier relationships. You share the risk with your customer. Your

customer depends on you to a high degree as a true business partner. You offer products and services that are completely aligned with your customer's needs, and individual buying centers within the customer's organization value your relationship.

THE SIGNIFICANCE OF THE CUSTOMER PROFILE: WHY IT DEFINES YOUR STAGE

Developing an understanding of customers' common needs allows you to move more easily along the evolutionary path. You know what your customers need from you. By meeting these needs you will be well on your way to establishing the type of strategic customer/supplier relationships that define Stage III customer care.

However, while research has established these needs to be common among most customers, one critical fact remains: not all customers are the same. In recognition of this crucial point, you now need to turn your thoughts to meeting your customers' unique needs. How? Through the diligent and conscientious collection of customer information; in other words, the **customer profile** (Appendix D).

The Customer Profile

What exactly is the customer profile? Ideally, it should be a structured representation of your key customers—a top-notch profile that would typically be prepared for each and every strategic customer. It would include two main areas: 1) corporate history/corporate overview and 2) customer budget/purchase capabilities.

1) Corporate history/corporate overview:
   - a general description of the customer's business
   - the customer's major products and services
   - the markets serviced by the customer
2) Customer budget/purchase capabilities:
   - the customer's ability to spend ("size of wallet")
   - competitive mapping (the share of the customer's business that you have relative to your competition, in the products and services you offer)
   - relationship targeting
   - constraints and impediments

Because organizations in different stages of the evolutionary process have different focuses when it comes to their customers, the customer profile will also be different depending on your current stage of evolution. At each stage, you should be developing customer profiles that will assist you in meeting your particular goals for that stage as well as establishing the foundation for your evolution into the next stage. Let's take a closer look at the customer profile from the perspective of each stage of the process.

Perspective from Stage I

Stage I organizations concentrate their efforts on acquiring customers. In this stage, your organization will most likely be concerned with the quantity of customers, not the quality. This, in and of itself, is a necessity for moving into Stage II. How else can you practice segmentation of your customers if you have no customers?

The customer profile at this stage of the evolutionary process tends to be simplified. Generally, the corporate history and a rudimentary overview of the customer will form the bulk of the information in the profile. Corporate history does not mean only the customer's name and address but also the key characteristics of the business.

In forming the customer profile at this stage of the process, ask yourself the following questions:
- Is the customer a local, national or multinational company?
- Is it a private or public corporation?
- What are its major divisions?
- Within each major division, what is the total number of employees?
- Within each major division, what is the total annual revenue?

The answers to these types of questions provide you with the base information of your customer profile. In most cases, this is the only type of information collected while in Stage I, as organizations focus on racking up the customer numbers and expanding the customer base. However, it's critical that these relatively limited profiles be developed at this stage, as they form the foundation for the more extensive profiles necessary to succeed as best practice organizations in Stages II and III.

The View from Stage II

The customer profile grows in importance for the company in Stage II of the evolutionary process. At this stage of the survival game, your organization must concentrate on feeding the vast information needs required before you can begin practicing customer segmentation. Because your organization's main concern at this point is retaining your customers, you must also collect this information in order to properly assess your customers' unique needs and formulate successful strategies to meet these needs.

In addition to the type of information collected in Stage I, key information in the Stage II organization's customer profiles should include a general description of the customer's business, its mission statement, as well as the names of the directors, the organizations represented by these directors and the positions they hold within these organizations. As well, your customer profiles should provide the answers to the following questions:

- What are the customer's major products and services?
- What are the market or industry sectors serviced by the customer?
- In which market segments does your customer have the strongest position?
- Who are your customer's major customers?
- Who are your customer's major competitors?

TIP

The Customer's Mission Statement

Next time you or your salespeople are in a customer's office, look around the reception area. You can usually find the customer's mission statement somewhere on a sign in the front lobby. Another place where such statements are generally prominently displayed is the annual report. These statements provide you with essential information that should be recorded in your customer profile.

For the Stage II organization that has a toehold on the next stage of the evolutionary process, take a look at the sidebar on the in-depth customer profile that follows. Developing this type of extensive customer profile provides you with a solid foundation of customer information and signals your company's increasing readiness to move into Stage III.

You will also find that an organizational chart can be of great assistance. Other sundry items that should not be overlooked include a file or list of key contacts within the customer's organization and their primary needs and possibly a financial profile.

The In-Depth Stage II Customer Profile

As you evolve towards Stage III, your customer profiles need to acquire more and more in-depth information. Take a look at them. If they include the following information about your most strategic customers, congratulations! Your organization is well on its way along the evolutionary process to Stage III.

Here's what the evolving Stage II organization needs to know about its customers:

- Brief customer history, including innovations, milestones, myths, legends and folklore, mottoes and themes
- Key sales and marketing activities to date
- Critical success factors for the customer's industry/market sector
- Critical success factors for the customer's organization

The Stage III Customer Profile: Focus on Customer Spend

TIP

What Is "Customer Spend"?

At Stage III, the concept of "Customer Spend" becomes very important, but what exactly is it? In a nutshell, customer spend is the amount that the customer is prepared to spend in total, in the current year or has spent in the previous fiscal year. In other words, the size of the customer's wallet—its budget or authorized expenditure.

Once you reach Stage III, you will find that the extensive customer profiles you developed in Stage II simply do not contain enough information. You must now go into more detail, with a particular emphasis on the customer's buying patterns.

What key questions should your customer profile answer at this stage of the process? Consider the following crucial information you will require to successfully tackle Stage III customer care concepts.

What Is the Size of Your Customer's Wallet?

This critical question is often overlooked. Every customer will have one or more buying centers that are responsible for purchasing a group of products or services, usually regionally rather than globally. Each buying center within the customer's organization operates on the basis of budgets, which they form each business cycle. Generally, budgets will not expand, unless sales exceed the target, and in such cases the next budget may be enlarged but will not likely have an impact on the current budget.

The customer's budget is a defined entity. With research, you can size it, and report it within your customer profile. Some customers will reveal the size of their budgets but generally only with those who they see as strategic partners. With other customers you may have to make an estimate based on extrapolations, research and perhaps even hearsay. Whether you obtain the actual figures or arrive at an estimate, it's vital that you have some knowledge of the size of the customer's wallet.

Is the Customer's Wallet Changing?

Remember that teeming corporate jungle? Change is everywhere around us. Markets expand, contract and die. You must stay on top of the changes occurring within the product and service groups you sell, and you must properly analyze the impact of these changes on your customer's wallet.

Your customer may be willing to tell you its purchasing forecasts, but you still need more background research. Independent research may reveal to you, for example, that while your customer's sales within a particular market category (or cell) are going up, the market itself may be declining and all of your customer's competitors have already bailed out. In such a situation, you must assess the impact of these market changes on your focus and your relationship with this particular customer's buying center and within this particular market cell.

In other words, changes to the business and market environment may force changes on your customer's wallet. It's best to remain aware and stay on top of any potentially explosive situations.

Your Goals with Regard to the Customer's Wallet?

What exactly do you want to achieve in terms of your customer's wallet? What issues do you currently "own" the way, say, FedEx owns next day delivery by 9:00AM? Which would you like to own? Are there areas in which you do not really want to compete?

Before you can think about trying to answer these questions, you must first have an answer to the first question—what is the size of your customer's wallet? Unless you know the size of the pie, you will not know if you are allocating the right level of resources to the customer's buying center.

You also need to examine your current share of sales from the customer. Do you think your current share is sufficient? Is there potential to achieve a greater share? Do you want to take advantage of this potential or is it more worthwhile to pursue other customers? It's important, however, that you don't simply look at your share of sales from the perspective of the customer's organization as a whole. Look instead at your share of sales by product or service grouping, or by specific buying centers within the organization. If you look at your share only from a total corporate perspective, you miss identifying where cross-selling and synergistic opportunities exist.

Calculate the Potential of the Opportunity

One important aspect of a customer's profitability centers on the expenses incurred in servicing the customer. Take a close look at the percentage of time and dollars spent on the account, categorized according to buying center and not simply by customer. In order to make the information more useful, do not look only at the effort of your sales force but also at the costs associated with after-sales service, research and development, promotion and technical service.

INFORMATION GATHERING BEST PRACTICES

Fortunately, much of the information you need to fill in your customer profiles is readily available and, in general, easily accessible. When compiling your profiles, you may want to access the resources listed below. Often, the information they offer consolidates information on your customer's business environment and can substantially enhance your customer profiling.

- Public databases. These are excellent resources for obtaining articles in magazines and newspapers around the world. You can generally access these databases at your local library and through the Internet. Databases such as Reuters, Business Week or Fortune can provide you with information on key executives, sales, new product introductions and strategic direction.

- **Brokers and analysts.** Don't overlook the usefulness of these professionals. Many of them cover a specific organization or a particular industry, trends in the industry, competitive activity and individual company performance. You can find them either through databases to which your organization already subscribes or directly from issuing brokers.

- **Trade associations and journals.** These can be veritable gold mines of information, as their main purpose is to provide industry-specific research, information, updates and trends. You will find trade publications for most industries and businesses, but remember that many of these publications are not held on the major databases. If you are having difficulty locating trade journals in your customer's industry, an Internet search or a call to the relevant association may prove worthwhile.

- **Customer's publications.** Reading the communications your customer publishes will give you a strong feel for the organization and a good sense of its values. It will also identify key corporate executives, possibly its strategic direction, and new product launches. It may also provide you with some information on key departments within the company and recent successes. Contact your customers' public relations or communications department for a wealth of material, including in-house journals, company histories and newsletters.

- **Industry associations and specialists.** These can sometimes be invaluable in providing briefings on industry-specific issues. They are also a good source of current trends, innovations and up-to-date news and innovations within their industries.

- **Research groups.** A surprising number of research groups exist that have the ability to provide you with customized reports or analysis on particular customers or industries. These are usually global in focus and provide forecasts of expected growth and key organizations that seem to be leading in innovation, sales or product launches.

- **Annual reports/10-K Reports/Standard & Poor Reports**. Read these reports carefully. They generally contain a bonanza of information and can add extensively to your customer profile. They usually provide full financial report and information on key executives and also strategic direction.
- **Customer's competitors**. Do some research on your customers' competitors. This will generally enhance your understanding of your customers' industry in general.

Where to Find All This Information

If you haven't given much thought to the collection of customer information, you're probably daunted by the sheer volume of data with which you'll have to deal as your organization follows its evolutionary course toward Stage III best practice status. Accumulating and maintaining such extensive customer profiling information is a formidable task that requires persistence and commitment.

The job may actually be more difficult than it looks. Not only must the information be collected, it must also be updated and usually by a number of different individuals. For example, personnel in sales, marketing and technical and customer service will likely all have valuable information to add to a customer's profile, from time to time. Finally, all of this information, collected, maintained and updated, must be distributed on a timely basis to others.

The globalization of our businesses creates even more complications. It's difficult enough dealing with the distribution of vital customer information when the recipients are in the same office. But often, the people who really need to access the data are in another geographic location completely—sometimes halfway across the globe. This is where a database and groupware applications come into play. Best practice organizations typically use groupware tools to their considerable advantage. Database technology allows best practice organizations to develop an accessible and standardized tool that effectively maintains and updates their constantly changing customer profile information.

Best Practices in Action

The following anecdotal studies provide you with an important perspective on information gathering and dissemination and demonstrates the knowledge pipeline in action. Information gathering is being used to shape the corporate culture, focus decision making and develop action plans for the customer.

THE HEWLETT-PACKARD EXPERIENCE

A leader in its specialized market, Hewlett-Packard demonstrates how adding strong information gathering programs emphasizing customer focus can breathe new life into an organization and into the processes that touch the customer. Even more important, this example highlights the importance of a standardized approach to information gathering and the profiling of the customer relationship. Hewlett-Packard is a testament to the concept of using feedback to inspire incremental change rather than discarding tried and true practices.

At the root of Hewlett-Packard's customer profiling approach is a management process in which each top Hewlett-Packard manager is given a key account to manage. This process serves a dual goal. First, it helps management keep in touch with the company's customers and their needs. Second, by giving the account manager overall responsibility for information collection and building and maintaining the customer profile, the information gathering forms part of a much larger purpose— the development of an annual business review process.

What considerations are of critical importance to Hewlett-Packard?

- **Consistency in reporting.** Hewlett-Packard's customer satisfaction and customer feedback processes are managed on a worldwide basis and are integrated and reported globally. The knowledge pipeline is being filled in a deliberate manner.
- **Teamwork.** Hewlett-Packard considers teamwork an integral element in keeping its focus on the customer. All employees' performance appraisals include measurements for both customer satisfaction and teamwork. While the account manager has overall accountability and responsibility for information collection, all team members share responsibility for the task.
- **Its corporate value system.** To ensure consistency of approach, all employees receive training in the "HP Way," a corporate value system that centers on giving attention to customers and their needs. Through this process information gathering and the customer profile itself is standardized, which assists management in making informed

decisions. In fact, the HP Way, along with the involvement and direction of Hewlett-Packard's top management, constitute the two key items that drive the company's corporate culture and keep its focus on the customer.

THE LEVI STRAUSS EXPERIENCE

Levi Strauss and Company adds another element to the best practices approach. While customer profiling is an important element, selectivity is an essential secondary consideration. The organization has centered attention primarily to the needs of its core customer, a Stage III approach, and does not try to produce a product that suits everyone. If a concept does not meet the needs of its core customer, it is dropped. At the heart of this is the need to gather sufficient relevant information that can facilitate this analysis.

Like Hewlett-Packard, Levi Strauss believes that information gathering will be of better quality if attention to teamwork and interpersonal skills is provided. The organization also realized that in its drive toward increased customer satisfaction, recognition of process problems as identified by the customer are not enough to satisfy the company's concerns. Instead, Levi Strauss focuses on extensive information sharing, which can only exist if there is a common approach to information gathering and customer profiling.

- The organization places flip charts that solicit employees' solutions to problems outside of busy access points in the office as a way of gathering input of all employees
- It uses its customer information to help it define which processes are "broke" and need to be fixed and then relates that to those customers requiring process "fixing." This can only be achieved if accurate information on customer needs are contained in the customer profile
- The organization leverages customer and market information systematically with the support of information systems.

Because it is in an industry driven by quickly changing trends, the company considers the sharing of customer information among its people a critical element of its success.

LESSONS LEARNED

Once you have established which stage of evolution you are in, the next step is to identify who your customers are and what they want. Customer profiles are the way to capture this in a consistent manner.

In building a customer profile, you must understand what customers need from an organization with which they would prefer to do business. With that in hand, you must collect and synthesize information that will help you address these issues. Customers can view you from a number of different perspectives from transactional supplier to strategic partner. Understanding where you currently stand on this continuum should help you target where you want to be and what information will assist you in getting there.

Building customer profiles is a Stage II or III activity. The fundamental difference lies with the type of information collected and for how many of your customers it is collected. Stage III organizations also focus more on "wallet sizing" to help them define their strategic targets. Information gathering should not be an arduous task, but certain disciplines and rigor should be exercised. Mine the information sources that are available and share best practices whenever possible.

In the next few chapters we'll continue building the foundation for your journey toward Stage III customer care. We'll examine other crucial points, including segmenting your customers, using the information you've collected in this chapter to understand your customers' unique needs and the role technology can play in your evolutionary process.

CHAPTER THREE

Segmentation

SOME CUSTOMERS ARE MORE IMPORTANT THAN OTHERS

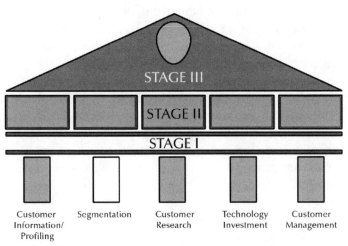

Figure 3.1: The Pillars of Strategic Customer Care—Segmentation

For years now the traditional pundits of customer care have expounded over and over again the virtues of exceptional customer service. You've heard the slogans—The customer is always right, We put our customers first, and several others along similar lines. Are they right?

Well, yes…and no. The fact is that you simply cannot afford to give exceptional customer service to all your customers. But does that mean you should give poor service to some customers?

Absolutely not. What it does mean is that you need to learn to be more selective in your choice of customers, and that is what this chapter will address—how to categorize customers to achieve strategic advantage—customer segmentation.

Let's start with an example and from that develop a structured approach to the concept of segmentation.

A HEALTH CARE ORGANIZATION

Developed a few years ago by a health care organization prominent in the Midwest, the following segmentation process and its implementation helped this organization achieve a 20 percent increase in sales and profits with a 10 percent reduction in its customer base.

The company distributed health care products to major hospitals and clinics throughout the United States. It had two major challenges. First, its sales force had become inefficient and costs per sales call were escalating. Second, it was receiving substantial complaints of slow response time on orders and poor shipment accuracy, particularly from its larger health care facilities/hospitals. Adding more sales staff was not an acceptable alternative. So the organization revisited the way in which it serviced its customers with a view to providing improved service to its best customers. But the challenge was to be able to clearly identify its customer groupings and then decide on how to align its inside sales staff with its external sales force to provide differentiated service.

To address this, customers were initially classified into the following five customer classifications:
• Level E: Transitional
• Level D: Maintenance
• Level C: Retention
• Level B: Base
• Level A: Strategic partners

These categories correspond roughly with the categories we will outline later in this chapter in the discussion of the Tier I to Tier V approach taken by best practice Stage III organizations. Let's take a more detailed look at how this organization considered these classifications:

Level E: Transitional
The organization regarded these accounts as mainly transaction oriented, with a primary focus on price rather than partnership. In general, customers in this category were high maintenance accounts but offered low potential. They tended to be less financially stable on a day-to-day basis. The company considered them potential candidates for "disengagement"—in plain English, they were about to be "fired" as customers.

Level D: Maintenance
The company described these accounts as lacking in management focus on the value of partnership. It also saw them as being vulnerable to market changes. In most cases, accounts in this group provided the organization with limited or even negative gross profit, but unlike the customers in the transitional category, they had the potential (based on knowledge of their total purchasing budget), with the application of slight additional attention, to move on to a positive, though limited, profit potential. Again, like the transitional ones, maintenance accounts were generally smaller and were likely to be resistant to changing market conditions.

Level C: Retention
The organization saw retention accounts as uncommitted or lacking full commitment to it as a supplier. As a group these accounts needed the organization's help to survive in the future. Generally, they provided the company with a constant gross profit stream but substantially lower than the accounts within base and strategic partner categories. The company's main objective in dealing with this group was to ensure that it did not consume inappropriate resources, particularly not at the expense of the two more desirable segments below (levels A and B below).

Level B: Base
The company defined this group as partnership-oriented accounts for which the organization had achieved low to medium penetration. These accounts showed a great potential for improvement, as they were recognized as having a strong

gross profit potential, if increased share could be achieved. While not necessarily progressive in outlook, they nevertheless constituted a stable and solid force in their industries. While these accounts were generally more focused on current market opportunities, they had the ability to become strategic partners. Therefore, they were candidates for the heavy investment of resources and time.

Level A: Strategic Partners
Accounts within this group had already entered into partnership with the organization. Each account represented a financially sound customer considered to be a major player in the future of its industry and with strong potential growth. In simple terms, customers in this group offered the organization the highest profit and provided the greatest potential for strategic partnership. Each customer in the group was considered a market innovator and leader in its industry. The organization also recognized that each of these accounts possessed a progressive mindset and a partner-oriented management system.

LESSONS LEARNED

The segmentation process described in this case study demonstrates a number of points. First, there is a desire for strategic partnership to the point where such partnership relationships are expressed as the goal of segmentation. Second, the organization understood a need to segment customers based on a broader range of criteria than simply revenues or geographic region. Lastly, which for the sake of simplicity was not explicitly discussed, the organization classified its customers based on a scoring and weighting process followed by a ranking based on multiple criteria. (These criteria included both the customer's potential and also its willingness to partner).

The discussion that follows provides guidance on how, regardless of your stage in the evolutionary process, you can and should address customer segmentation to achieve success.

BUILDING THE FOUNDATION: NOT ALL CUSTOMERS ARE CREATED EQUAL

The concept of giving different customers different levels of service can be a difficult one to accept, particularly among Stage II organizations. After all, companies make the move to Stage II once they recognize that retaining their customers is half the battle in the survival of the fittest. Moving on to Stage III therefore requires that these Stage II organizations make a large leap in the way they think: from focusing on nurturing each of their customers and placing all their efforts on making sure their customers stay with them, they must move on to a more nontraditional mindset.

Stage II organizations need to learn to let go of some of their customers, provide a core level of care to others, and give a restricted, select group of customers an exceptional level of service. At first glance, this new understanding of customers as assets, each of whom have different values, may appear to be very much at odds with the driving force behind the evolution through Stage II: maintaining your customer base. And in many ways, it is. After all, you worked hard to acquire a good solid group of customers, and now you're being told that rather than nurture all of them, you must focus your best efforts on giving exceptional service to only a portion of them.

But going from the mindset required for Stage II to the type of thinking needed to survive in Stage III does not really require such a large leap of faith. You've heard all the statistics. Just as entering Stage II required you to recognize that it costs five to ten times as much to acquire a new customer as it does to maintain a current one, moving into Stage III simply requires you to accept that most of your profits will be derived from a small, select group of customers.

But how do you determine which customers to place in this select group? How do you ensure that you accurately determine the potential of each customer? Do other factors, like customer needs, have an impact on the segmentation process? How do you decide who should receive merely good service, and who should be given exceptional service?

Stage I and Stage II organizations need to learn certain things in order to equip themselves with the necessary tools to move into Stage III—where they must accurately determine which customers belong in their select group of most profitable customers. The crucial tool that can make or break your customer selection process is **customer segmentation**.

THE IMPORTANCE OF CUSTOMER SEGMENTATION

Once you've acquired that basic database of invaluable customer information, that we discussed in Chapter 2, you can begin practicing segmentation. But there are many ways in which you can categorize customers. Below we provide you with a high level overview, followed by a detailed analysis of the stages.

An Overview on Segmentation

Stage I Segmentation: The Traditional Way. This is segmentation by geography, revenue or industry sector. On its own it's not very helpful, but it does play a limited role in the Stage III segmentation process.

Stage II Segmentation: The Evolution toward Best Practices. Some customers are just more profitable than others. Whether it's a decreased expense in servicing their account, the volume of their repeat business or any of the other various and critical factors, you can't hide from the fact that in terms of their impact on your revenue potential, all customers are emphatically *not* the same. Focusing on customer needs allows you to practice differentiated service. Customers in the same grouping, when categorized by needs, will demonstrate similar needs. Classifying your customers based on needs paves the way for the substantial benefits of successful differentiated service.

Stage III Segmentation: Strategic Tiering. This is the ultimate approach. It basically encompasses a little of everything above and works amazingly well in helping you to find those customers who really qualify as your strategic customers—crown jewels.

Stage I Customer Segmentation: The Traditional Way

Most organizations, particularly those in Stage I, start with the most traditional—and most common—approach to customer segmentation, sorting customers by geography or sales volume. Granted, this approach represents a very low level of sophistication, but on the other hand, at this stage it's often all that's required.

Learning to Walk

Why don't these Stage I companies employ more successful forms of segmentation? Organizations in Stage I direct their energies to acquiring customers. This means that these organizations are unlikely to see the need for more sophisticated forms of segmentation, and unlikely to have the skills and personnel required to properly utilize the more sophisticated approaches even if the necessary technologies were given to them. Remember, you can't run before you learn how to walk.

The 80/20 Rule

Using these traditional segmentation approaches also means that Stage I organizations tend to focus on the **80/20 rule**. Their segmentation process directs all their attention to the top 20 percent of their customers, which will provide about 80 percent of revenues. Unfortunately, by focusing on actual revenue generation, Stage I organizations may miss opportunities among the remaining customers who may have enormous untapped future potential.

Though the 80/20 rule can be quite short-sighted, it is generally appropriate for those in Stage I of the evolutionary process. After all, their focus is on customer quantity and current revenues.

Stage II Customer Segmentation: The Evolution toward Best Practices

The Stage II organization will generally find itself, at some point of its evolution, poised on the brink of more sophisticated segmentation, customer profitability. At this point the focus switches from revenues to profit. You can't get away from the fact that not all customers are equally profitable, nor do they all have the potential to become your most profitable customers.

Taking this to its logical conclusion, not all customers deserve the same level of service. You need to work toward reserving your premium service for your premium customers. You may not be able to charge them more for this service, but the long-term benefits to you are substantial. The bottom line will most likely be an increase in customer profitability, a decrease in costs, and a corresponding increase in profits. Not a bad result for simply making the leap from directing all your energies to all your customers to directing most of your energies to a small segment of them.

Getting Started—Research, Research and More Research

Consider this the starting point. You will need a substantial amount of research and analysis when it comes to your customer information database (see Chapter 2). The information you collected during Stage I provides a good start, but this material is very basic. You need to go far beyond the simple facts that helped you through Stage I.

You also need to introduce your sales force to the importance of this research and provide them with some tools of analysis which may be as simple as basic spreadsheet and sorting software. More sophisticated tools are commonly known as decision support tools, and there are a plethora of these software packages available. As your front line, your salespeople need to know how to define a customer's potential and current and future needs.

Don't just assume that you have sufficient information about your customers' needs. Direct customer research is not only mandatory, it's crucial to success. Ask your customers directly. Let them confirm the accuracy of the material you've collected.

Taking Action—Customer Profitability and Customer Needs

Three basic views on customer categories are set out below. For the Stage II organization, these three views, called customer supplier types, will provide you with a basic starting point. As you read through them, you're likely to react with a spark of recognition to the description of each type of customer. Most likely, you can probably name off the top of your head a few customers for each category.

Type I Transaction Focused Customers—No Profitability, No Potential

Mainly focused on best price and availability, these customers are commodity buyers and your least profitable customers. Look beyond revenues to the customer's actual impact on your profit margins and you'll understand what is meant by least profitable. Transaction focused customers offer you limited profit potential and low volume. On the other hand, you will find that they tend to provide you with regular repeat business.

You should be able to identify the majority of your transaction focused customers simply with a quick review of your customer list. On average, the following characteristics define them:

- They tend to be commodity purchasers.
- They are expensive to service.
- They are always on the look-out for the lowest price possible.
- They do not expect a high level of service.
- They seek an easy way to place their commodity orders.

The most cost-effective way of dealing with these customers is to give them low-cost service. Remember, they don't expect a high level of service and want attention only when they request it. So you should usually provide limited sales calls—or none at all.

Don't let your transaction focused customers consume too much of your energies—ideally less than 10 percent of the available time of your sales force and your customer service representatives. These customers warrant the lowest level of service, which is in accord with their expectations. True, some may demand disproportionate attention, but you will have to manage this.

TIP

Training Your New Customer Service Reps

Once you have segmented your customers into the basic levels, you will find that your transaction focused customers will provide the ideal early training ground for your new customer service reps. Because they expect a lower level of service, the inevitable beginners' mistakes will be less likely to disrupt your relationship with these customers.

Type II Customers—Some Profitability, Strong Potential

Type II customers have a singular market focus and therefore concentrate on a limited product offering. You'll find that most Type II customers are moderately profitable and, in fact, you may find that some of them provide you with substantial profits. What are their defining characteristics?

- Moderate profitability. The ones who provide substantial profitability and potential likely purchase from you in only one or two product groups.

- They view you as only one of a cluster of suppliers providing the service or product.
- There is a strong possibility of obtaining a dominant share of their purchase potential.
- They expect a little more than just basic service, which generally translates into expanded hours of operation or localized service access.
- They will occasionally request information regarding inventory availability, order status, pricing and account status.

How should you service your Type II customers? In general, it's not profitable to provide them with "one-stop" service for all their customer needs. But you should provide them with sufficient customer service that allows you the opportunity to up-sell or cross-sell other products or services.

How much of your energies should be directed to servicing them? Unlike Type I customers, Type II customers demand slightly more service. You should aim to meet their increased service needs. Ideally, your customer service representatives should devote between 30 to 40 percent of their time servicing them.

TIP

Assessing Potential

While profitability is a key issue in segmentation, you need to move beyond mere profitability and assess your customers' potential to purchase additional products and services that will enable you to achieve higher profits from the relationship. You need to consider these important factors:

- Have you taken advantage of opportunities to cross-sell?
- Can you create opportunities to cross-sell if none currently exist?
- Can you see yourself working toward obtaining a dominant share in each of their buying centers?

Type III Customers—The Strategic Partner

You will run into this phrase again and again throughout this book. The concept of the strategic partner is a critical element of the route map to success in customer care. It represents those customers that are willing to share risk for mutual benefit. This customer type includes those with the highest profit potential and with whom you have already formed a strategic partnership.

The defining characteristics of the strategic partner include:

- If you don't already enjoy a dominant market share position with this customer, there's a high probability of achieving it.
- True partnership most accurately describes your relationship with this customer, who has made you a complete and open participant in the detailed and long-term conduct of the business.
- The customer demands a proactive relationship from you, and you generally operate as an extension of the customer's sales force. This could include identifying new product or customer opportunities or simply providing competitive information that will help them in developing strategy.

Type III customers require very personalized and knowledgeable customer support when they contact your customer service center. Assign a specific customer service representative or a team to be responsible for meeting their needs. These representatives should be knowledgeable in a variety of areas, including order entry, accounts receivable and inventory management.

Understandably, you want to devote the bulk of your energies toward servicing your strategic customers. In general, between 50 and 60 percent of your customer service time should be directed to addressing their needs.

TIP

Flexibility as Added Service

You will find that Type III customers generally expect and appreciate the flexibility of being able to conduct their business with you in a form that will be most convenient to them at any given time, in any given situation. By all means, provide them access to your services by fax, phone, Internet, or whatever means will make it easier to do business with you.

TIP

Your Customer Service Representative and the Strategic Customer

When providing "one-and-done" support to your Type III customers, your customer service representatives must also function as quasi-sales representatives. In addition to traditional customer service, your representatives should be able to offer your strategic partners sales assistance as well and should be competent in anticipating the customer's needs and providing a variety of services that keep the customer informed.

Stage III: Strategic Tiering

This is the best practice approach to customer segmentation for Stage III organizations. It combines components of each of the other methodologies: the traditional methods, profitability segmentation and assessment of the customers' needs. Only your premium customers deserve your premium service, but who are these premium customers? Remember our discussion of the different types of customer/supplier relationships in the previous chapter? Let's look at these classifications again, but this time, let's explore from a more qualitative basis, so that we can provide both a qualitative and a quantitative approach to the definition of each of these categories.

In this case, there are five categories you can use to describe your current relationship with each of your customers:

1. **Tier V Transactional/Competitive Relationship**

2. **Tier IV Niche Relationship**

3. **Tier III Diversified Relationship (Sustaining Customers)**

4. **Tier II Major Provider Relationship**

5. **Tier I Strategic Partnership**

You may find it helpful to think of each of these customer/supplier relationships in terms of tiers in a pyramid. At the bottom—Tier V—you place your transactional/competitive relationships, while in the top, the narrowest and more exclusive tier—Tier I—you will find your strategic partnerships.

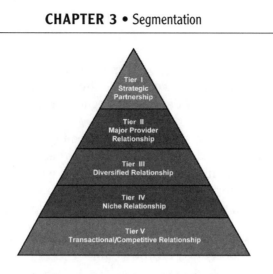

Figure 3.2: The Concept of Strategic Tiering

Tier V: The Transactional/Competitive Relationship

The word "transactional" best describes customers in this relationship category. To them, you are merely a "me-too" supplier, and it's unlikely that you compete against other suppliers for their business on anything more sophisticated than a price level. These customers tend to be transitional in the true sense of the word, and because price is their main concern, they usually have little hesitation in switching loyalties at a moment's notice.

These customers are similar to the transaction focused customers we discussed under Stage II segmentation:

• They have the lowest level of customer expectation.
• They have the lowest customer service requirements.
• They have a limited desire or need for direct access lines to your customer service department.
• They usually require limited or even no customer service support.

Despite these common needs, you'll find that, paradoxically, your "transactional" customers have a tendency to be high maintenance, because they demand a disproportionate amount of time from your customer service people compared to the profit you obtain from the relationship. Often they'll demand multiple quotes, extra sales visits and then, frequently they'll be late payers. The effort required to service their demands is not proportional to the potential return.

For the average organization, transactional/competitive supplier relationships represent approximately 20 to 25 percent of the total customer base. The group's potential drain on customer service resources warrants careful monitoring, and best practice organizations at Stage III develop strategies to keep a close eye on this segment.

What should your strategy be for dealing with this group? Because they can be exhausting to service, the best strategy is "up or out." That is, if you find that your relationship with them does not move up to the next level within a reasonable period of time, you need to seriously consider "firing" them, "transitioning them out" as customers.

What Makes Customers "Transactional"?

On a deeper analysis of your transactional/competitive supplier relationships, you'll likely find a number of negative factors. In all probability, for each of your "transactional" customers, you'll probably discover that:

1. To date, you've only managed to achieve a low or perhaps even a negative profitability with these customers.

2. The potential for any future increased profits from them is extremely low, if it exists at all.

3. The customers themselves are not financially sound. In fact, they probably find themselves challenged financially on a day-to-day basis.

4. Despite their negative profitability for your company, they are high maintenance accounts, very demanding and vocal in their demands. The effort expended to keep these companies happy, despite their low expectation of service, is usually disproportionate to the potential return on your effort.

5. The customers themselves do not operate with sophisticated processes or systems. They tend to think on a short-term basis, as they are generally transaction or product oriented.

6. They respond negatively to changing market conditions, either displaying resistance or an inability to adapt to the changes.

7. Finally, this type of customer typically represents a small account.

Tier IV: The Niche Relationship

These niche customers are "limited investment" customers. While they have more value than Tier V customers, their potential is not that much greater. They will regard you as a niche supplier and allow you little or no opportunities to cross-sell your products or services. You're unlikely to move beyond the niche label with this customer unless you develop new products or services. And, even with something new to offer them, the likelihood of expanding on their potential as a customer remains low.

Identifying the Niche Relationship

How do you identify the niche relationships in your customer base? In general, these customers exhibit the following characteristics:

1. They represent a medium to low gross profit level and a medium to low potential for your organization.
2. They are not considered to be highly profitable themselves.
3. You may find that some of them may be in a shaky financial condition.
4. They operate internally with less than sophisticated processes and systems.
5. They tend to be transaction or product oriented.
6. You may consider them to be resistant to changing market conditions.
7. They tend to represent a smaller account in terms of sales than other higher level customers.

You will also find a common set of needs among the customers falling into this tier. In general, they require:
• Services associated primarily with the core products and services purchased
• Basic and reliable services
• Limited need for customer support services

Generally, niche relationships are self-sufficient, although their potential for increased profit is generally low. In many organizations, these relationships represent approximately 25 to 35 percent of the total customer base. While their future profit potential will not likely increase, they should be considered to have, in general, a neutral impact on your customer service energies, given their self-sufficiency. In other words, you won't make much profit from them but neither will you spend a lot to maintain the accounts.

Tier III: The Diversified Relationship (Sustaining Customers

Identifying Diversified Customers

How should you identify your sustaining customers, the ones with whom you have formed a diversified relationship? On analysis, you'll find a number of defining characteristics:

1. The sustaining customer exhibits solid gross profitability and high potential for your organization.

2. The customer will tend to be both profitable and financially sound.

3. In a diversified relationship, the customer will see you as just one of a number of suppliers.

4. Despite being one of a number, the customer also views you as a significant supplier who is well respected.

5. Like those in the niche and transactional/competitive supplier relationships, the sustaining customer still tends to be price and service oriented.

6. Again, like the two previous categories of customers, this customer will also be reactive rather than proactive when it comes to changes in the marketplace.

Diversified relationship customers are "sustaining" customers. They see you as a value-added supplier, but you haven't yet attained the pinnacle of strategic partnership. You're well on your way, though. The sustaining customer values your judgment, and ample opportunity exists to increase profitability by cross-selling products and services among the customer's buying centers.

Often you will find that you hold a home base position with one of the customer's buying centers, and that increases the probability that you can expand your position into other buying centers. This generally occurs through increased opportunities to cross-sell, particularly as the loyalty of your home base buying center improves.

Home Base: This is the buying centre in which you have a dominant market share. You should be able to move from this position into other buying centres by having your contacts introduce you to the other centres or provide references or testimonials.

Devoting a certain amount of resources to servicing these customers makes sound business sense. With a bit of effort, you can succeed in bringing them forward, hopefully into the next category of customer relationship. Among best practice organizations, this group of customers typically represents approximately 15 to 20 percent of the total customer base.

As a group, customers in a diversified relationship with you have some common needs. They need a supplier who can provide general advice and information that can potentially lead to customer growth, but they need lower level customer support only occasionally.

Tier II: The Major Provider Relationship

> ### Defining the Major Provider Relationship
>
> How can you tell when you have established a major provider relationship with a customer? Take a look at the defining characteristics of high potential customers. They:
>
> 1. contribute a high gross profitability to the total profit picture of your organization.
> 2. represent a large potential for greatly increased profitability for you.
> 3. are profitable companies that are financially sound.
> 4. have granted you hold a dominant customer share position within their organizations.
> 5. tend to be partnership-oriented in their relationship with you.
> 6. are not as aggressive and progressive in the face of market changes as the Tier V group of customers, but they nevertheless brave market changes solidly. In effect, they also are evolving toward adaptability, sharpening their ability to remain flexible as the markets undergo continuous and rapid changes all around them.

Welcome to the big leagues! The customers in this category are "high potential" accounts, and the name says it all. They, together with the next group of customers, deserve the greatest portion of your focus and efforts. With these customers, you are just short of forming a strategic partnership, and by focusing on them you stand a good chance of pushing your relationship with them forward into Tier V.

In this category, the customers consider you a valued supplier. Unlike those customers with whom you have formed a diversified relationship (Tier III), you tend to have at least two home bases with the high potential customer's buying centers, and usually there's further potential for cross-selling.

Among best practice organizations, this group of customers form approximately 10 to 15 percent of the total customer base. It's important that you devote a solid portion of your resources and energies to caring for these customers, as well as the ones in the next level. The high potential customer could possibly number among your crown jewels—your most profitable customers.

As a group, you will find that these customers have a number of common needs. In particular, they will rely on you to:

- Be proactive and knowledgeable not only about their own needs but also about market conditions and the current state of their industry.
- Provide directional business solutions and innovative problem-solving capabilities.
- Give them responsive customer support whenever they require it.

Tier I: Strategic Partnership

The Quest for the Crown Jewels

With strategic partnerships so important to the future of your organization, it's crucial that you can determine who exactly among your customers deserves the title crown jewel. These special, strategic customers have a number of distinguishing characteristics:

1. They contribute the highest proportion of gross profitability.
2. They have the potential to add further to the gross profit they provide you.
3. They are quite profitable organizations themselves and without a doubt financially sound.
4. They are customers who have permitted you to achieve a dominant share position in your product and service categories, and if you haven't yet, there's a very high likelihood that you will achieve a dominant position soon.

> 5. Savvy and intelligent, these customers are themselves aware of the continuous changes taking place in market conditions and are ready and eager to form strategic alliances.
>
> 6. Conscious of the need to be flexible and show adaptability, they are both market innovators and industry leaders.

These customers represent the ultimate stage in customer relations. Consider them to be the crown jewels of your customer base. What happens once a customer reaches the strategic partnership stage with you? You share your customer's risk, and your operations become horizontally and vertically integrated with theirs. Your strategic partners depend on you to help them prosper.

Among best practice organizations, these strategic customers constitute up to 5 percent of the customer base but between 30 to 50 percent of the organizations' profits. These numbers alone reveal the importance of these customers to your organization. They are indeed your true crown jewels, premium customers who deserve premium care.

> *TIP*
>
> *Crown Jewels*
> As the name indicates, your crown jewel customers constitute a very rare asset. You won't have many of them but the ones that you have will play a critical role in your organization's success.
>
> Crown jewels are customers that offer the greatest potential for a win-win relationship. They are Type I customers that are willing to share risk, partner and grow through your product and service offerings.

As a group, your Type I customers have a number of common needs. You will find that they will look to you to be:
- Proactive and knowledgeable about market conditions and their own unique customer needs.
- Willing to operate in true partnership with them.
- Prepared to provide them with extensive customer support.
- Ready to give them the very best service available.
- Innovative, particularly in helping them develop practical and efficient solutions to their problems.

GETTING STARTED: A STEP-BY-STEP GUIDE TO SEGMENTATION BEST PRACTICES

Knowing the importance of segmentation is really only half the battle. So much rests on the ability of your organization to properly segment its customers. Unless that is done accurately, you can end up in more of a muddle than when you first started.

So, have you accepted the basic principles underlying segmentation? Do you understand the importance of properly categorizing your customers? If so, then let's examine a structural process by which you can allocate your customers to the five important tiers of customer relationships outlined above.

The following step-by-step approach is based on practical application, not just theory—and it works.

Step 1: Customers and the Revenues They Generate for You

Generate a list of all current customers. If your customers cut across multiple divisions or product groups, make sure you include them in each division's list. For each customer, in each division, identify total revenues based on most recent annual revenue figures. Categorize your list on two levels: First, rank the entire list of customers based on revenues generated, from highest to lowest. Second, sort the list of customers by business unit or product grouping. If a customer buys from more than one business unit, classify that customer under the business unit for which it generates the highest revenues. Then, within each business unit, rank the customers based on revenues generated from highest to lowest.

Step 2: Segmentation by Revenues Generated

Based on the revenue figures generated in Step 1, select the customers representing the top 70 percent of your total revenues. This isolates the transaction-focused and market-focused customers (remember them from our discussion of Stage II segmentation in the early portion of this chapter) from further segmentation and simplifies and expedites the segmentation analysis.

For all the customers that fall within the lower 30 percent of total revenues, identify and select any customers that have a high future profit potential, possibly based on current products or current volume purchases. These are customers you believe have the most potential to move from lower to higher tiers, for example, from Tier II to Tier I.

Step 3: Rank Your Selected Customers

The customers selected in Step 2 are now ready to be ranked according to a list of criteria. In order to further categorize these customers, you will have to use some of the more extensive information you've been collecting as part of your Stage III customer research. Using a scoring template similar to that described in Figure 3.3 (on page 66), rate *each* of your selected customers High, Medium or Low for each of the following criteria:

- willingness to become a partner
- trend of increased revenues generated for your organization
- your current share of customer's business
- potential for this customer to represent a significant share of your organization's business
- significance of your company's product or service to the customer's business
- current gross profit achieved from this customer
- customer's gross profit potential
- potential to cross-sell additional products and services
- customer's degree of innovation orientation

Step 4: Final Classification

Finally, using the result of the ranking exercise in Step 3, classify each of your selected customers into one of the five segmentation tiers (Tier I to V) by matching the ranking results to the criteria shown in Figure 3.4 (on page 67).

Note in the figure, that each tier has distinct minimum criteria, with the most stringent criteria reserved for Tier I. Together with the secondary criteria, the ranking will establish each customer and rank them appropriately by tier.

Customer	Willingness to partner HML	Increasing trend for revenue HML	Current customer share HML	Increasing trend for customer share HML	Significance of company's products HML	Current gross profit HML	Customer gross profit potential HML	Potential for integration HML	Degree innovation oriented HML	Tier I-V

Figure 3.3: Strategic Customer Care Scoring Template

Segment	Minimum Criteria	Secondary Criteria
Tier I Strategic Relationship	Must rank high for: • Willingness to partner • Current gross profit achieved • Customer gross profit potential • Innovation oriented	Must rank high for one of either: • Customer share or • Increasing trend for customer care And must rank medium to high for at least two of the remaining three criteria.
Tier II Major Provider Relationship	Must rank high for: • Current gross profit achieved • Customer gross profit potential	Must rank at least medium for either or both of: • Customer share • Increasing trend for customer care • And Medium for innovation Plus medium to high for at least two of the remaining three criteria
Tier III Diversified Relationship	Must rank medium for: • Current gross profit achieved • Customer gross profit potential	And medium for at least four of the remaining seven criteria
Tier IV Niche Relationship	Must rank medium for one of either: • Current gross profit achieved • Customer gross profit potential	And medium for at least two of the remaining seven criteria
Tier V Transactional/ Competitive Relationship	Must rank low for both: • Current gross profit achieved • Customer gross profit potential	And low for at least four of the remaining seven criteria

Figure 3.4: Strategic Customer Care Criteria for Tiering

DEVELOPING STRATEGIC PARTNERSHIPS

The ABB Group, a global engineering company primarily serving customers in electric power generation, transmission and distribution industries, recognizes the importance of developing long-term partnerships with its most important customers. In fact, its corporate strategy states: "ABB contributes to the success of its customers by developing mutually beneficial long-term relationships." How did ABB translate this statement into action? The organization recognized that customers can be positioned on a "partnering continuum" as shown below.

You will note that this is a variant of the customer relationship categories discussed earlier in this chapter and in Chapter 1. However, in this case, ABB had six categories of classification ranging from the commodity supplier to the strategic partnership.

In creating its segmentation, ABB relied on an interesting dynamic. It reasoned that, as its relationship and involvement with selected customers grew and matured, so too did the

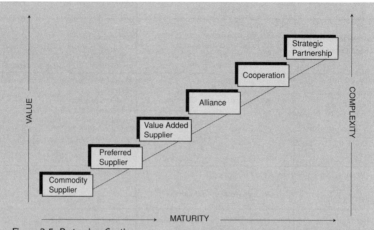

Figure 3.5: Partnering Continuum

customers themselves. As the customer organization became more complex, ABB's value to them also grew.

With this in mind ABB's segmentation process looked at the following questions:

- Where is the customer today?
- What is the customer's potential in moving up the partnering continuum?
- If the potential existed, how could ABB best align its resources to encourage the customer to make the move up the continuum?

With the answers to these questions, ABB began the arduous task of classifying its customers. It identified four key areas to create its segmentation criteria:

1. Current size of account
2. Potential size of account
3. Strategic importance of account to ABB
4. Current relationship with account

Within each of these major categories, ABB assigned relative weightings and scores. These scores allowed the organization to develop three major customer groupings: Class I, II and III.

Class I. Customers placed within this classification merited special coverage. An account manager was assigned to each of these customers, a specific account strategy defined, and the current relationship mapped to identify points where the relationships were strong, weak or required reassessment. ABB performed periodic progress reviews on the accounts in this tier in order to determine if specified targets and objectives were being met.

Class II. Customers within this category required active coverage, on a project by project basis. Unlike Tier I, the company developed a project rather than an account strategy to handle each customer in the tier. Specifically, recognizing that projects were more short-term than in a multiyear Class I relationship, a dedicated account manager was not assigned. The account manager shared responsibility for an account within this tier with an account representative, and Class I initiatives were introduced on a trial basis.

Class III. The company did not actively seek out accounts in this category as they were less loyal and less willing to become strategic Class I partners. These customers required more reactive coverage; the decision whether to bid on any particular job offered by these accounts was made on an opportunity by opportunity basis.

LESSONS LEARNED

ABB and the pharmaceutical organization discussed at the beginning of this chapter reinforce the potential that can be achieved with a well-structured segmentation process. But it is not just the process that strengthens the pillar, but also your recognition of customers as assets, each unique and having different values, some more important than others. You must also accept the need to focus efforts on your most profitable customers and less on the less strategic customers. This starts with a recognition and acceptance of the five categories you use to describe your current relationship with each of your customers:
1. Tier V Transactional/Competitive Relationship
2. Tier IV Niche Relationship
3. Tier III Diversified Relationship
4. Tier II Major Provider Relationship
5. Tier I Strategic Partnership,

and a process to classify your customers into each of these categories. With limited finite resources this can be the only strategy.

After an in-depth analysis you begin to focus on those that display the greatest potential, even if they are not currently the most profitable. You must recognize that all customers not being equal, some simply may not be worth the time and effort required to maintain them.

Our case studies demonstrated the successful use of segmentation practice to achieve its stated goals. Revenues and profits increased in excess of 20 percent through a structured segmentation process and resulting action plans. The conclusion? Segmentation is a powerful tool in the hands of a best practice organization that fully understands the potential benefits of offering differentiated service to its customers.

CHAPTER FOUR

Focusing on Customer Needs through the Voice of the Customer

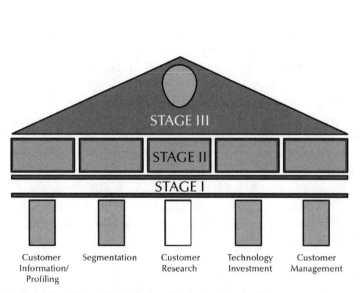

Figure 4.1: The Pillars of Strategic Customer Care—Customer Research

Everyone agrees that it's important to listen to our customers; the only disagreement is on how we can best do that. For a long time, experts judged that a more or less intuitive style of managing relationships was sufficient to enable us to listen to the voice of the customer. Lately, however, more and more organizations are finding merit in using a more structured approach to assess the true state of their customer relationships. While a number of reasons exist to explain this trend, the use of this more structured approach—voice of the customer measurement, our next pillar—is, in essence, driven by competition.

Today we must do more, and do it better, if we want to keep and expand on our customer relationships. This includes being more aggressive in seeking input—asking our customers for their concerns and opinions rather than waiting...and waiting...and waiting to be told—as well as listening better to the answers we receive.

As we have done in other chapters, it is best to start with an example, and there are few better in this area than IBM's AS/400 division, based out of Rochester, Minnesota.

IBM
ALL CUSTOMERS ARE NOT CREATED EQUAL

IBM considers the voice of the customer (VOC) a critical measure for its long-term success. As highlighted in Chapter 1, the results of a 1990 research study conducted by the company[1] showed that a one percentage point increase in overall customer satisfaction rating translated into an additional $257 million yield over five years. The study was based on actual customer satisfaction and revenue data from 1988 to 1990, with the basis for the revenue gain derived from the average purchase price of an AS/400. In 1996 the company recalculated the correlation between customer satisfaction and revenue and found that the numbers still held true.

Customer satisfaction has become the guiding principle for the AS/400 division. More importantly, both executives and employees have accepted this direct correlation between customer satisfaction and revenues.

Consider these statistics:

- Customers do not just buy an AS/400 product but also associated hardware (printers, monitors, displays) software, service and financing.
- For every dollar a customer spends on an AS/400, they also spend another three dollars, most often for the purchase of IBM products or services.
- With the exception of the second and third quarters of 1997, the AS/400 division has increased its revenues by double digit figures for 21 consecutive quarters.

---

[1] IBM AS/400 Division, Rochester, Mn.

- The AS/400 division has doubled its business from 1990 to 1996.

- Do the math, and you will see that the correlation between customer satisfaction and revenue holds true. IBM's customer satisfaction levels have improved ten percentage points since 1990.

A Rigorous Approach to VOC Measurement

Given the importance of customer satisfaction to its revenues, it's not surprising that IBM takes VOC measurement very seriously. Research has told them that all customers are not the same, and some customers warrant specialized attention. For example, 95 percent of its business comes from customers who have rated them a four or five on a five-point customer satisfaction scale.

In light of their research, IBM has placed a great emphasis on the development of a rigorous approach to VOC measurement, involving:

- **Segmentation.** The company segments first by worldwide geography, then by industry, sub-industry and also by what it calls "application opportunity segments"— segments of the market that have a particular need and use for the AS/400 equipment. Then, within each industry segment, it further divides its customers by number of employees, industry growth projections, local, regional, national and multicultural mark-up and major industry classification. Finally, it segments by current position versus the competition.

- **Research.** Through surveys, interviews, literature searches and attendance at industry-specific conferences, IBM collects the required information needed to achieve success within each of its industry segments.

- **Cross-comparisons.** IBM uses cross-comparisons with other key data and information to validate the accuracy of prioritized processes, gain additional detail on crucial quality features and stay aware of current customer satisfaction and market and competitive dynamics.

- **Continuous data collection.** The company continuously gathers together information from customer satisfaction surveys, consultant reports, complaints, gain and loss reports (reports that identify new customer gains and customers lost by each of the segments identified earlier) and feedback from customer councils (customers that meet several times a year to review IBM's plans for research and development as well as marketing initiatives).

- **The customer partnership call process.** This enables IBM to take a proactive role in ensuring customers easy access to the company to make comments, seek assistance and voice their complaints.

IBM's Customer Partnership Call Process

The customer partnership call process provides an excellent example of how to seek out VOC input proactively. IBM calls every AS/400 customer 90 days after the system is installed and asks about their satisfaction. The process identifies customer dissatisfaction early and helps the company measure the effects of its improvements. If a customer expresses dissatisfaction with any aspect of his or her relationship with IBM, the process invokes a series of follow-up actions to resolve the customer's concerns and restore complete satisfaction. Thirty days after resolving a customer's concern, the company calls the customer again to confirm their satisfaction—a follow-up procedure that ensures that the customer has the final say.

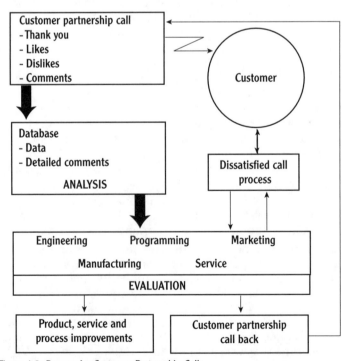

Figure 4.2: Process for Customer Partnership Calls

BUILDING THE FOUNDATION: THE VOC INTERVIEW AND SUMMARY

First things first. Why the focus on VOC? Just because other organizations have begun measuring and recording the voice of the customer or gauging customer satisfaction on a large scale is not, in and of itself, a reason to focus on VOC. Let's look instead at the merits of VOC. Starting with the premise that the quality of service represents a critical variable—and one entirely within your control—that can win or lose business for you, consider the following benefits of VOC measurement:

- VOC enables you to get closer to your customers. For many organizations, this is a goal of their organizational strategy.
- When you obtain the customer's opinion, you can base your strategy and your actions on fact not mere intuition.
- By forcing you to take the initiative and go to the customer directly, VOC prompts you to use a service strategy rather than merely reaction.
- Measuring VOC allows you to meet the expectations of an increasing number of customers who have VOC initiatives of their own and, moreover, who consider the employment of VOC measurement a mark of a progressive organization.
- Effective VOC programs produce information previously unknown, no matter how much your service team thought of itself as in touch with the customer.
- VOC data provides a baseline against which to gauge future improvement, providing you with an invaluable ability to measure that improvement.

BEST PRACTICES IN THE VOC

Voice of the customer (VOC) measurement is broader than just asking customers to rate you on how satisfied they are on the quality of service you provided, the traditional approach to customer satisfaction measurement. VOC measurement is more probing and focused on both customer satisfiers, what makes the customer pleased to do business with you, and dissatisfiers, what may cause them to defect. It is focused on processes that touch the customer (after-sales service, billing, order processing, delivery, etc.) and seeks to improve these points of contact. This form of research provides us with a broader method of measurement: an important point of differentiation when we all feel the driving need to measure, record and respond to what the customer is saying or thinking at each point of contact.

Traditional customer satisfaction measurement (CSM) can tell you that your customers are satisfied or dissatisfied, in general, but it cannot tell you what action you must take to improve and it cannot tell you what changes are necessary for your more strategic crown jewels. Accordingly, you need a more focused, probing method to capture customer needs efficiently and effectively, and that is where the broader based VOC research plays a role. Also, while focused customer service and its end result, customer satisfaction, is a basis of competition, there may be a more fundamental foundation to the growth and appeal of VOC measurement.

TIP

Why Measure Customer Satisfaction?
Management guru, Peter Drucker, put it most succinctly when he said, "What doesn't get measured, doesn't get done."

To obtain the VOC, you will need a questionnaire that addresses the key customer touch points (and we will give you some pointers shortly). The method you will use to obtain this information will vary depending on your stage in the evolution, but the basic questionnaire remains the same. In Stage I, most organizations use a mailed questionnaire to obtain customer input simply because the customer base is too large to do it any other way. Stage II organizations use a combination of telephone surveying and personal interviews, focusing primarily on those customers that are essential to retain. In Stage III, it is done exclusively by personal, face-to-face interviews and only with the strategic Tier I and II customers.

Developing the Questionnaire

In developing your questionnaire, try to think backwards. Think of what you will do with the result first, then determine the questions and sequencing that will get you there. Specifically, address these five questions in the following order:

1. What You Need to Know
2. The Design of the VOC Questionnaire
3. Relevant Questions

4. How to Present the Data
5. Assessing the Accuracy of Your VOC Findings

Let's go through these questions one by one. Once you understand them—and often this requires some preliminary internal and possibly external research in order to identify key issues—then specific questions and the flow of the questionnaire can be started.

1. What You Need to Know

The best way to answer this question is to consider what VOC measurement research should ideally provide.

- **Customer Satisfaction Index (CSI) Measurements.** CSI tells you where you stand in the minds of particular groupings of customers on particular issues. It can be as simple as your rating, on a five-point scale, as to how your customers rate your organization on the service it delivers to you. Some organizations (note the FedEx example that follows) create a number of such CSIs and weight each of these. While CSI is an important measure, it is only one measure, and not the most important. The results obtained from CSI measurements can tell you only where you are at a given point in time. It cannot point to or give you advice as to what your organization must do to improve.

- **Customer Action Measures (CAM).** This measure helps you to predict the likely future behavior of your customers. It requires specific questions to understand the customer's likely future behavior, degree of loyalty and willingness to recommend.

- **Important Actions (IA).** Using this measure you can find out how your organization can best focus its efforts to achieve customer-desired improvements. The questionnaire must specifically address and probe the interviewee on the most important actions that the organization should take to improve its positioning (this is usually limited to the three most critical items).

FEDERAL EXPRESS
A BEST PRACTICE EXAMPLE

While the use of a CSI is still an important measure for Federal Express, the results obtained from CSI measurements can tell you only where you are at a given point in time. It cannot point to or give you advice as to what your organization must do to improve.

Since its early years, Federal Express has provided a best practice example of the development and establishment of a CSI. Recently, with a view to continuing its progress toward the ultimate target of 100 percent customer satisfaction, the company replaced its old measure of quality performance—percentage of on-time deliveries—with a new measurement, a 12-component index, or service quality indicator (SQI), that comprehensively describes how its customers view its performance.

The company weighted each item in the SQI to reflect how significantly each factor affected overall customer satisfaction. Using its advanced computer and tracking systems, including the SuperTracker, a hand-held computer used for scanning a shipment's bar code every time the package changes hands between pick-up and delivery, the company is able to gather extensive performance data. Rapid analysis of this data from all of the company's operations provides daily SQI reports. These reports are then transmitted to workers at all Federal Express sites.

How is the data generated in the SQI reports used by the company?

- Federal Express management meets daily to discuss the previous day's performance, and to track weekly, monthly and annual trends.
- Quality action teams analyze data contained in the company's more than 30 major databases to locate root causes of problems, possibly delays, lost or damaged packages, etc., that surface in the daily SQI reviews.
- Cross-functional teams use the extensive customer and internal data generated by the SQI to assist the company's new product introduction process.
- SQI measurements have been linked directly to the corporate planning process, beginning with the CEO, the COO, and an executive planning committee.
- SQI results form the basis on which Federal Express executives are evaluated, with individual performance objectives established and monitored through SQI measurements.
- Executive bonuses rest on the performance of the entire corporation in meeting performance improvement goals.

Also, all executives do not receive year-end bonuses unless employees rank their leadership at least as high as the year before.

To reach its aggressive quality goals, the company has set up several cross-functional teams for each service component in the SQI. A senior executive heads each team and ensures the involvement of front-line employees, support personnel and managers from all parts of the corporation as needed. In fact, two of these corporate-wide teams contain a network of over 1,000 employees working on improvements to customer service.

2. The Design of the VOC Questionnaire

The most effective VOC measurement questionnaires need to be designed to include both qualitative and quantitative components. Ratings and importance rankings also play a large role in the successful VOC program. Other considerations include:

- **Confidentiality**. You must inform all respondents that their individual responses will remain confidential. Respondents are more open and honest when that guarantee is provided. Nevertheless, they may want you to take immediate action on some items and waive the confidentiality later.

- **Probes**. Probes are secondary questions that are asked to obtain clarification. In some cases they are planned in advance and built into the questionnaire—"if the score is less than three on a five-point scale ask…" Give consideration to the types of answers you may get in response to your questions and areas which may require further probing or clarification. You should include a number of probes and suggested prompts. An effective prompt would be the lead sentence, "What one thing could Organization X do to…" If additional comments are not forthcoming after the respondent's initial response, you may also want to ask whether he or she could suggest any other items that would assist Organization X in improving in this particular area.

- **The Occupied Interviewee.** Involve the customer as an active participant during the interview itself. One method of keeping the interviewee occupied during the interview session is to ask him or her to enter their ratings and rankings directly onto the questionnaire. The more they feel a part of the process, the more committed they will be to its success.

- **Length of the interview.** For the personal, face-to-face interview, it's best to keep the session under 90 minutes in length. You should commit to this time frame when you book the interview, and promise to keep to it when you sit down with the interviewee. Some respondents will give you more time, and some will give you less. When you are under time constraints, focus on the central deliverables, as well as the most important actions that your organization can take to improve. Get to the heart of the issues. If you are unable to complete your questionnaire because of a restriction in timing, try to arrange a second interview, either by phone or in person.

Developing the VOC Interviews

Interviews are an important part of a VOC. When you incorporate them in your VOC program, keep the following points in mind:

- Interviews conducted in person are less impersonal but can present logistical problems; that is, arranging convenient times particularly when there are multiple locations and several individuals that have to be interviewed—it's on their timetable, not yours.
- Interviews conducted by telephone are more impersonal but present fewer logistical problems.
- The interviewer should, as a rule, use a prepared outline.
- Often an outside professional within a market research or consulting organization will be called in to conduct the interviews.

Advantages:

1. The interviewer-customer dialogue allows the opportunity to branch out into areas not covered in the interviewer's outline.
2. The process permits a more extensive and in-depth explorations of topics.
3. Some executives may accord the interview more weight than they give to surveys and may therefore put more thought into their responses.

Limitations:

1. Interviews cannot target as many people—whether in person or by telephone—as can be reached by the mail survey.
2. Studies have indicated that subjects may be more inhibited and less forthright in a personal interview than they are when filling out a survey in the privacy of their offices.

3. Busy executives tend to find the interview process time-consuming, making scheduling and performing the actual interview more difficult.
4. Because of the likelihood of a broader range of responses, summarizing, categorizing or otherwise arranging the findings can be more difficult.

Developing the Mailed VOC Survey Questionnaire

Survey questionnaires are important for structuring the VOC interview. While a relatively small number of them are done by voice-response telephone or through e-mail, the majority continue to be performed through printed forms. If you decide to employ the survey approach in developing your VOC, keep the following in mind:

- The surveys are usually best kept short, from four to eight pages, because the longer they are, the less likely customers will complete them.
- The most common format is to provide the respondent with boxes to be checked in several rating categories along with space for written comments.
- Forms are typically distributed to customers by mail or, when possible, in person.
- Rating categories used in the survey tend to address soft values of service quality such as responsiveness, understanding of the customer's objectives or business, creativity, initiative, people skills, communication and attitude.
- Rating categories are frequently developed through organized focus groups of customers, sometimes with the participation of the customer's sales and marketing vice presidents.
- Using focus groups to develop rating categories can help to promote acceptance of your questionnaire within the organization.
- Most commonly, an outside organization will be used for some or all of the following: process design, form creation, handling of incoming customer responses, creation of statistical database, reporting back to the sponsor and interpretation of data.

Advantages:
1. The mailed form can reach a much larger number of customers than the personal interview.
2. The larger number of responses possible with the survey means greater statistical validity for the resulting data.

3. Surveys enable you to evaluate a larger number of customer relationships.
4. In some cases, a customer may be more forthright filling out a form than they would be in a face-to-face interview, particularly if the interviewer is from the organization conducting the VOC program.
5. Survey findings are easier to summarize and period-to-period comparisons to measure progress are easier to prepare.

Limitations:
1. The customer's executives may be more likely to dismiss a form as being unworthy of their time and attention. This shortcoming can be mitigated by gaining commitment before delivering the survey questionnaire.
2. Feedback is confined to the material and questions on the form. There is no opportunity to deviate into other areas.

3. Relevant Questions

The Stage I Questionnaire. If your organization operates within Stage I, you may find a more simplified version of the questionnaire to be more helpful. Your key questions will relate to the development and establishment of a customer satisfaction index (CSI).

In most "command and control" Stage I organizations, VOC measurement results will be distributed primarily to senior management who will use the results primarily to focus on tracking performance of front-line staff. Middle management and front-line staff will usually see the results only as part of a "carrot and stick" approach. They are provided information only on a need to know basis.

The Stage II Questionnaire. Stage II organizations must address the issue of customer retention, and the factors affecting it generally relate to processes that touch the customer and thus make it easy (or hard) for the customer to do business with you. VOC measurement therefore becomes a means of addressing the issues driving internal process improvement and alignment. For an example of how one best practice organization has developed a VOC measurement approach to meet the need to improve internal process, see the case study on the Kodak Corporation.

KODAK CORPORATION
FROM THE INSIDE OUT

Kodak Corporation provides an excellent example of a best practice use of VOC measurement to assess and improve on the processes that ultimately touch the customer.

To start, the company takes a much broader view of VOC and includes customer panels, market research customer feedback and more into its VOC measurement. As set out in Figure 4.3 on page 84, the organization has recognized that it will need VOC input as input to four critical processes that drive its action with the customer. These are the processes that drive strategic direction, creative focus, implementation and reaction to market feedback. For each of these process categories it has identified the VOC information required and the most common sources of that information.

Once this information is collected, and it is extensive, the organization can then identify which process activities are deficient, and which meet or exceed customer expectations. It can also identify customer priorities and assess the impact that process improvement can bring. And by sharing this information throughout the organization it can achieve organization-wide alignment. Staff realize customer priorities and issues and understand why their support is essential.

The Stage III Questionnaire. At Stage III, organizations have completely shifted focus. The goal becomes the identification of a customer-by-customer approach to addressing the issues affecting customer satisfaction and the improvement of value in the customer relationship.

To start, you must understand the major issues that drive customer satisfaction and dissatisfaction. Create a shopping list of issues, and then, with a select group of customers prioritize this list, expanding or contracting as appropriate. This will get you down to a more manageable group of issues that you can now group and represent on a performance wheel, similar to the one that follows.

Figure 4.4 shows a performance wheel with four quadrants that relate to key customer care issues. You may choose to describe them

Voc Level	What It Is	Most Common Sources of Information
VOC 1 **Strategic Direction**	VOC 1 is the higher-level customer understanding that identifies basic market needs and trends and shapes the strategies for broad-scale technology and business investments. This understanding is essential input to broad portfolio decisions and definitions of market participation strategies.	• Learning bank information (high-level organizational learning and market understanding) • Historical data, knowledge, and experience • Market situation analyses • External experts • Futures research and secondary research
VOC 2 **Creative Focus**	VOC 2 is the processed customer information that is the basis for creatively defining new product concepts, product families, and services. Business management coordinates the use of market research techniques to identify specific customer product and service needs. With other functional areas, management also uses this information to shape product family and technology and product platform strategies.	• Customer panels • Customer visits • Market research • Trade shows • Sales calls
VOC 3 **Implementation**	VOC 3 is the processed customer information that represents the stated and implied customer requirements for product performance, features, and benefits that drive product definition activities. Thus, it drives implementation or commercialization activities beyond the ideational stage. For example, product commercialization teams use this information as input for the Quality Function Deployment (QFD) product definition.	• Customer panels and site visits • Test markets (trade trials) • Market research • Quality Function Deployment (QFD) • Customer feedback
VOC 4 **Reaction to Market Feedback**	VOC 4 is the processed information that results from customer responses to our products, services, and marketing activities. This market feedback drives corrective action to existing and future products and services, and it is used to improve all Kodak value propositions and marketing programs.	• Customer feedback, as from Kodak Information Center (KIC) • Sales education and customer interface (Kodak Education and Development Center) • Customer satisfaction studies, including lost sale studies • Customer visits • Sales calls

Figure 4.3: Kodak: Voice of the Customer—A Guidebook

differently, once you group your issues; however, in this case, they are:

- Customer focus
- Fiscal/financial focus
- Operations/logistics focus
- Product/services focus

Within each quadrant, the wheel shows a number of issues that reflect the organization's performance in that quadrant.

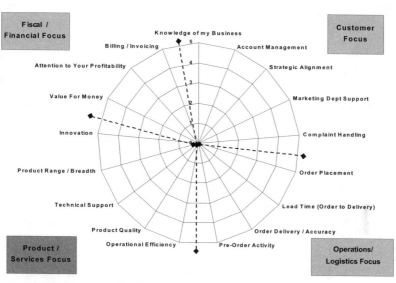

Figure 4.4: Measurement Wheel

Developing the Stage III Performance Wheel

One best practice organization arrived at its performance wheel using a series of overview questions. Not intended to be used as part of the questionnaire, these questions represented problems for which the organization sought answers—in essence, the answers that the VOC measurement could potentially provide.

Relationship with the Client

- Have all team members developed relationships with top management, integral departments and operational staff?
- Has a "client map" been established so that we may better understand the power issues within the client company?
- Do we meet regularly enough with the decision makers within the customer's firm?
- Do all team members have a precise idea of the products and services being sold in other divisions or departments within the customer's organization?
- Do we use our publications actively to reinforce the customer relationship?
- Do we know what our competitors are doing in the areas in which we have a product or service?

Service quality:

- Have we delivered on our promises in terms of creativity, deadlines, technical and industry-specific knowledge?
- Has the client specifically told us we've been delivering the service it expected?
- Do we know the two or three main challenges facing our customer today?
- Do we know which problems the customer may be looking to us to help solve?
- Have we offered ideas on how our customer might solve its main problems?
- Have we taken into account the customer's global needs?
- Have key members of the account team visited the customer's key operating sites?
- Have we demonstrated to the customer areas in which we can sell additional product or service lines during the past year?
- Have we warned the client sufficiently in advance of changes in our account management team?

Pricing/Value for Money

- Have we provided a detailed explanation of the prices we charge?
- Have we considered offering free or discounted service—for example, in training or technological support—in order to demonstrate our long-term commitment to the client?
- Have we demonstrated how our pricing structure has saved the customer as a result of our recommendations or suggestions?
- Do we let the customer know quickly about impending price changes?

Once it had listed these issues, the company identified which questions would best be answered through VOC formal research, which could be tracked and which required development by the account team.

The performance wheel in the following section *How to Present the Data* shows the results of the process just outlined.

4. How to Present the Data

How the data should be presented will depend in large part on the stage of evolution of your organization. Stage III organizations, for example, focus not on quantity but rather on quality. The measurement process applies to each customer individually, and customer needs are considered unique. Because of this focus, grouping of customers' responses has very little relevance. Based on the result of the VOC summary, an action plan is made. Each action plan will be different, as it reflects the immediate needs of each unique customer. Summarizing the data has no immediate value as it will not and cannot affect the customer plan. This is more of a nice to have analysis, rather than one that is a pressing need to have.

The performance wheel on page 88 shows the VOC results for one customer. It represents the collective interviews with six senior managers within a customer organization. This summary wheel reflects the customer organization's specific needs, rather than a watered-down generalization. While the research findings reveal significant back-up detail, the key issues that needed to be addressed can still appear in a one-page snapshot like a performance wheel. Let's review what this representation provides:

- CSI Rating 3.0—This reflects the response to the customer satisfaction question that was posed at the beginning of the questionnaire. The question read:

  "Overall, based on the products and services you receive from XYZ, please rate your overall level of satisfaction (where 1 is not at all satisfied and 5 is very satisfied).

Not at all Satisfied				Very Satisfied"
1	2	3	4	5

  On average, the customer has indicated that there is significant room for improvement.

- There are no areas where this organization is superior to the customer's best supplier. There are three areas—technical support, order placement, order delivery accuracy and billing/invoicing—where it is equal to competition (where the "x" and "o" overlap). This is in response to the following question that was asked for each spoke in the wheel:

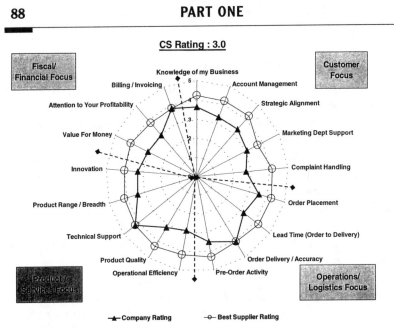

Figure 4.5: Performance Measurement

"On this wheel, I will ask you to rate the best supplier that you deal with (with an O on the same scale of 1 to 5). For example, if Company XYZ is the best supplier or equal to another best supplier, you should give the same score for both XYZ and best supplier questions (X and O should therefore be on top of each other)."

If one of your suppliers is particularly strong in the category being discussed you should give this best supplier a score higher than the one you gave to Company XYZ. There should never be any Os below the Xs since if Company XYZ is the best supplier, the O and X should overlap, and we are not asking about suppliers who are worse than Company XYZ.

- The organization is substantially weaker than the best supplier in all other areas.
- The three most important areas that the customer sees as critical action items based on the analysis of results are account management, market support and attention to customer profitability, and in all these cases, Company XYZ is performing at satisfaction levels of 3 or lower, a less than exemplary performance.

5. Assessing the Accuracy of Your VOC Findings

Once you have VOC input, you need to ensure that the results accurately reflect the customer's thoughts and opinions. In other words, did you hear them right? As a result, there's a strong need to involve the client in the team's assessment of the VOC results and the prioritization of the issues developed. The main objective of VOC feedback is to analyze the information obtained in order to enable your account teams to strengthen your customer relationships. So, how do you go about doing this?

You must create learning relationships with your customers. Here's the underlying idea, simply put: the customer teaches the provider to give it the service it wants, and that works to make the bond between the customer and the provider extremely tight. A learning relationship—in other words, a relationship that gets "smarter" with every interaction between customer and provider— is the lynchpin of customer loyalty.

The follow-up process of reviewing the findings with the customer is the most important part of the VOC initiative. Without performing follow-up, you cannot ensure that you have truly heard the voice of your customer and fully understand its operating challenges. Of course, it's risky to ask your customer, "How did we do?" They might very well respond with criticism simply because you've asked for their comments. But when that happens, it gives you an opportunity to address these criticisms as well.

Follow-up needs to be incorporated into the very fabric of your organization. For example, whenever you plan site visits and meetings, ensure that you've allocated time to follow up on the VOC survey. Resist the temptation to consider that you already know how the customer feels, because you have done the survey. Customers' needs change, and you must be ready to listen and respond.

Finally, if there's any one point in the service provided that demands the investment of your resources, it's the period after you've followed up and collected customer feedback. A senior executive once said, "Customers are always happy to take part in the survey. They're even happier when they see that we've responded."

USING YOUR DATA

In fashioning your VOC initiative, you need to take it beyond questionnaire development and the actual collection of data. Too often, organizations implement VOC measurement programs that effectively obtain good, solid customer data only to falter when attempting to use the results for maximum effect.

How can you avoid this? In order to make full use of your VOC results, it's essential that you establish a formal, management-enforced commitment, *prior to the VOC measurement launch*, to the following three principles:

1. You will follow up on responses from individual customers and act on your follow-up findings.
2. You will aggregate your findings to form the basis for strategic change at the organizational level.
3. You will ensure that management at all levels will take active, personal, continuous and visible ownership of the VOC measurement process.

While all three principles are critical, the third one counts the most. Senior and field management must be willing to invest their time and energy in the VOC measurement initiative and the importance of the initiative must be communicated to all levels of the organization. With such a commitment, your VOC initiative will be an engine for action. Without it, you simply have data.

The Need for a Customer Bill of Rights

Frequently, I've spoken about the concept of the customer bill of rights (the CBR), and it still amazes me the number of organizations that express reluctance to establish and publish a CBR. In my previous book,[2] I asked my readers some important questions that highlight the need for an organization to develop, publish and distribute a CBR:

- Do your customers know what they can expect from you?
- Do they know what you offer as your core service?
- Do your internal customers, your employees, know the standards of customer service you expect them to deliver? Do they know what standards your management will meet in delivering quality service to them?
- Do you have a service strategy and a customer bill of rights?
- Do you proudly post your CBR on the wall in full sight of your customers?

---

[2] Stanley A. Brown, *What Customers Value Most*, John Wiley & Sons, Toronto: 1995.

Why is the CBR important and what does it have to do with our discussion of VOC? Consider this. Regardless of the industry in which you operate, your CBR will fulfill two purposes. First, it tells your employees what you expect of them as a routine standard of performance. Second, as a service policy the CBR makes a bold commitment of service to your customers.

Unlike the mission or vision statement, a traditionally top-down document usually prepared by senior management with limited, if any, input from the front-line, the CBR is generally a bottom-up document. It represents significant input from both your customers and your front-line staff. It clearly states what your company will deliver to the customer—in other words, the service commitment for which you want to be known. The CBR also makes a clear statement that you, as a committed and concerned supplier organization, are anxious to obtain VOC input into how you're meeting your service commitment.

Organizations that have developed the CBR usually evidence a strong sense of pride in the document, sending it out to customers, and in some cases, printing it on the back of invoices and business cards.

The CBR represents a significant opportunity to place your commitment to your customers out in the open for all to see. The section that follows provides you with some tips on how your organization can develop its own customer bill of rights.

Building the Customer Bill of Rights

It's astonishing that many organizations do not see the value of establishing and publishing a CBR. What better way can an organization express its commitment to the customer than making its customer care policy an open document for all to see? If you're ready to make a commitment to your customers, here are a few tips for developing a CBR for your organization.

Start inside your organization. Ensure that you enlist the assistance of those individuals within your organization who "touch" the customer to help you identify the critical issues. This allows you to tap into their reservoir of customer-related knowledge and lets them be a part of the process.

Use a customer focus group. It's always wisest to develop your CBR with the help of your customers, but make sure that your customer group represents a true baseline cross-section of your customer base.

Validate. Go to a sample of your customers and validate that the issues you have pinpointed really are essential.

Do a reality check. Ensure that each item you make a part of the CBR:

- Is measurable (quantitatively)
- Is deliverable as part of a process that "touches" the customer
- Has a minimum acceptable standard
- Has meaning in the eyes of the customer

Prepare a "gap analysis." A gap analysis should summarize the results of the above activities and draw conclusions as to the gap between the customer, staff and management expectations along the key dimensions of customer care center performance and capabilities. The gap analysis should detail where differences exist.

This is the point at which senior management must get involved, as some tough decisions will need to be made. Are you willing, and can you afford, to meet all of these expectations? And for those promises to which you're willing to commit, what will your minimum acceptable standard be?

Start the culture change. Once you've prepared your first draft of the customer bill of rights, review this document with the organization as a whole. Explain why each term of the CBR has been chosen, how conforming to the standards will be measured and the implications of the document for your organization. Hear everyone's comments and make modifications and additions as appropriate. Repeat this exercise with a select group of customers. Then set out an action plan to ensure that your organization will be able to deliver service that meets the terms of your new CBR.

Be prepared to communicate your CBR and solicit the VOC. Once you have demonstrated your consistent ability to deliver the service promised in your CBR, you should begin to aggressively communicate your message. Post it on your walls, print it on the back of your invoices and send it out as a special communication, possibly through a newsletter, to your customers. Remember, the CBR will be your standard against which you will constantly be measuring your performance. Listen to customer complaints and take corrective action as appropriate. Perform research constantly to identify your effectiveness in meeting the terms of the CBR and the areas in which you need improvement. In order to be successful, the CBR must be respected by both your organization and your customer base—and this respect can come only through a consistent demonstration of your commitment to the promises you have made in the CBR.

The customer bill of rights stands for your commitment to your customers, but in order to be effective, your entire organization must stand behind your promise to deliver. After all, nobody likes to admit failure, and this fear of failure itself may do more to encourage excellence, and align your organization, than anything else.

Your CBR will clearly establish the minimum standards of customer care your organization is prepared to provide to all of its customers. This does not, of course, mean that you will not raise these standards for a select group of customers—in fact, the Stage III organization generally becomes adept at tailoring the promises in its CBR to meet individual customer needs. Nevertheless, your customers in general do need to know that you have a set of standards to which you have made a public commitment and against which you are prepared to be measured.

The Customer Bill of Rights

Your customer bill of rights should state, clearly and concisely, the customer care you are prepared to deliver to all of your customers. Take a look at the following example for an idea as to how you may want to prepare your CBR.

Mount Sinai Hospital, Toronto, Canada—Our Philosophy of Patient Care

It is our objective and commitment that:

1. All patients should receive considerate and respectful care.

2. All patients know the name(s) of the physician(s) in charge of their care.

3. Medical staff keep patients informed about their care, their diagnosis, anticipated treatment and prognosis. This information should be made understandable to the patient. When it is not, in the opinion of the physician, advisable to give such information to the patient, the information should be made available to the appropriate person on his or her behalf, when so requested.

4. The right of the patient to refuse treatment be recognized after the patient has been informed of the possible medical consequences of such refusal.

5. The hospital and its staff ensure that there is not undue invasion of patient privacy in delivery of medical care.

6. Confidentiality of patient information be preserved. The patient should be apprised of the fact that Mount Sinai Hospital is a University affiliated hospital, undergraduate and postgraduate medical students may be involved in his or her care under supervision of his or her own physician.

7. Within the capacity of the hospital, patients' requests for services be respected.

8. Coordination of patient care be ensured.

9. Policies and procedures affecting patient conduct within the hospital be made known to the patient on admission.

Here's another example that reinforces the importance of the customer bill of rights as a focal point. New York has been criticized often for its taxi industry. While the clean-up was massive, there is one other change that occurred that had a marked impact on obtaining the VOC and assessing performance.

Found Inside a Taxi in New York

As a taxi rider, you have the right to:
- Direct the destination and route to use
- A courteous English speaking driver who knows the streets of Manhattan and the way to major outer-borough destinations
- A driver that knows and obeys all traffic laws
- Air conditioning on demand
- A radio-free (silent) trip
- Smoke and incense-free air
- A clean passenger seat area
- A clean trunk
- Refuse a tip if the above is not complied with

Now that drives attention and focus!

VOC and the Best Practice Organizations

In the examples that follow, notice the variety of methods being used to obtain the VOC.

There is no one best method, but the underlying reasons driving the use of VOC have some degree of consistency. Best practices organizations use VOC measurement to:

• Identify processes or failure points that need attention
• Set corporate direction
• Ensure consistency of practice
• Maintain customer focus

Notice how each of the organizations that follow achieve this.

TOYOTA USA
READING THE PULSE OF ITS CUSTOMER

Toyota USA has implemented a best practice approach to understanding the needs of its customers that has, at its core:

• The creation of a customer satisfaction index (CSI)
• A drive toward consistent improvement
• Attention to customer complaints and factors leading to customer dissatisfaction factors.

Like most car manufacturers, Toyota has a fundamental need to keep close to its customers in each of the many segments of its business. In developing its best practices, the company found that one measurement system by itself was insufficient to assist the company in coming to a better understanding of how their customers view their vehicles, how the customers view the dealers from whom they have made their most recent purchase, what customers think of product enhancements, the likelihood of a customer returning, and finally, how their customers view the service department. Because of the multiple points of contact that customers have with the company and its franchised dealers, the mechanic, sales staff, warranty claims department, marketing, customer service centre and so on, Toyota turned to a variety of means to collect an authentic VOC.

Rising to the challenge before them, the organization developed two distinct surveys:

• **The new sale mail-in survey.** This survey focuses on the new sale experience and is given to each customer immediately after a new car purchase. The information collected by the survey tracks customer satisfaction by dealer and individual sales representative. Summarized daily, dealers can view their own data on Toyota's Intranet. Different summaries are made available to Toyota's senior management, again through the Intranet.

- **The service telephone survey.** Conducted through its in-house teleservices unit, the telephone survey measures customer satisfaction by specific dealer and individual service technician. To ensure that customers do not feel inundated by survey requests, this service survey is not conducted within the first 60 days after the sale, and following the initial telephone survey, the respondent cannot be surveyed again for a six-month period.

The two surveys developed by Toyota effectively combine customer satisfaction with the buying process, delivery experience, service experience, and product quality. Both surveys are analyzed on a similar basis, with each question attracting a rating on a five-point scale, from "1" (very dissatisfied) to "3" (neutral) to "5" (very satisfied). The company then prepares an index to track overall customer satisfaction that is computed by the responses.

Why VOC Research?

Toyota's demonstrated passion for conducting VOC research stems from findings from a variety of studies it has conducted on customer satisfaction. It has found that:

- A direct correlation exists between a customer's perception of the quality of the service provided and his or her willingness to recommend a dealer to others.
- A direct correlation exists between overall satisfaction and both customer loyalty and customer recommendation.
- A direct correlation also exists between customer loyalty and customer recommendations and the company's market share and size of its revenues.
- A customer's intention to purchase a Toyota product again was based on the customer's level of satisfaction with both the sale—in terms of both the dealer and the product—and the service.
- Other reasons for the company's reliance on VOC are that in a blind survey of its customers, conducted by a third party research firm, it discovered that customer satisfaction was actually 20 points higher among those customers

surveyed, compared to those customers who were not. Why is this? All customers want to feel wanted, and the best way to make them feel wanted is to let them know that their opinions count. The chart below demonstrates the impact of dissatisfaction:

Customer Satisfaction Findings			
Satisfaction Level with Sale		Intention to Buy Again	Sales per 1000 customers
Sales	Service		
Satisfied	Satisfied	87.1 percent	871
Dissatisfied	Dissatisfied	22.9 percent	229

Figure 4.6: The Impact of Customer Dissatisfaction

Clearly, the more satisfied the customers are with both the sales and service component, the more likely they are to repurchase. To further emphasize the point, look at how that translates to the average number of purchases per 1000 people and multiply this figure by $20,000 or more. Would you put attention to customer satisfaction if this was at stake?

The Customer Assist Center

Toyota also receives comments and complaints through its customer assist center. Using complaint management software, Toyota collects all inquiries and complaints, which are then traced, summarized and routed to those personnel most affected by the complaints. It publicizes its 1-800 customer assist center number widely and actively seeks questions, comments or complaints. In fact, the number is included on every piece of documentation given to the customer.

Let's review the core principle of Toyota's program once again:

- **The creation of a customer satisfaction index (CSI)**. The index is based on two key surveys, the new sale and service survey that are constantly under review. This index, and the monthly trend analysis established from it, forms the basis of annual dealer planning meetings, meetings designed to make change rather than keep the status quo.

- **A drive toward consistent improvement**. For Toyota, this can only be accomplished through not only the dissemination of the survey information back to the dealer network promptly so that appropriate action can be taken, but also feeding that information internally to new product development, marketing and others that can effect change.

- **Attention to customer complaints and factors leading to customer dissatisfaction factors.** Its customer assist center makes it easy for customers to complain. Toyota also tracks customer complaints using sophisticated contact management software. It sifts through this information and disseminates the results throughout the organization.

KODAK
A MULTIDIMENSIONAL VIEW OF THE CUSTOMER

Kodak has made best practices in VOC research and information sharing a part of the very fabric of its organization. Each of its operating divisions exhibits a passion for VOC research, and the company encourages a diversity of approaches.

As one Kodak senior executive put it, "Each one of us must play a role in making Kodak a truly customer-focused organization. We consider this a critical part of the cultural change that needs to take place. Our success as a company depends on it. We believe that achieving a voice of the customer capability won't simply help us improve our marketing ability. We see the voice of the customer as a basic business focus that will also help us work to improve quality, control costs and grow our revenues and our profitability."

Kodak's best practices include:

- Occasionally "getting in" and "living with" the customer. "Shadowing" the customer—literally following them around as they do their jobs—allows Kodak to see through the customer's eyes how the product is used and how it performs, how easy it is to install and to maintain.

- Establishing a marketing goal requiring 100 percent of all critical decisions to be made using VOC information.

- Creating a process that leverages VOC data from other regions to establish a "hit list" of top VOC opportunities.

- Gathering and analyzing VOC information through customer site visits, use of standing customer panels/councils and establishment of customer user groups.

- Identifying individual customer issues through the VOC

survey process and resolving identified problems by local field management, at times while a survey is still in progress.

- Including VOC/customer satisfaction results in business reviews.
- Using VOC information to monitor the effect of actions taken.
- Hosting engineers within its product divisions and other interested parties who wish to listen to—and help answer—real-time customer questions.
- Establishing an index to monitor worldwide customer satisfaction measurement activity and drive follow-up action for areas in need of improvement. This index has become a part of management's performance plan and has regional, business unit, and country components.

LESSONS LEARNED

As we have found throughout this chapter, organizations must learn to recognize the importance of listening to the voice of the customer. But having acknowledged that VOC is essential, executing effective research is the next hurdle to overcome, followed closely by analysis and action planning. There are several things that can help you strengthen this pillar. For example, recognizing your stage in the customer care evolution is essential. Where you are in your evolution has an important impact on the types of questions you will ask in the VOC questionnaire and how the questionnaire will be administered. The closer you get to Stage III the more focused you should be on conducting face-to-face interviews and truly hearing the voice (and seeing the face) of the customer.

Questionnaires have to be designed keeping in mind how you will be using the results of the research. You must concentrate only on need to know information bits on which you can take action, and ignore nice to know luxuries. You will only have a limited amount of interview time with the customer, so make it count.

The VOC questionnaire must include more than customer satisfaction measurement. IBM provides an excellent Stage III example of why a process view must be taken when designing the questionnaire, and as FedEx demonstrates, it is essential that you identify whether the customer is satisfied or dissatisfied with the processes that touch them. Even as important, you must be able to uncover customer priorities so that you will be able to take immediate action.

The information must be distributed throughout the organization. As our Toyota example points out, those who have the most contact with the customer need current reliable information that addresses customer needs, but even those who have limited contact need to be informed and involved.

All of the best practices organizations that we discussed in this chapter did not rely on one single means of obtaining the voice of the customer—multiple methods were used. Kodak clearly demonstrated that with careful thought, each of these means can be compatible and synergistic and can lead to a multidimensional view of the customer and the issues facing them.

Keep the VOC simple and focused. This chapter provided you with some simple effective tools that can help you achieve meaningful results, among them the customer bill of rights and the performance wheel. Each of these can clearly show you where you are today and direct you to where you must be tomorrow.

Regardless of your stage of evolution, you can develop best practices in VOC measurement. With care and a commitment to gathering VOC input and implementing improvements based on the VOC process, your organization can join the ranks of leaders such as IBM, Toyota, FedEx and Kodak.

CHAPTER FIVE

The Importance of Technology

A KEY ENABLER

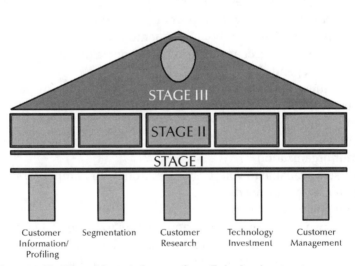

Figure 5.1: The Pillars of Strategic Customer Care—Technology Investment

Technological advances play a large role in shaping the business revolution we all face as we approach the twenty-first century. To a large degree the new corporate environment is the result of changes in technology that include the proliferation of intelligent devices both in the home and at the office, a rapidly developing electronic commerce infrastructure that is effectively modernizing the traditional supply chain, lower entry barriers and the public's insatiable desire for even more advanced technology.

According to a recent Yankee Group report,[1] there is no question that there is no alternative to technology. As product cycles get shorter and markets get more competitive, companies that employ best of breed customer acquisition and retention tools will hold a substantial advantage. In addition, as companies integrate their internal operations and business partners to create the extended enterprise, their customer management process will need to adapt to new team and virtual selling models.

Does this mean we should go out and buy the latest and greatest technology? Do we force the newest advances on our customers or our organization? Or do we first ask ourselves, "What is the right technology for my organization at this stage of its customer care evolution?"

You must always look first at the stage of evolution you're in, because even the quickest, most efficient, greatest piece of technology will not do you any good if your organization has not evolved to the point where it can be implemented seamlessly and used properly. So the correct answer to all of the questions above is, quite simply, "It depends."

Whether or not your organization should invest in any particular new technology will depend on a number of factors:

- Your stage of evolution
- The effect of the technology in driving or enabling change in your organization
- What is available to your customers from your competitors
- Your customers' needs
- Your goals and strategies

The last two are the most important factors to be considered: you must assess the impact of the technology in light of your customers' needs and the goals and strategies of your organization.

BUILDING THE FOUNDATION: CHOOSING YOUR TECHNOLOGY CAREFULLY

In this chapter, we'll continue exploring the principles underlying the customer care process by focusing on the ways that best practice organizations at each stage of the evolutionary process have

---

[1] Yankee Group, Volume 2, No. 12, June 1997.

dealt with technological advances. Most importantly, to help you in preparing for your evolutionary journey, we've included a four-step process that identifies the best way for you to make your technological choices. Finally, to round the chapter off, we will discuss a variety of tools for success, many of which you may find suitable for your organization today.

THE ROLE OF TECHNOLOGY: MATCHING IT TO YOUR STAGE OF EVOLUTION

A comparison of research results from IDEAS 97 and IDEAS 96 shows that the major questions facing us have not changed at all. As you can see in Figure 5.2 below, we still face the same pressing issues: improved use of technology to enhance customer service, statistical real-time and historical reporting and centralization/consolidation to achieve improvement—all technology related issues.

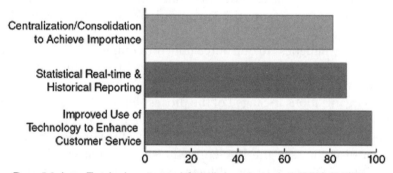

Figure 5.2: Issues That Are Important and Critically Important in both IDEAS 96 & 97

Like a deer caught in the headlights of an oncoming car, we are frozen, not knowing which way to go. For your organizations these issues, just like the deer's predicament, can be considered matters of life and death. After all, our quest is for survival.

How *do* you decide which way to go? The wrong choice means that the deer gets flattened by the car and the organization by the changing economy. How can you avoid making mistakes? Usually it's a case of organizational maturity. Depending on your stage in the evolution, your "best technological bet" will be different. That's because organizations in each stage have different goals, needs and different focuses. And we've come far enough now to recognize that, as with everything else, no technology can claim a "one size fits all" answer.

Stage I—The Desire for Internal Control

Organizations in Stage I exhibit a number of common operating characteristics:

- An attitude that's best described as internal command and control rather than a shift of power to those personnel who are closest to the customer—the sales force.
- A preference for "homegrown" applications—internally developed and configured software applications with limited support tools—rather than choosing well-defined, packaged solutions.
- A lack of connection between the buyer of the technological solution—management—and the ultimate user—sales and customer service staff. The result is the purchase of support tools that drive internal efficiency but which frequently have a negative impact on the organization's interaction with the customer.
- An unwillingness to outsource noncore competencies, including customer care. This is the direct result of the command and control management mindset.

Organizations in Stage I of the process tend to have primarily a behind-sight-of-vision focus, as shown in Figure 5.3. For a more in-depth discussion of the concept of sight-of-vision and behind-sight-of-vision, see the box entitled *"Focus on the Visible or the Invisible?"* Often this type of focus stems from a basic inferiority complex at this stage about the organization's ability to effectively control its front-line staff. As a result, the organization becomes more internally focused and technological applications with a command and control, or silo, mentality appear more important.

However, keep in mind that regardless of where your organization is in the evolution, you can always develop best practices appropriate to your particular stage. Since the focus at this stage is appropriately on command and control issues, a best practice organization at this stage would:

- Invest heavily in software, hardware and training that add efficiency and effectiveness. Granted, the applications will be much

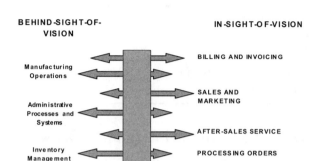

Figure 5.3: The Meaning of Sight-of-Vision

more silo-oriented and more focused on the sales functions from a primarily internal perspective, but again, this is an appropriate orientation and focus for a Stage I organization concerned with command and control.

- Automate their processes. At this stage most organizations have a strong need for executive information systems (EIS) in particular. An EIS will help you analyze your data and present it in a readily useable format—graphs, charts and control panels.
- Limit its focus almost exclusively to monitoring and control purposes, because the goals and strategies of the organization rely primarily on such a focus.
- Make investments in e-commerce or the Internet that focus on e-mail and static applications such as lead qualification (which customers are most likely to want to buy your products), contact management (tracking customer contacts, brochures and sales literature sent), sales reports, expense reports and sales/customer acquisition reporting and monitoring.

Focus on the Visible or the Invisible?

Exactly what is "sight-of-vision" and "behind-sight-of-vision"? As you can see in Figure 5.3 some of the processes in your organization will be more visible to your customers than others. A behind-sight-of-vision process typically focuses on your organization's administrative processes, as well as on your product and/or service production processes. On the other hand, sight-of-vision processes are those in your organization that in fact "touch" the customer in some way or other. Examples of sight-of-vision processes include:

- Sales contact processes
- After-sales service
- Technical service
- Order processing and billing
- Customer complaint process

Stage II: The Need for Information Sharing

At Stage II of the evolution, organizations become most interested in the integration of organizational functions in order to achieve synergy and efficiency. An organization that is taking its first steps in the Stage II evolutionary transformation is usually beginning to utilize the lessons it has learned in its Stage I experience.

In this stage, organizations share some common characteristics:
- A focus on interaction with the customer.
- An undifferentiated emphasis on the importance of all customers and interactions with them.
- A keen interest in knowledge management, the sharing of current, reliable information throughout the organization for better informed decision making.
- A growing concern to become more interactive with the customer.
- A move toward increased cross-functionality; that is, having front-line staff responsible for a combination of tasks. For example, the customer service staff will be responsible for order entry and billing inquiries, the net result being that the customer is not transferred on multiple occasions and receives improved service from informed staff.
- An integration of front office processes—such as sales, inside sales, after-sales—with back office procedures such as billing and credit. In this case, the systems that the front-line staff use have access to all the systems required to handle the above tasks simplifying inquiries and file updating capabilities.

The Stage II organization generally undergoes a transformation in its regard for its sales force and experiences a new desire to make its salespeople more efficient and effective. This can be done only by placing more information and decision-making power in their hands, that in turn implies a shift in the power base and a greater willingness to share customer-related information with the front-line staff.

In Stage II, the beginnings of a change in corporate culture become evident. Examples of technology best practices at this stage include:

- Investment in technology that focuses on applications that interact with the customer, such as interactive, Web-enabled order entry systems (providing immediate acknowledgment of the order, or if the product is out of stock, providing suggestions or delivery options to consider).
- A more aggressive use of the Internet for functions like order status inquiries and interactive order processing.
- Cooperation between internal and external sales forces.
- Greater investment in technology that supports teamwork such as groupware tools.
- Increased activity in development of programs that promote customer loyalty and customer retention.

The best practice organization in Stage II recognizes that one of its greatest challenges is balancing the desires of management—cost efficiency, productivity, improved performance and control—with the needs of its customers—quality customer service, ease of access and customer control.

Organizations successfully meet the challenge of meeting this delicate balance by breaking with the principles of traditional customer care and delivering differentiated service and varying levels of customer support to different customer segments. The result is improved profitability and, more importantly, enhanced customer satisfaction.

Best practice organizations recognize that managing the customer relationship is built around two main concepts:

1. "Know me"—know who the customer is when they call you, and know the customer's needs.
2. "Hear me"—when the customer has cause to complain or wishes to give you ideas.

Stage II: Focus on Teamwork

As the Stage II organization begins to recognize the benefits of teamwork among its internal and external sales forces, software applications that allow it to share databases such as customer files become increasingly important. These applications assist in shifting power and experience/knowledge to both the customer and front-line personnel who

"touch" the customer and include applications in areas such as:
- Product configuration
- Presentations, proposals and recommendations
- Electronic catalogs
- Order management
- Customer service

Stage III: The Focus on Knowledge Management

Organizations operating within Stage III think within a new paradigm—an enterprise-wide paradigm that moves them beyond the concept of customer retention to that of strategic customer care. In other words, Stage III organizations understand that:
- Not all customers are the same and not all customers deserve the same level of service.
- Technology and efficiency will drive success.
- Internal competencies may not be sufficient and strategic alliances may have to be considered in order to provide the customer with a total solution.
- Customers, as highlighted in Chapter 1, beome more valuable the longer they remain customers, but to reap the benefits of this requires customer profit maximization.
- Satisfied customers lead to higher profits.

At this stage, organizations focus on enterprise applications that share knowledge, react more responsively to their customers and permit the organization to be proactive. They recognize as well that one of the keys to success is customer longevity.

Some best practices in the use of technology among Stage III organizations include:
- Proactive database marketing systems that identify those accounts that should be most receptive to certain products and services and that leverage the organization's information sources.
- The ability to analyze profitability, by customer and group of customers (more on this in Chapter 9).
- The use of the "knowledge pipeline" as a key strategic tool for information sharing across the organization.
- Executive information systems (EIS) that are more robust than Stage I applications in that they allow the organization to be more responsive to changes and shifts in both market sectors

and customer profitability performance.

- Applications tools specifically geared to support the functions of the organization's sales force, including sales, customer support, external help desk, field service, quality assurance and competitive and customer intelligence.

Restructuring undertaken by the Stage III organization usually results in a more centralized hub and spoke environment. By re-engineering the sales process and empowering the sales representatives, sales management becomes free to focus on recruiting, hiring and training new representatives, a more efficient and productive use of time.

TIP

The Best Practice Stage III Information System

Best practice organizations in Stage III should generally look for information systems that focus on:

- Shared data, to be used by both customer support and customer service staff
- The ability to collect and share information for the continuous improvement of customer service, business processes, products and services
- Enabling customer contact representatives to act as the starting point for corporate product development, customer retention and quality management initiatives

---

A STEP-BY-STEP APPROACH TO TECHNOLOGY INVESTMENTS

Now that we have discussed the various best practices in technology for the three stages of the evolutionary process, we will next outline a step-by-step approach to show you how to make the best technology investment choices for your organization.

To begin with, you must remember that your organization cannot be all things to all people, nor can you invest in everything that's available. You therefore must take a step-wise approach to transforming customer care.

Step 1: Readiness vs. Customer Needs Assessment

In this initial step, you must review not only your internal practices—where you are today, how silo focused you are and your readiness to change—you must also assess the needs of your customers. And, as discussed in Chapter 3, not all customers are the same, nor do they all want or deserve the same level of service or the same access to your technology. Therefore, you should review the needs of your targeted customer base in particular.

The point of this analysis is to assist you to:

- **Identify gaps in perspective.** These gaps, which relate to who should have access to certain data and how the data should be used, affect the type of technology and systems that may be required. Gaps can exist between the customer and customer support, between customer support and other functions within the organization such as sales and billing, credit and inventory management and between senior, middle and front-line service providers. The best technology in the world will not improve your customer service, enhance revenues and increase customer retention, if the organization—and for that matter, the customer—is not ready to accept it.
- **Establish priorities.** The fact is, most organizations simply do not have the manpower capacity nor the financial means to absorb dramatic change and move immediately to Stage III customer care. Your most important segments will define your priorities for change and the speed with which you can introduce new processes and technology, so you must remember to pay attention to them.
- **Identify change management issues.** Do not underestimate the impact of change on your employees. Readiness assessment is a highly underrated tool. Such an assessment helps you to identify change issues and the hurdles you must overcome when introducing a new approach to customer care.

You must remember that, while you can design the best processes in the world enabled by state-of-the-art technology, you are doomed to failure if your people do not buy into the project with you. To succeed, you must get everyone on board.

Step 2: Change Identification

In Step 1 above, you identified the change management issues facing your introduction of a new customer care process. Now, you must identify the changes in process or technology that you need to address—that is, key changes that your organization must undergo. These often include:

- **Re-engineering of processes that touch the customer**. These often include marketing, sales acquisition, order entry, after-sales service and the customer complaints/comments process.
- **Software solution selection**. A number of choices exist, including enterprise solutions (a Stage III requirement), sales force automation tools (used effectively by Stage II and Stage III organizations) and application specific Stage I tools such as contact management software.

Step 3: Transition/Migration Strategy

Most organizations fail in this step because of their do-it-yourself attitude. When you need help, get help. Don't try to do it all yourself. Most people cannot objectively balance priorities. If you pay for a service from a qualified third party integrator/consultant, you are more likely to meet your budget and timetables.

Most organizations need help in:

- **Best practices reviews**. Your time is better spent learning from both the mistakes and the successes of others who have made them before you.
- **Implementation planning**. Do not underestimate the power of a proper project plan and the identification of critical milestones, dates when deliverables are due or testing must be completed. You simply will not succeed without assistance from an objective and qualified third party who can push you beyond your limits when necessary.

Step 4: Implementation and Pilot Testing

This is the big step when true transformation occurs. You must determine here how you want to appear to your various customer segments and be able to achieve that transformation from your current state. Pilot testing is used because it's always better to test with a select group of customers before making wholesale changes.

TOOLS FOR SUCCESS

There are a number of important tools that you should consider using in order to move forward along the evolutionary path. And as you move forward, these tools will also evolve and provide you more functionality and allow you to be closer to the customer. These tools include:

- The Internet

- Sales force automation
- Enterprise customer care (more likely a Stage III application)
- Virtual selling

The Role of the Internet in Providing Customer Care

The World Wide Web today offers an increasingly effective way to interact with your customers. When an interaction takes place on the Web, the cost to you as the supplier is zero. That's right. *Nothing*. Compare this with the telephone. For example, every call you make to Federal Express to ask them to track your package costs them between two and three dollars. They lose money on that package. But if you go to their Web site and track the package yourself, it doesn't cost them anything. They make money. The more customers who use their Web site, the more cost-efficient their business becomes.

The Role of the Internet in Customer Care

Marketing on the Internet backed by personal response handling has become an increasingly common customer care/call center application. According to a recent Economist Intelligence Unit (EIU) study, 63 percent of businesses feel that in the next five years, the Internet will be the most important technology available for dealing with customers. The study predicts that the Internet will replace voice mail as the number one technology used by companies for customer management.

Here are the rankings found by the EIU study:
- The Internet (63%)
- Electronic document interchange (EDI) (58%)
- E-mail (54%)
- Direct database access (49%)
- Voice mail (45%)

More and more companies today are combining a personal response handling system with their marketing on the Internet. The customer's demand for call center based response to Internet-generated inquiries is certain to increase rapidly.

Many companies find that an external supplier can often handle telephone responses in a more efficient and cost-effective way. Similarly, this rationale will apply to responses generated by

Internet inquiries, whether the response is made by telephone, e-mail, Internet "chat" or via the merging technology of the Internet and the telephone.

The On-line Bookstore

Marketing on the Internet has become increasingly common. Leading the charge in this area are Internet bookstores. Internet users shop more and more using the Internet, and books remain one of the products that achieve the highest sales in this medium. Not surprisingly, the on-line book market is also one of the sectors in which competition is the toughest.

What's the advantage for the consumer? Buying books on the Internet can be much faster and cheaper than traditional channels. Technology becomes an important enabler in this thriving new industry, linking data-processing systems, order entry and tracking systems.

The prudent on-line bookstore also recognizes that not everyone has access to the Internet or is familiar with using it. Some people prefer to speak with a person rather than communicate with the supplier solely by electronic means. Even though orders can be taken on-line and all necessary information is available on the bookstores' Web sites, most electronic bookstores will also set up a call center from the outset.

Critical Factors for Success on the Net

To be successful on the Internet, however, you need to do more than simply create a Web page. Consider the following five critical factors for success on the Net:

1. **You must target the right customers**. Not all of your customers are either ready or willing to use the Internet. You may have to invest time and money in educating those who will benefit the most from using the Internet. You may even have to go an extra step and actually install the internet software on their system. Make Internet use accessible and easy for your customers. And remember, you may not want certain customers to have access to certain internal databases, for security and confidentiality reasons. Use Internet technology to your advantage as well as your customers'.

2. **You must manage the customers' total experience.** Limited functionality, the inability to place orders or leave e-mail messages on your Web site is a customer turn-off. Customers want the ability to browse, place orders, access inventory, change their order quantities and revise their delivery dates.

3. **You must streamline the processes that touch the customer.** A disappointed customer? In 85 percent of the cases, the customer is disappointed because the process—such as the credit or order process and not the service representative—failed. Remember, then, that when you take away the service representative, all you have left is the process. Make sure it's in good working order. How easy is it for your customers to place an order, make a complaint or get promotional or pricing information? Make it easy, and they will be less likely to be disappointed.

4. **You must help your customers do their jobs.** Your Web page can be a two-way device if used properly. What information can you send to your customers to help them compete? New product information? Leading trends? Competitive intelligence? "Push" the technology to them and enable them to respond to their market conditions more rapidly. Help them to stay ahead of the curve, not behind it.

5. **You must deliver personalized services.** When your customers sign on, introduce them to the products and services that will meet their needs. Have the screen laid out in ways that make it easy for them to place repeat orders and look for related products and services. Solicit VOC—let them complete the interaction by leaving you messages on how you can improve.

When you apply today's technologies to streamline your customer interactions, you make it easier for your customers to do business with you. While most technologies require systems to talk to one another seamlessly, reliably and securely, across company boundaries, geographic boundaries and time zones, remember that the Internet is not restricted by any of these.

The New Meaning of Sales Force Automation

Sales force automation (SFA) has taken on a whole new meaning today, because organizations in a wide variety of industries—financial services, pharmaceutical and health care, packaged goods and distribution—have found it to be an effective means of building customer loyalty and generating repeat business. Here's one example.

GLOBAL COMPUTER
SALES FORCE TRANSFORMATION

Global, a multibillion dollar computer manufacturing company, faced fierce competition in the undifferentiated commodity hardware industry. In order to compete in this new environment, Global had to realign its sales organization around a solutions-based sales strategy. This meant turning its hardware-oriented sales force into an integrated team capable of meeting its customers' needs through the use of higher-margin integrated computing solutions.

Three specific actions had to be taken. First, the company created a new vision and strategy for the sales force, with measures and targets attached. Second, it developed a model describing the cause-and-effect drivers of success in selling solutions to customers' needs rather than just products. This model also reflected the knowledge and skills required to excel as an integrated solutions provider. Lastly, the company created an integrated knowledge management system that delivered the right knowledge to the right people at the right time, every step of the way through the new, integrated sales process.

Global's sales organization expects tangible improvements including a 50 percent improvement in sales, attributable to better industry positioning, better problem/solution definition and improved cross-selling to clients and a 25 percent decrease in operational costs, driven by quicker go/no-go decisions on opportunities.

The key to this turnaround from the days of old when SFA was considered merely a means of improving administrative efficiency is, in a nutshell, the linkage of SFA to customer service systems. Properly deployed, an SFA solution linked to a customer service system can:

• Automatically collect and update customer information.
• Create a customer knowledge base that helps your sales force to be more proactive in its customer interactions.
• Enhance sales productivity and marketing effectiveness.
• Create competitive advantage.

According to a research study by the Insight Technology Group, successful customer service initiatives that involve SFA translated into revenues per representative increasing by up to 50 percent, sales costs decreasing by as much as 35 percent, sell cycle lengths (the length of time it takes to close a sale) dropping by 25 percent and retention rates and margins on sales increasing by 2 to 3 percent.

Sales Force Automation (SFA)—Five Years Ago

Five years ago, sales force automation was seen as a tool to reduce paperwork, streamline transactions, allow salespeople to spend more time selling and less time on producing. In short, SFA represented increased administrative efficiency. The essential elements of an effective SFA tool included:

- Contact management
- E-mail
- Word processing call plan/report
- Presentations
- Lead tracking and proposal systems

The Challenges Facing SFA Initiatives

Success, however, does not come without its own challenges. Most significant of all the challenges facing the implementation of SFA are cost, time and the sometimes forgotten *"what is the customer willing to accept?"* Most organizations have found that costs exceed planned estimates and projects take an additional six to nine months completion time. This is because, to function at its optimum, SFA can seldom operate on a single software system alone, and more time is needed to integrate multiple software systems.

While current SFA systems have improved functionality, the need still exists to tie together:

- Word processing, desktop publishing, spreadsheets and e-mail
- Contact management
- Multimedia presentation development
- Remote sales rep communications management
- Ad hoc report generation
- Product configuration
- Hotline support and customer issues tracking
- Executive information systems

Another challenge is the need to give multiple users access to data, with the capabilities to create, review and update the sales information database. Not only are field sales staff provided with access but so are marketing, sales management, customer support, telesales, senior management, channel partners and finance individuals. More users means that more time is invested in ensuring that a proper interface has been put into place.

What about Customer Acceptance?

A 1995 TARP (Technical Assistance Research Program) survey asked 20 high-tech and pharmaceutical companies how they handle calls to sales representatives who were not in the office. According to the results, accessibility to sales representatives was poor and sales forces had insufficient back-up. Over the last several years, improvements in call center technology have made access by the customer to the organization significantly easier. Self-help features such as interactive voice response (IVRs), 24-hour service availability and the Internet have made this channel more attractive to use and thus taken a significant burden from the sales representative.

Consider the following. Companies that have backed up their sales representatives with high-level call centers—using SFA tools that provide access to common databases—have seen improvements in customer satisfaction by as much as 30 percent, along with increases in sales force productivity in the order of 20 to 39 percent.

Benefits of Linking Sales to Behind-Sight-of-Vision Processes

What are the benefits of linking the sales process to those administrative processes, such as billing, order processing and inventory mangement?

- Improvements in efficiency of estimating, bidding and proposals.
- Easy and fast access to corporate data, including inventory, production, customer service and accounting and financial records.
- Reduction in design and order delivery lead times.
- Faster, more effective problem resolution and customer service.
- Improvement in conversion of specific customer requirements into future product specifications.
- Improvements in the ability to define and refine future products and customer relationships, as well as continuously improve quality control via customer feedback.

Investment in SFA

One of the biggest challenges facing organizations today is the need to justify the investment in sales force automation. The costs for the software alone can run from $5,000 to $20,000 per license, or per salesperson. A more formal cost benefit analysis must be conducted to ensure that the investment is warranted. One tool that has received considerable use is an application effectiveness assessment,[2] shown in the box below.

SFA Assessment Process

1) Model the Sales Process
If no prior modeling has been done:
- Clearly define the boundaries of the process(es) of interest.
- Identify the individuals most familiar with the process(es) and assemble them in a workshop to model process(es) and assess effectiveness.
- Have individuals compile and prioritize Must-Do-Wells associated with each part of the process(es).
- Capture and record data about opportunities for process improvement while the process model is constructed.
- Capture information about various applications and systems to create a technical quality questionnaire for IS staff.

2) Assess the Application(s)
- In the workshop, have users estimate the level of support provided by the various technologies to conduct a business activity.
- Estimate how much activity that is currently manual and can be automated.
- Have users answer functional questionnaires to assess the effectiveness of each application and tally average scores.
- Have IS staff answer technical questionnaires to assess architectural and operational characteristics of system and tally average scores.
- Plot together average scores from both questionnaires.

3) Interpret the Findings
- If expectations are not being met, ask whether there are actual problems or if functionality was never properly aligned with system objectives.
- Address and correct technical issues (system upgrades, etc.).
- Address opportunities for further automation functionality.
- Establish measures to continually monitor and improve the system.

---

[2] Jay Bitsack, Chris Leibfried and Mike Thomas, *Sales and Field Force Automation*, pp. 34-40, PricewaterhouseCoopers, October 1998.

Living Up to Expectations

How can you determine if SFA is living up to your expectations? One way is to perform an effectiveness study. Taking a structured approach toward identifying the problems and interpreting the results can help an organization realize dramatic improvements in its SFA system.

The Importance of Enterprise Customer Care

You may have heard some people say that sales force automation is dead. It isn't. What's happening is that for the "great" company, SFA becomes instead sales force optimization. Great companies are agile and entrepreneurial. They have the ability to harness both the speed of small enterprises and the scale of large organizations as needed. Great companies thrive on independence, yet have the cross-functionality and encourage the independence needed to act quickly and seize opportunities.

For the great company, technology is a key enabler, but it alone does not provide the solution. Instead, great companies turn to the integration of technology, functions, information databases and customer focus.

USAA
A GOOD EXAMPLE

USAA represents one of the best examples of an organization dedicated to the principle of customer-centric solutions by bringing in line technology, cross-functionality and information sharing. The company has transformed itself from an automobile insurer of US Army officers to a worldwide provider of products and services including property and casualty insurance, life and health insurance, annuities, no-load mutual funds, relocation services and a discount brokerage service.

Its core strategy is "know thy customer," and the root of its success is its commitment to being on the cutting edge of information technology. The company has invested heavily in sophisticated capabilities, particularly in the areas of document management and customer information capture and management. In an average year, the company handles 90 million calls, 35 million pieces of inbound mail and 100 million pieces of outbound mail. Each line of business (property and casualty insurance, life insurance, savings bank, investment management, alliance services) has its own application system. One corporate system has the key data elements to "know the customer." This allows all agents handling calls to immediately identify the customer and at a high level, the relationship that customer has with USAA.

Data in this central system includes: demographics, address, activity in other accounts at an aggregate level, (but not all product data), and data on customers' children. Depending on the nature of the call, the agent handling the initial call may be able to provide all information required or may need to pass the member onto a line of business specialist. The quality and nature of the data selected for the corporate system, coupled with the high availability of documentation concerning customer requests, allows USAA to deliver highly efficient transaction processing services to their customers.

In short, USAA uses technology not only to serve its customers but also to enhance its ability to listen.

Integration: The Key in Today's Technological Environment

With its primary focus on customer-centricity, integration plays a key role in today's technological environment. Integrated technology/software packages are available that can provide you with one or all of the following modules in the form of a single integrated package:

- **Campaign management:** capability for planning, implementing and tracking the effectiveness of sales and marketing campaigns.
- **Computer telephony integration:** automatically routes calls to the appropriate representative while providing that person with personalized information about the customer.
- **Literature fulfillment and inventory management:** allows representatives to quickly mail, e-mail or fax literature to customers and to track inventory as it is used.
- **Desktop reports:** allows the analysis of results to identify opportunities to improve profitability.
- **Quotation management:** helps representatives to quickly and easily develop and send customer quotes.
- **Customer databases:** provides vital data about your customers and the products they own.

MICROSOFT
THE TECHNICAL HELP DESK

In the field of high-tech support, there is no bigger player than Microsoft. In 1996, the company received over 30,000 calls a day and employed over 2,500 support professionals. Today, these numbers are significantly higher. Now, in addition to these calls, Microsoft also receives an even larger number of requests via electronic services like the Internet and e-mail. Why the increase in volume of requests? Microsoft realized that the stand-alone consumers of their technologies had significantly different customer requirements than their medium to large organizational customers. So, in March 1996, they segmented their support business into these two distinct categories.

To provide the type of technical service that their customers expect, Microsoft has re-engineered its service delivery process and also implemented enterprise contact management software and a full-text search engine. The system provides full case, contact and billing management and call coding ability so Microsoft can capture the necessary technical information during the support process and reuse this information to continuously improve its products and services.

All actions taken on behalf of the customer, are tracked and managed by the system. Since implementing the system and undergoing significant process re-engineering, the percentage of "very satisfied" customers at Microsoft has increased dramatically while at the same time, the average time spent on each call has been reduced by 10 percent. The decreased time spent on customer calls has been attributed to better flow and better capturing and sharing of technical information during the problem resolution process.

Many organizations today recognize the need to help their sales force acquire and close more business. Many enterprise organizations, in fact, have collaborative selling environments where sales teams work together to manage opportunities throughout the sales cycle. Within this team-selling environment, telemarketing representatives qualify leads and distribute them to sales staff who then manage the lead. In the case of existing customers, opportunities for up-selling and cross-selling exist.

Enterprise customer care solutions facilitate this process of tracking opportunities and customer needs. When that next opportunity comes along, the ability to "wow" the customer, increase revenues and create loyalty becomes a reality, not an unfulfilled dream.

TEXAS COMMERCE BANK
COORDINATED CUSTOMER CARE

Texas Commerce Bank (TCB) meets its competition head-on with a coordinated sales organization that focuses on achieving total customer satisfaction. More than 800 bank sales representatives at TCB utilize an enterprise customer care information system that enables them to access all the information that they require about specific customers, products and events. With this system, the TCB sales representatives are not only more productive, they are also more effective—a crucial factor in today's highly competitive financial services industry.

TCB is just one example of the increasing number of forward-looking companies that use customer relationship management (CRM) to help them maintain key customers, increase sales and lower marketing costs through improved targeting. Like other leading organizations, it has realized that, after decades of cost cutting and downsizing, only a customer-focused organization will survive.

The Art of Virtual Selling

Speaking of dreams, look at the following example of virtual selling. As you read through it, remember that this is not something out of the *Twilight Zone* or *Star Trek*. Technology exists that enables all of the things you'll read about in the following pages. Remember, too, as you read this virtual selling example, that regardless of the technology available, to be effective in closing business, a salesperson still needs to be effective in front of the customer. Some things never change!

Brian Edwards sat at his desk, preparing for what would be one of the most important sales calls of his career. Sure, every sales call was important, but today, Brian needed to have all the bases covered. And he believed he had. He was about to make a call on Lowell Matthews, one of the most demanding buyers at Wolff Technologies.

Before venturing out on the call, Brian turned on his computer, typed in his password and waited just moments for his wireless modem to access his home office network. Within seconds he was able to view the latest news and stock reports on Wolff Technologies. What a lucky break! It appeared that Wolff Technologies was about to introduce new satellite technology for the digital TV market. Scanning through the article, Brian noted that his company, NCE, was able to enhance Wolff's product with their innovative new cellular control. The key was to get the message across that NCE could deliver on its promises.

Using the company's sales force automation tool, Brian accessed the presentation packages available to him and rebuilt his sales presentation. He reviewed his technical library and updated himself on the technical features of the cellular control product. He accessed Wolff's previous sales purchases to date and the tracking reports on previous calls and reviewed the complaint/comment tracking system. He looked in particular at the concerns Wolff had expressed in relation to the previous trials. Lastly, he reviewed the pricing templates and reconstructed possible pricing options.

Remembering that Wolff Technologies had moved offices, Brian clicked on his contact management system, and double clicked the map icon to obtain a route map to the new site. Now he was ready. Brian arrived at Wolff Technologies with time to spare. Checking his contact management system again before entering the office, he noted that Lowell Matthews' assistant, Elena—who really controlled Lowell's allotted time with suppliers—was a fan of the Boston Celtics. Fortunately, he had tickets to next week's game in his briefcase. Luck or just good planning?

Within minutes Brian was ushered into Lowell's office. Lowell, a man of few words, was extremely bright and always well-prepared. Without wasting a moment, Brian got right to the heart of the matter. He mentioned Wolff Technologies' newly announced foray into the digital TV market and told Lowell that he wanted to show him how NCE could add value to the product launch. Placing his laptop in front of Lowell, he proceeded to run through his presentation.

He followed up his presentation by going into split screen mode. One side of the screen displayed the product spec for the as yet unannounced NCE cellular control and on the other side was a 3-D revolving image of the product.

"Impressive," said Lowell. "Can I get a copy of the specs?"

Without hesitation, Brian punched the print key on the laptop, and the portable printer in his briefcase hummed as it printed off color copies of the six-page product specification.

"But what are the results of the Beta tests," Lowell wanted to know. Again, within seconds, the results came on the screen, followed by a video testimony from the general manager of the organization that had conducted the Beta test, a respected electronics assembler.

Brian was now ready for the close. He had one more trick to pull out of his hat. "Would you like to speak directly to our VP Operations and assure yourself of our delivery and quality capabilities?" he asked.

"Of course I would, but I don't have time to set up interview after interview," Lowell said.

"Not to worry," said Brian. He punched another key on the laptop and his wireless modem kicked in. The computer dialed a number and the call was answered by Cynthia Leigh, VP Operations. Brian spoke to the screen directly and asked Cynthia if she could switch him to video conference mode. He then introduced Cynthia to Lowell and opened up the dialogue.

"I have just been acquainting Mr. Matthews with our new xj14 cellular product and would appreciate it if you could give him some information on product availability and quality control."

On the laptop, Brian and Lowell watched as Cynthia's image shifted to split screen. She remained on one side of the screen and on the other she proceeded to take Lowell on a tour of the operating plant, inventory system and quality control procedures, all in vivid color. She then introduced him to a number of the people on the plant floor.

Lowell Matthews was visibly impressed. He thanked Cynthia Leigh and looked up at Brian. "I'm willing to give your product a test if you can meet our pricing needs," he told him.

Brian thanked Cynthia for her time and signed off. He then returned to his presentation and worked through the pricing options. Because time was of the essence, Wolff Technologies would need a trial run by next week. Brian once again crossed his fingers. He connected his wireless modem again and dialed through to inventory control to access product availability. He was in luck. The product was in trial at 14 organizations, and one, RMB Semi-Conductors Industries, had a production delay that had put their requirements back about four weeks, more than enough time to produce a new production run. With the tap of a few keys, Brian rerouted the product to Wolff Technologies. A credit note was issued to RMB Semi-Conductors and a bill of lading issued to Wolff Technologies.

Within six months, Wolff Technologies had become the largest single buyer of NCE Industries' xj14 cellular control.

It might read like science fiction, but in reality, every single piece of technology wizardry in this story is available right now. Technology is far ahead of the traditional corporate mindset. All we need is a vision and a roadmap and the willingness to be bold.

LESSONS LEARNED

As you can see from the analysis in this chapter, when it comes to technology, you truly cannot run before you learn to walk. In making their technological investments, organizations must stay true to the distinct goals of the stage they're in. For those in Stage I, technology must be able to assist you in acquiring new customers. For Stage II organizations, technology must be used to enhance customer satisfaction and drive loyalty. Stage III organizations must use all of these and more. They must be able to offer differentiated service to their strategic customers and be sufficiently knowledgeable about them to create a win-win situation through the relationship.

If you do not identify the stage you are in and make the appropriate technology investments, you will court failure. This doesn't mean, either, that you cannot make use of the different tools for success outlined in this chapter—all organizations can utilize these tools, provided they keep their focus on their own needs and whether the cost of the new technology justifies the expenditure.

To help you on this path, remember that your organization cannot be all things to all people, nor can you invest in everything that's available. You therefore must take a step-wise approach to transforming customer care. This starts with a review of not only your internal practices but also the needs of your customers. To succeed, you must understand both. Next you must identify the changes in process or technology that you need to address—that is, key changes that your organization must undergo. Be careful. Don't try to do it all yourself. Most people cannot objectively balance priorities. If you pay for a service from a qualified third party integrator/consultant, you are more likely to meet your budget and timetables. Last, determine how you want to appear to your various customer segments and be able to achieve that transformation from your current state. Pilot testing must be used because it's always better to test with a select group of customers before making wholesale changes.

When organizations do keep their needs in sight and understand the decision making and implementation steps, technology can prove a powerful tool in the customer care evolution. As you prepare yourself for your journey, give some thought to this very important question: what technology do you need to possess right now to get to where you want to go?

Staged Customer Management

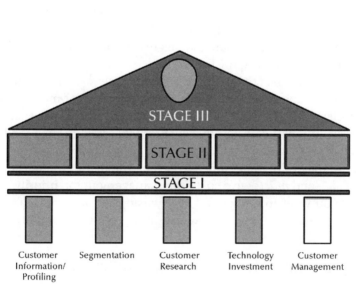

Customer
Information/
Profiling

Segmentation

Customer
Research

Technology
Investment

Customer
Management

Figure 6.1: The Pillars of Strategic Customer Care—Customer Management

In tomorrow's competitive environment customers will expect to be serviced in a manner appropriate to their status, their needs and their desired method of contact. Not convinced? Consider this. According to Frederick Reichheld,[1] a noted Harvard professor, the average US corporation loses half its customers every five years.

---

[1] *Harvard Business Review*, March-April 1996.

Peppers and Rogers[2] estimated that most businesses lose about 25 percent of their customers annually.

The reality is that customers are a scarce and valuable resources, and they do *not* want to be treated like a commodity. Instead, they want specialized care, differentiated and focused to their individual, unique needs. How an organization achieves this is the topic of this chapter.

BUILDING THE FOUNDATION: CUSTOMER MANAGEMENT MUST FIT THE STAGE

In order to effectively compete in today's marketplace, companies must focus on their customers—the ones they have right now. In the last decade, too many companies have assumed that their product or service was so superior in quality that customers would buy it and come back for more—no matter how they were treated. In today's highly competitive marketplace, however, you can no longer tolerate this kind of complacency. The fact is, customers have become increasingly bold and aggressive in their demand for superb quality and responsive service.

Despite the fact that each stage of customer care has a different set of goals and needs, you must focus on customer management regardless of which stage your organization is in. As you prepare for your evolutionary journey, this chapter takes you through the best practices for customer management that are appropriate to each stage of the evolutionary process. Because no matter where you are, you can—and *must*—give customer management top priority.

If you want to attract and keep customers, ask yourself these fundamental questions and see if your responses support your business objectives.

Do you treat different customers differently?

You must differentiate customers first by their value to you and then by their needs. It's simple: you don't want to waste time differentiating low-value customers by their needs, because you don't want to create a high-cost relationship with a low-value customer. So figure out who your highest-value customers are, then differentiate this select group according to what they need.

---

[2] Don Peppers and Martha Rogers, *The One to One Future: Building Relationships One Customer at a Time*, New York: Doubleday Currency, 1993.

Do you create learning relationships with your customers?

Remember the discussion of learning relationships in Chapter 4? The basic underlying concept of a learning relationship is simple: your customers teach you how to give them the service they want and that makes the bond between you and your customer even tighter. Your relationship with your customer gets smarter with every new interaction. In other words, the learning relationship represents the key to creating customer loyalty.

Do you keep your customers?

Customers' needs change over time. In some cases, in order to keep the customer relationship, you must meet new customer requirements, which may or may not be within your capabilities. When this happens, do you let the customer walk away or do you form strategic alliances in order to offer your customer a complete solution? Looking at it from another angle, ask yourself this: Would you pay to have alliances with other high-quality companies and professionals who *could* deliver the services your customer needs? If you can answer yes to this question, you can continue to own the customer relationship. This is an example of Stage III customer management.

On the other hand, you can't just hire someone to do a better job of keeping your customers longer and growing them into bigger, more loyal customers. The desire to do this must permeate your organization. You must consider this task as simply your way of doing business.

Do you organize around customers?

The firm of the future will be organized around individual customer relationships. However, most of today's companies aren't organized for this new way of working and don't have anyone in charge of making it happen. You may not be able to make the changes overnight. In fact, it's unlikely that any organization could, but you can make a start by identifying your highest-value customers and putting somebody in charge of them. It's an incremental step that can work wonders. It speaks to three issues: organization, time and money. You'll find that as long as no one is responsible, no one is going to have the money or find the time. But once you put someone in charge, you *will* make more money and suddenly you'll also find the time.

The fact is each customer wants something different. Some really do want individualized service and will gladly off-load functions to you if you perform them competently—and will remain loyal to you forever. Others simply want the best price. These customers will always award contracts strictly according to bids: they don't want a relationship with you.

A STAGED PERSPECTIVE ON CUSTOMER MANAGEMENT PRACTICES

Stage I—Proactive Customer Management

As we have seen, organizations operating in Stage I place their primary focus on customer acquisition and command and control issues. The Stage I company must therefore meet the challenge of finding tools that deliver on these goals against a backdrop of low customer loyalty and low levels of customer retention.

Some of the most effective tools that a Stage I organization can use are teleservices and the call center. Consumer habits have always been subject to a process of constant evolution dictated by prevailing market conditions. Our customers today face an ever increasing choice in terms of the range of products and services available to meet their needs. This means tougher competition for businesses and increases the importance of adopting an interactive approach to customer management. Such a strategy demands the ability to communicate easily and quickly with the organization's entire universe of customers and potential customers.

In today's competitive markets, you must deliver higher standards of customer service in order to increase customer satisfaction and create customer loyalty. Thankfully, advances in both computer and telecommunications technology allow us to keep pace with these increasing customer demands for quality service.

TIP

What Do Customers Want?

Today's consumers want more from their suppliers. They have become increasingly receptive to the establishment of a relationship that is:

- Direct
- Personalized
- Immediate
- Convenient

Teleservices Is an Answer

Teleservices, or telemarketing, represents a tangible response to our customers' new demands, and many organizations have used teleservices to both win and retain customers. At a number of stages of customer interaction during the customer cycle—presales, sales and post-sales—teleservices operates as an integral component in the profitable management of customers for organizations in Stage I of the evolutionary process.

1. **The pre-sales phase.** Applications of customer management teleservices at this phase of the customer cycle typically address activities such as:
   - Qualifying and quantifying the prospect and its need for your product or service
   - Describing and presenting the added value of your product or service—a good telemarketer should be able to highlight benefits that are tailored to the potential customer's needs
   - Verbally demonstrating the competitive advantages of your product or service, again tailored to the unique customer needs, where appropriate
   - Guiding the prospect toward the most convenient purchasing option
   - Dispatching relevant supporting information or materials (fulfillment)

TIP

Making Buying Easy

One important step in teleservices is to guide your prospect to the most convenient purchasing option. These include:

- **Sales force**: arranging for a sales call and dispatching the appropriate sales team member.
- **Local outlet**: providing the name and address of the closest outlet.
- **Direct sale**: concluding the sale or cross-sale opportunity directly on the call.

---

2. **Sales phase.** During this phase of the customer cycle, telemarketing can also provide some substantial benefits. Your telephone sales representatives can be your most effective means of:
   - Reassuring the new customer on all aspects of the product or service and outlining featured benefits and uses.

- Reinforcing the customer's identification with the product—with, for example, a "Welcome Pack" made available through the phone, mail, fax or e-mail. This welcome pack might contain a letter from the president thanking them for the order or instructions on how to use the product, or the names of key personnel in the company to contact.

- Providing the necessary follow-up, by phone or other means, to reassure the customer that it has made the right choice.

- Updating customers regarding delivery arrangements and dates. Consider this one of the best opportunities to promote customer satisfaction and customer loyalty for your organization. Remember, customers do not like surprises. They want assurances that your product will arrive on time, as promised. They may forgive you for late delivery if they are forewarned, but they will become irritated, and may leave you, if they are surprised or disappointed. The worst case scenario? Disappointed customers will also tell others of their bad experience.

3. **Post-sales phase.** During this phase, your inside customer service representatives can play an equally important role by:

   - Providing product/service support on how to use the product, sometimes while the customer is actually in the process of using it. Often, your representatives can be effective in selling additional services or accessories. In many cases they may even work with customers to identify new uses and therefore created an increased demand for the product.

   - Providing administrative support for the product in areas such as billing, accounts receivable or inventory control. You will find that the Internet provides a very cost-effective means of providing this type of customer service. They can find answers to their questions at their convenience from home or office. When they have difficulty getting that information however, they need access to a friendly voice that can guide them or provide the answers in a timely, reliable manner.

   - Dealing with complaints. Complaint handling is an area critical to the success of your organization. The customer service representative must be responsible not only for the overall handling of each complaint but also for the tracking and liaising with the different departments involved in meeting the customer's needs. Your representative will also generally be responsible for making the decision about how each complaint should be resolved and ensuring that the complaint is handled to the customer's ultimate satisfaction. (For more on customers who do not complain, *see* Customer Complaint Management later in this chapter.)

- Minimizing customer attrition. The financial services and telecommunications sectors are most attuned to this concept. Organizations within these two sectors have created "save" centers to minimize customer attrition when the customer announces its intention to depart. In such situations, the service representative will transfer the call to the "save" department where the representatives are skilled in identifying the root cause of the discontent and offering incentives to stay. Some organizations even have mathematical models that can identify imminent departures and make proactive calls to keep the customer by addressing the relevant issues. The potential in such situations is to turn potential cancellations into repeat sales.

Call Centers

What attributes must an organization's call center have? Call centers have applicability in all stages of the customer care process, although they are also more evolved as the organizations evolve through the stages. In general, however, the primary attributes regardless of stage are:

1. **Accessibility**

   Because call centers communicate directly with the customer via a central point, you can ensure a consistent and high-quality flow of information in both directions. This in turn gives you greater flexibility in terms of implementing strategies required for winning new customers and retaining existing ones. You also gain an invaluable "listening post" for gathering market intelligence.

   Specifically, your call center should:

   - Provide a central point to which all telephone numbers used for customer communication can be directed.
   - Offer high levels of flexibility and service—for example, operation 24 hours, seven days a week.
   - Handle the variety of media that may be used by your customers—telephone, mail, fax or e-mail.
   - Provide access to a unified and coherent source of information that allows for a full dialogue with each customer or potential customer.

2. **Integrated use of main resources**
   In order to establish this attribute, your first step should be to define clearly:
   - The overall and specific objectives of your call center.

- The performance benchmarks you will be using by reference to market standards.
- The nature and behavior of the customer or prospect base being served.

Because it is a direct channel of communication with the market, your call center is a service in its own right and an essential part of the marketing mix. Therefore, its successful implementation requires a high degree of organizational skill and professionalism.

3. **Procedures to ensure quality and an appropriate system for reporting and control.**

   Procedures for ensuring quality performance must be well documented and monitored. All members of the call center operation, from senior manager and supervisor to customer service representative, must know their role in the organization. Like actors on a stage, each part must be played to perfection for the performance to be successful. The requirements to ensure that this occurs include:

   - A strong training program, not only for initial training of all staff, but also for ongoing refreshing and training as new products and services are introduced.

   - A coaching or mentoring system. Staff need ongoing support from supervisors and mentor to discuss the right way to handle customer issues and best practices in responding to customer needs. Formal training can go only so far. What happens after that is what will ensure consistency and conformance.

   - A quality monitoring system that may take a number of forms such as remote monitoring of calls by a member of the training staff, customer surveys to assess perceived quality of the call, and mystery calling through to the call center itself (a third party would call into the call center to assess various aspects of the quality and accuracy of the call).

   - A reporting system that tracks performance against critical quality and service levels. The following chart represents a variety of aspects that may be measured. We have not included the best practices column of this chart as this varies by industry sector and type of call center.

Performance Measures		Definition	Best Practices	Goal	Current Source of Information
1.	QUALITY/CUSTOMER SERVICE MEASURES				
a.	Quality of service rating	The quality of service rating measures the accuracy of the information being provided to the customer by the customer service representative (CSR)			
b.	Customer satisfaction rating	The percent of customers who rate the service good, very good or excellent			
c.	Event based survey	The rating of the call experience			
d.	Percent of calls resolved on first contact	Percent of call assisted by CSRs (less the number of externally transferred calls)			
e.	Internal transfer rate	Percentage of callers who are transferred to another CSR (Escalation)			
f.	External transfer rate	Percentage of callers who are transferred to another department outside the call center			
g.	Number of CSRs to supervisors	Ratio of CSRs to supervisors.			
h.	Complaint rate	Number of complaints received compared with total number of calls received			
i.	Training hours per CSR per year	The number of hours provided to CSRs each year (up training), not including initial training.			
j.	Number of calls monitored per CSR per month.	Supervisors are supposed to monitor 'x' calls per CSR per week for supervision.			
2	CALL HANDLING MEASURES				
a.	Number of calls offered per CSR per month	Number of available incoming calls per CSR per month			
b.	Number of calls handled per CSR per month	Number of incoming calls successfully answered by CSR per month			
c.	Call blockage rate	Percentage of callers who receive a busy signal.			
d.	IVR completion rate	Percentage of callers who are satisfied with the automated information and do not select live assistance.			
e..	Average time in IVR	The average amount of time a customer spends in the IVR.			
f.	Average abandoned rate	Percentage of callers who hang-up before reaching a CSR.			
g.	Average speed of answer (seconds)	The amount of time the average customer waits on hold before his or her call is answered by a CSR (doesn't include abandoned calls).			
h.	Average queue time (seconds)	The amount of time a customer waits in queue (includes abandoned calls).			
i.	Average call handle time	How long on average a CSR spends on each call, including after call work.			

Table 6.1: Performance Measures and Definitions

j.	Average call talk time	The average amount of time the CSR spends talking to the customer. Usually timed from when the call arrives at the CSR station to when the CSR releases the call.			
k.	Average after call work time	The time a CSR spends completing a transaction after the call has been disconnected.			
l.	Average time on hold	The average time the customers is on hold while waiting for the CSR to locate the appropriate answer.			
m.	Service level	Percentage of calls acted on within a certain timeframe (80 percent in 20 seconds) Formula being used is (Total calls handled within 20 seconds plus total calls abandoned in less than 20 seconds)/Total calls queued			
3.	**COST/PRODUCTIVITY MEASURES**				
a.	Average cost per minute	Average cost of telecommunications, agents, facilities, equipment, information systems and all other costs associated with assisting customers.			
b.	CSR productivity rate	Productivity = percent (time handling calls + after call work + logged in time)/ total time available			
c.	Attrition rate	Percentage of the CSRs who leave during the year.			
d.	Absentee rate	Percentage of CSRs who are on sick leave during the month.			

Table 6.1: Performance Measures and Definitions

Customer support plays a vital role in the competitive success of organizations across a broad range of industry segments. Your customer support process provides your company with the critical link to your customer through the entire length of the customer relationship. The effectiveness of your support system can have a substantial impact on revenues and profits. Satisfied customers will be more likely to upgrade than switch suppliers, and you will find increased opportunities for cross-selling additional products. Remember, too, that the satisfied customer is also your advocate and can help expand your customer base.

Stage II—Integrated Customer Care

Stage II companies understand this principle: the longer a customer stays with a company, the more the customer is worth. Long-term customers buy more, take up less company time, express less sensitivity to price and bring in other customers. But Stage II organizations remember that these customers were not always that way and that bringing their customers to this state was often an extremely long, hard haul.

In Stage II, organizations obsess about maximizing their customer relationships and are most concerned about customer retention. Their concern stems from a renewed respect for the customer, motivated by a number of factors:

- Intensifying global competition
- The transition from a manufacturing economy to a service economy
- Shorter product cycles and saturated markets
- Less opportunity for product differentiation
- An increasing sensitivity toward service on the part of the consumer

At the same time, the complexity of today's products and services requires businesses to interact more effectively with customers at every level.

The Long-Term Customer—Stability in Today's Changing Environment

Today, top executives see forging long-term relationships with their organization's best customers as the key to establishing stability in an increasingly dynamic market. Customer management on a more intense level has surfaced as a crucial factor to organizations' survival. These executives focus on driving their organizations to becoming customer-centric both in thought and deed.

In fact, in the Economist Intelligence Unit (EIU) study mentioned earlier, the management of customer relationships at 200 companies around the world was examined. Customer relationship management (CRM) emerged as the discipline currently driving fundamental changes at leading global organizations.

Customer Relationship Management (CRM)

CRM places the customer's needs first, and its success depends on two fundamental building blocks:

1. **You must understand your customers deeply.** This way of managing customer relationships, when combined with insight into

customer values, can help companies consistently boost customer retention, increase customer loyalty, expand referrals,
increase revenues and profits per sale, lower direct costs by optimizing channels and lower marketing costs through improved
targeting.

2. **You must align your organization's capabilities.** This enables
you to better deliver value to your customers. Such alignment
can be accomplished through an integrated approach to customer management, in which multiple functional departments
act as one in order to seamlessly support your customer's needs.
The result is an organization that is more focused on quickly and
effectively identifying and addressing the customer's needs from
multiple departmental perspectives, including marketing, sales,
support and quality.

   Working in tandem, your marketing and sales departments
   can stay focused on attracting and acquiring customers while
   inside sales, after-sales service, new product development and
   order processing functions can concentrate on retaining and
   leveraging the customer relationship. This complete integrated
   customer relationship cycle, with its components of "attract,
   acquire, retain and grow," provides the framework that supports
   Stage II customer management.

The heart and soul of CRM lies in its ability to establish and effectively use enterprise customer care information systems, because
the real challenge lies not in attracting customers but in retaining
and leveraging customer relationships.In order to address this challenge, you need a proper approach to enterprise-wide customer
care information systems.

Enterprise-Wide Customer Care Information Systems

An enterprise-wide customer care information system allows your
organization to integrate:

• All aspects of your company's customer interactions—sales,
marketing, customer service, field service and product quality—
thus enabling your organization to present a single face to your
customer.

• Back-office systems—manufacturing, finance, human resources
and accounting—resulting in a number of effects. It allows
functional departments with behind-sight-of-vision customer

contact to reap the benefits of being closer to the customer. It gives front-line customer support personnel more access to back-office information. It enables your entire enterprise to look at how the customer interacts with the business.

Interactions with the customer can also be tracked and treated as an important part of the information file on the customer, rather than being discreet occurrences with no coordinated resolution mechanism. This enables you to create a searchable knowledge base that can be accessed by employees of various skill levels. Such access can then provide immediate details regarding customers, products, enhancement suggestions, sales opportunities and resolution of customer issues.

Stage III—Strategic Account Management

One major difference between the way a Stage II and a Stage III organization views customer management lies in the latter's focus on strategic account management. In many ways, for the Stage III organization, strategic account management can be as much a philosophy as it is a practice.

TIP

Strategic Account Management: Certain customers require special treatment and rather than having just an individual salesperson responsible to them, warrant a team. This team is focused on customer needs and a desire to create a "win-win" relationship with the customer. If the customer can improve its profitability by working with your organization, they will be more loyal and dependent on you, and you will, in turn, achieve increased profitability.

After all, if only 20 percent of your customers represent between 40 percent to 60 percent of your potential, you need to find a way to form strategic partnerships with those select customers in order to further nurture the relationship for mutual benefit.

In Stage I, organizations consider all customers to be important, and continuous customer acquisition is the goal. At Stage II, customer relationship management and limited differentiation becomes the goal. Stage III switches the focus to differentiated service for their select, crown jewel customers and the mutual benefits of partnership with these key customers.

Basic Principles

How does the Stage III organization meet the goals of differentiated service and strategic partnership? Let's take a look at the basic principles driving effective strategic account management.

- **Revitalize, modify and systematically apply a streamlined account management process to all strategic customers.**

  Strategic customers offer a very strong potential for the Stage III organization. After all, these customers are organizations within which you could potentially establish a dominant, if not exclusive, relationship with regard to the products and services you sell. But you cannot afford a haphazard approach. Rather, you need a route map to guide you through the process of building the relationship. Remember that your customer may see you from a number of different views—for example, they may operate both regionally or globally. You must be able to respond to these differences, yet provide a consistency in operating practices.

- **Create an environment where strategic customer account management receives priority through ongoing senior management sponsorship.**

  You must ensure that your senior management plays an active part in this process. After all, they are part of the account team, champions of the cause and the individuals who ensure that the proper resources have been allocated to the strategic account teams. They must remain highly aware of the integral role they play and accord your strategic customer account management the proper priority needed to meet your goals and objectives.

- **Give their strategic account teams objective measurement criteria to provide benchmarks for assessing success.**

  As the Mad Hatter said to Alice in *Alice in Wonderland*, "Any road will take you there if you don't know where you are going." With effective customer profiling and VOC questioning, you can discover the critical questions that need to be addressed in order for you to assist your customer in overcoming tomorrow's challenges. No other measure will be more important than your success in helping them jump these hurdles.

Guide to Successful Implementation

Organizations that successfully implement a strategic approach to customer management recognize the following elements of managing strategic accounts:

1. Why We Need a Common Approach
2. Understanding the Role of the Team
3. Recognizing the Customers' Strategic Needs
4. Developing the Strategic Action Plan
5. Developing an Implementation Plan

Let's take a look at each of these components individually.

1. Why We Need a Common Approach

Strategic account management requires that we think about our strategic customer's needs from a strategic perspective. As a strategic partner, you need to manage your customers *proactively* and consistently—if you don't, you may find them managing you. The strategic customer provides you with growing customer service opportunities—while their demands are higher, the rewards will be proportional to your efforts.

Strategic account management also requires you to use a common language to discuss customers and use a common process to identify issues important to the strength and vitality of your strategic relationship with the customer.

2. Understanding the Role of the Team

I am convinced that nothing that we do is more important than hiring and developing people. At the end of the day, you bet on people, not strategies.

—Larry Bossidy, Chairman and CEO, AlliedSignal

Teams have—and create—strength. A single candle burns brightly, but when you put two candles together the flame is four times brighter. In a similar analogy, a flashlight may not work with only one battery, but when you put two batteries together back to back, you have light. Simplistic examples? Of course. But they tell the tale. Teams have power—as long as they are properly aligned. Individual effort, while exemplary, will not be as effective.

So, if all this about the power of teamwork is true, why aren't more organizations using teams effectively? There are two main reasons:

- Organizations tend to undervalue the importance of people and how people can work to "strengthen the flame."
- Organizations do not know how to build teams for effectiveness—in other words, they do not know how to align the batteries to create the necessary power.

According to a seven-year study sponsored by the Institute of Personnel and Development (IPD) of more than 100 medium-size manufacturing firms in the United Kingdom, companies often neglect their real moneymakers—their people—in favor of more exciting improvements. The study reveals that when it comes to improving the bottom line, focusing on the ways employees are managed and developed far outstrips the gains reaped from either investments in technology, research and development or a focus on strategy and/or quality.

The study, conducted for the IPD by the Institute of Work Psychology at the University of Sheffield and the Center for Economic Performance at the London School of Economics, found that the way people are managed and developed accounts for 19 percent of the variation in profitability between companies and 18 percent of the variation in productivity. These are astounding figures, especially when you consider that investment in research and development accounts for only 8 percent of the variation in profitability and 6 percent of the variation in productivity. An emphasis on quality, new technology and competitive strategy barely crept above 1 percent in terms of their contribution to the bottom line. Another significant finding is that the more satisfied workers are with their jobs, the better the company is likely to perform in terms of profitability and, particularly, productivity. These results are consistent with the IBM research results discussed in Chapter 1. Many of the firms in the study did not make a causal connection between good people management practices and business success. Too often, companies regarded "people issues" as a luxury relevant only to larger firms, or as something to be considered only when the "real" business issues had been effectively dealt with.

But, as the study results demonstrate, this is simply not so. You have a lot at stake in your employees. Without good people in your organization, you simply won't be a success—and may not survive.

3. Recognizing the Customers' Strategic Needs

You need to address the crucial question: *What is happening on this account?* More specifically, understanding your customers strategic needs requires you to identify:

- **The context in which your customer competes.** This context may be regional or global. Understanding your customers' challenges in this area enables you to identify opportunities for the development of new products and services as well as areas in which you may need to form strategic alliances with other suppliers in order to help your customers compete.
- **The underlying issues driving future customer spending.** Understanding issues such as customers' strategic needs will help you to realign your resources as required in order to support your customers' future direction.
- **The customer's major buying centers.** Each of your customer's buying centers presents an opportunity to establish a relationship and deepen the overall strategic link. However, keep in mind that not all of a customer's buying centers may be in a growth mode—while some may be strategic, others may be declining.
- **Your current position relative to the customer's buying centers.** Where do you have strong relationships? Where are they weak? Examine which relationships can be leveraged the most.
- **Your competitors' positions relative to the customer's buying centers.** What market share does your competitor have relative to your position and why?
- **Issues concerning your customers' customers.** Helping your customers to be more successful with their customers will most likely make them more dependent on you for their continued future success.

4. Developing the Strategic Action Plan

You need to develop a strategic plan that balances your organization's capabilities with those of your customers' needs—*What do we (the customer and supplier as a team) want out of this account?* You must articulate an overall strategy and establish concrete actions for realizing that strategy.

Your strategy should:
- Summarize the customer's critical issues/problems, needs and opportunities.
- Identify your current and your desired relationships with the customer.

- Define a strategy for measuring the quality of the relationship.
- Consider the economic implications of the relationship.
- Outline alternative strategies for reaching the target relationship.
- Confront identified constraints—how you are currently viewed in the eyes of the customer.

5. Developing an Implementation Plan

Lastly, you need to develop an implementation plan that addresses the question—*How will we achieve what we want?* Implementation plans should include:

- Critical objectives and who, what and when milestones: who is responsible, what is to be done and by when must it be accomplished.
- Performance measurements.
- A process for objective customer feedback.
- Revenue and financial forecasts. Protecting the core revenue is an important task.
  In particular, you need to focus on three points:

1. **Defend your home base.** You must defend the buying center in the customer's organization in which you are strongest by maintaining customer commitment to the core service or product and providing your customer with higher value than it can receive from other suppliers. At the same time, you must be driven to expand your home base and expand your position into other buying centers.

2. **Avoid "cross kill."** Do not cross-sell into very high-risk areas when you already have large, growing and profitable home bases. If you are not successful, you may lose your existing strong position in your most important home base.

3. **Manage change.** This ensures that your relationship survives changes in management of the buying center and other key relationships that exist within the strategic customer organization. That means that you must build insulation against potential departures and changes.

Always remember that your customer relationships are built from the inside out. Begin by consolidating your home base and then move out to other buying centers.

CUSTOMER COMPLAINT MANAGEMENT

Most companies spend millions of dollars collecting customer feedback but seldom analyze or use this data when making decisions. This doesn't make any sense. When they complain to you or give you constructive feedback, your customers are, in effect, reaching out to you, and if you do nothing with this data, you are essentially turning your back on this golden lifeline. You must recognize the importance of customer feedback and then effectively manage it to assist in the customer management process.

Most organizations honestly believe that they understand the customer. When they do receive the odd complaint, they respond quickly and do not believe that customer complaints are an issue. Nothing could be further from the truth. As the box below demonstrates, most customers, whether individuals or organizations, do not complain; they simply walk straight to your competitors.

Most People Do Not Complain

It's important that you don't jump to the conclusion that all's well just because your company has not been receiving many customer complaints. It's actually a well-documented and proven fact that most people—and organizations, for that matter—do not bother to complain. It's simply easier to walk away than to confront the problem. With so many suppliers available to service your customers' needs, why go to the bother of confronting an annoying situation and becoming aggravated? Many customers just shrug and ask "Who really cares?" How many letters of complaint or comment cards have you yourself written or filled out, without effect.

Customers will ask, " Who do I complain to? Who do I get in touch with? "There's usually not much sense complaining to a front-line customer service representative. Most customers want to complain to the most senior individual who has accountability and responsibility. But how do they find that person? Then there is the fear of retribution. Customers may sometimes wonder, will my supplier get back at me when things are in short supply or hold up my production line with late deliveries? After all, we've all heard the slogan, "Don't get mad...get even."

What's the value of encouraging and resolving complaints? According to a National Consumer Survey conducted by the US OCA/White House (Figure 6.2), 95 percent of customers will buy from you again if you resolve their complaints quickly. Among those who are dissatisfied but do not complain, only 37 percent are likely to buy from you again. These are powerful numbers.

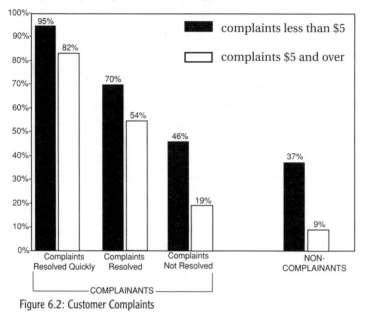

Figure 6.2: Customer Complaints

How easy is it for a customer to make a complaint to your organization? Research has found that the greater the number of people that a customer must go to in order to resolve a problem, the lower the loyalty. But, far from being an annoyance, customer complaints offer you an exceptional opportunity to increase customer loyalty, reduce defections and learn more about what your customers value most. If you do not handle them properly, however, you stand to put a minimum of 8 to 10 percent of your revenues at risk. Consider the lifetime value of this lost relationship.

Ironically, satisfied customers tend to complain more, because they believe that complaining is worthwhile. So an increase in complaints may actually indicate that you're doing a better job at satisfying your customers!

Technology and the Customer Complaint System

Since complaint handling can be such an important factor in your organization's success, you should track, log and respond to customer complaints in as efficient and effective a way as possible. Luckily, a number of software packages are available today which provide you with the ability to manage the data related to complaints.

These software solutions support the enterprise-wide distribution of knowledge. Generally speaking, each complaint is recorded as if it were an ordinary request for assistance or information. A new case is created for each complaint and assigned a code or reference number that identifies the type of complaint. This code is then used to categorize it in the database for future reporting purposes. Depending on the severity or frequency of the complaint, the issue will become a priority issue or be handled in due course.

Most complaint management software includes the ability to:

- Create a file for the complaint.
- Provide a solution (if the complaint is product specific, this could include searching the database for a solution).
- Attach the solution to the customer.
- Distribute the complaint information to the appropriate department or individual for action or resolution.
- Maintain a database of these complaints as a valuable tool for improving customer satisfaction.

LESSONS LEARNED

The wave of the future lies in a customer-centric orientation. Ask yourself these four fundamental questions once again:

Do you treat different customers differently?
You must differentiate customers first by their value to you and then by their needs.

Do you create learning relationships with your customers?
The basic underlying concept of a learning relationship is simple: your customers teach you how to give them the service they want and that makes the bond between you and them even tighter.

Do you keep your customers?
Customers' needs change over time. In some cases, in order to keep

the customer relationship, you must meet new customer requirements, which you may or may not be able to do.

Do you organize around customers?

The firm of the future will be organized around individual customer relationships.

By working today to establish best practices in customer management that are appropriate to your stage in the evolutionary process, you will build a solid foundation for your transition into the next stage of evolution. But regardless of the stage in which your organization operates, you can—and should—develop best practices that meet the needs of your organization in that particular stage of the evolutionary process.

In Stage I, because of the focus on customer acquisition and command and control issues, the call center begins to come into play. Customer care must be provided to all customers in an effort to maintain the customer base for as long as possible. But strict quality and performance measures must be put in place to ensure that your customers receive a consistent level of reliable service.

In Stage II there is a greater focus on integrated customer care and the desire to manage the customer's entire experience with the organization. Accordingly, you must align the organization's capabilities to better deliver value to the customer. This requires an integrated approach to customer management in which multiple functional departments are acting as one to seamlessly support customers' needs.

In Stage III the focus becomes differentiated, strategic customer care through principles such as strategic account management, a team-based approach to the customer and individualized strategic account plans.

While you must recognize your stage in the evolution, at the same time you must pave the way to the next stage in the process. As you can see in your preparation for the evolutionary journey, your experience through each stage of the process must not be wasted. While the goal of Stage III customer care beckons alluringly, remember that it becomes much more difficult to achieve without proper practices developed at each stage of the evolutionary process through which you've already journeyed.

Part Two

The Route Map to Stage III Customer Care

THE 12 STEPS TO GET YOU TO YOUR DESTINATION

In previous chapters we saw the three different stages in the evolution of customer care, drew your attention to the focus and goals unique to each stage and provided examples of best practices of organizations at each of the three stages. Now that we have provided you with the foundation pillars, you must decide how evolved you want these pillars to be and how well-developed a customer care process you require. The remaining chapters of this book will focus primarily on Stage III customer care, the survival strategy for the future, although we will not ignore Stage II.

In this and succeeding chapters, the route map to success will take you through a proven process to achieve improved customer care. For most organizations this should mean Stage III strategic customer care. Why the insistence on striving for Stage III? If you do not identify, acquire and keep customers that warrant Stage III care, you may be doomed to mediocrity or worse. In today's fast-paced environment of rapid change, mediocrity spells failure.

Part II of this book thus concentrates on the 12 steps that organizations must follow in order to complete their evolution to Stage III customer care. To succeed in Stage III, you need to change your focus. You can no longer be all things to all people and must concentrate instead on adding value to your most important customer relationships. Armed with the skills you acquired in Part I of this book and the evolutionary route map, you will be able to develop initiatives unique to the special circumstances of your company and your strategic customers.

The customer care process described in this part of the book might seem to you as if it were just common sense. Perhaps. But as Voltaire said, "If common sense were very common, more people would have more of it."

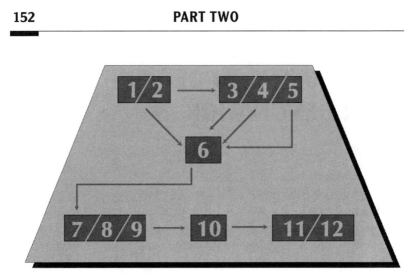

Strategic Customer Care Process

THE ROUTE MAP

The 12 steps of the customer care process incorporate some of the best practices described earlier in Part I. These steps form the route of your journey to Stage III customer care and are described as follows:

1. **Management alignment and mobilization.** This step enables you to gain the buy-in, understanding and consent of your management team. It is a critical first step in which alignment between senior management and the balance of the organization must be achieved. Without proper alignment, the customer care process will be less than optimal.

2. **Change readiness assessment.** With this step the readiness for change of management and organization is assessed. This serves a dual role, first in pinpointing potential constraints and relevant issues that must be addressed proactively, and second, to assist in selecting the composition of the strategic account management teams (Step 7) that are needed to support the customer action plan (Step 8).

3. **Customer segmentation.** Customer segmentation allows you to concentrate on a select few—your strategic customers. These are the ones for whom you can add value and with whom you can increase profitability (both yours and theirs). It is therefore essential that you use the right criteria and develop the

appropriate models for this segmentation exercise. Remember, not all customers are the same and not all customers contribute equal value to the organization.

4. **Customer profiling**. With this step you will assemble information that will help you understand the characteristics of your strategic customers. There is much information that must be collected, analyzed and shared, and technology will play an important role in this process. Stage III organizations require more depth and detail than Stage II organizations.

5. **Voice of the Customer (VOC) intervention**. This is a critical step and one that also distinguishes Stage III from Stage II customer care efforts. Obtaining the voice of the strategic customer enables you to identify, from the customer's perspective, the areas in which you require improvement and where you should concentrate your efforts. It is also essential for identifying the key team building blocks that you must assemble.

6. **Gap analysis**. This step allows you to identify where gaps exist, both internally and externally, between your senior management, middle management, front-line support staff and your customers. Remember that many areas of potential disconnection can exist. This step helps to facilitate this identification and cause pause before proceeding with customer action plans.

7. **Management call to action/Strategic account team mobilization**. Within this step, your task is to determine the composition of the strategic account management teams, one for each strategic (Tier I or II) customer. You will use input from the previous gap analysis stage, with particular attention to customer needs, as identified in Step 5. It is important that you identify and select members who will be best able to manage the development and implementation of a customer care strategy and define roles and responsibilities for those that will interface with and support these teams.

8. **Strategic action planning**. In this step you plan and document specific action in which to address these items that are most important to the customer. This is the heart and soul of the customer care process.

9. **Customer alignment**. Aligning your customers enables you to gain both customer input and support of your draft strategic action plan. This is critical to the Stage III customer care process as it signals a one-to-one alignment between the strategic customer and the organization.

10. **Team training**. Proper training is essential to effect the changes necessary to address customer issues and the management of change internally. While training will occur throughout the customer care process, team training must be completed by this point to ensure that a cohesive, knowledgeable team is prepared to implement the customer care action plan.

11. **Implementation mobilization**. This step enables you to effectively design the implementation strategies and activities that you have previously identified and agreed with your strategic customers. It is important to recognize that some of these activities may not be provided by the organization, and that is where outsourcing and strategic alliances play a role.

12. **Performance monitoring and adjustment**. This step is both the end and start of the journey to strategic customer care. It is a necessary tool for conducting ongoing, repetitive evaluation of the existing state of affairs and the tracking of performance against goals. Remember, customer expectations are progressive.

As the chart below demonstrates, the process steps fall into natural groupings, each of which will be covered in the chapters that follow. We have also provided a cross-reference to the pillars described in Part I of this book.

Steps 1, 2, 7 and 10 deal with alignment—alignment of senior and middle management as well as the front-line forces (Chapter 8).

Steps 3 to 6 focus on information gathering and analysis. You cannot move forward without knowing where you are today (Chapter 9).

Steps 8 to 12 deal with action planning and recalibration. A good plan must be developed with the customer, and you must measure your progress continuously (Chapter 10).

Process Steps	Process Chapters					Foundation Chapters			Appendices					
	7	8	9	10	11	2	3	4	A	B	C	D		
1	X	X			X				X					
2	X	X			X				X		X			
3	X		X		X	X								
4	X		X		X	X								
5	X		X		X			X						
6	X		X		X									
7	X	X			X									
8	X			X	X					X	X			
9	X			X	X							X		
10	X	X			X									
11	X			X	X									
12	X			X	X									

The Strategic Customer Care Process

ARE YOU READY?

As you read through the chapters that follow, consider:

- What stage are you in today and to what stage do you want to evolve? For some organizations, striving beyond Stage II customer care is inappropriate; for others, Stage III is a survival strategy.

- For those that are in Stage I and wish to evolve to Stage II or Stage III, the process that follows will guide you through this evolution.

- For those currently in Stage II and who wish to remain there, the process will help strengthen those foundation pillars. In its present state, the route map that follows is overbuilt for Stage II organizations and must be streamlined a bit, although the process steps should stay pretty much intact. Review the pillars described earlier and make adjustments. Your needs in the area of segmentation (Chapter 3) and customer profiling (Chapter 2) will be reduced. Your customer research needs (Chapter 4) can be less rigorous, but research remains a critical component. Technology investments (Chapter 5) are less demanding. As well, action planning/customer management (Chapter 6) will be done at a more general, market segment level, rather than at a strategic customer level. In the chapters that follow, we will try to alert you to Stage II related issues where appropriate.

• If your goal is to move to Stage III, the route map that follows will provide you with a proven blueprint.

Remember, you'll face a number of obstacles as you progress along the evolutionary route to Stage III customer care. With this route map as a guide, you *will* succeed, provided you meet the challenges ahead of you with resolve and commitment. If you're ready, let's start on the path to Stage III—*strategic customer care.*

CHAPTER SEVEN

Your Survival Strategy for the Future

WHY THE ROUTE MAP IS ESSENTIAL

There is only one boss: the customer. And he can fire everybody, from the chairman on down, simply by spending his money somewhere else.
—*Sam Walton, Wal-mart*

USING THE ROUTE MAP: PERSPECTIVES ON STRATEGIC CUSTOMER CARE

If you don't want to be simply another commodity supplier with limited customer loyalty and retention—and a significantly limited profitability potential—you must gather together your resources and march solidly along to Stage III of the evolutionary process.

So, let's start with an example, a case study of an organization, PHH, that has put its process in place to achieve Stage III, strategic customer care. Let's look at what it accomplished and the steps that it took to get there. As you read through this example, look at how evolved the foundation pillars are:

- Customer profiling
- Customer segmentation
- Customer research
- Technology investment
- Customer management

Also consider how knowledge management (a common database that allows for information sharing) and strategic account management (a focus on the most significant customers based on potential) play such a strong role in these organizations' drive to success.

PHH SUCCESS THROUGH PARTNERSHIP

Founded in 1946, PHH is a North American and European leader in the fields of vehicle management solutions for corporate, government and utility fleets. The organization has designed its services to lower costs, increase productivity and help its customers meet their strategic objectives.

The organization has used a "Partnership Approach" with respect to customer care, the foundation of which is based on creative partnering with both suppliers and customers, innovative thinking to use technology to reduce costs and create improved customer satisfaction, teamwork, effective listening to customer needs, and global service capabilities.

How effective is partnership? Consider this. It has allowed PHH to retain its Fortune 500 clients for more than 50 years. In addition, the company has kept almost 300 clients for 20 years or more.

One of PHH's strengths has been its ability to understand the industries in which it operates and to use its expertise in creative ways to identify solutions to solve customer problems. Within the PHH process, technology plays an important role not only in managing internal information but also in disseminating and simplifying the information that the company distributes to its clients. PHH's electronic commerce helps its clients to streamline operations, reduce errors and improve quality. These include both static and active applications such as electronic data interchange (EDI), electronic funds transfer (EFT), electronic mail and electronic billing.

At the heart of PHH's electronic commerce strategy is a data warehouse that allows the organization to centralize and integrate databases designed specifically for reporting information, enables users—internal and external—to analyze trends and generate flexible reports, and provides easy access to comprehensive information through both Internet and Intranet applications.

Over the years the organization has re-engineered its customer "touch" process and the way it adds value to its client base. These elements together represent a cornerstone of PHH's promise to the customer.

Let's take a closer look at one of the key areas the company restructured: role segmentation. The process involved the creation of three functional and separate yet intertwined roles:

- **New Business Development (Acquisition).** PHH's new business development associates call on prospects with a strategic message directed at senior leadership levels of the prospect organization.

- **New Business Activation (Integration).** Once the prospect has decided to do business with PHH, the new business associate then works to ensure a smooth and timely integration between PHH and the new client.

- **Client Relations (Service).** The company assigns a two-person service delivery team, composed of an account executive and an account consultant, to every client. The account executive—the relationship marketing contact—is responsible for networking with the client organization, the sale of additional services, consulting on fleet policy and enhancing the client's profitability.

Another cornerstone of its operating strategy is customer segmentation. By customizing its service levels based on the size of the customer and importantly, their potential, PHH focuses its energies on the customers that can possibly contribute the most to its own success. It does not try to be all things to all people—that is, it does not try to give the same service to all customers. On the other hand, for its key customers, it will customize its services to meet their individual needs and help the customer improve its bottom line. By doing this, PHH effectively concentrates on an issue that is often ignored by most organizations—creating the dependent customer. Let's not skip over this point. PHH's goal is to help its customers become more profitable. If it is successful in continuously driving costs out of the customer's expense structure, the customer will be more profitable and able to concentrate on its core capabilities, another factor that will improve profitability. When PHH is successful in this, the customer has no need to leave, in fact, it becomes dependent on PHH to help ensure its success. This is more important than customer loyalty; it is customer dependency.

Ways to Survive

An ever changing landscape greets us whenever we look to the future to see what we can make of the new business environment. A simple glimpse forward tells us that the rules are no longer the same. Traditional notions of customer care no longer work. What's the key to the survival of your organization? There is one simple answer, as PHH so aptly demonstrates—dependency. The dependent customer comes back to you again and again, seeking your help in increasing its prosperity and becoming an advocate of your services and products.

Ask yourself, *"What can I do to make my customers depend on me for their survival and growth?"* Consider this. A recent research study conducted by Cornerstone Research and Cornell University highlighted the importance of a strategic focus on the customer. The study found that customers that bought more products from a supplier tended to be more loyal than those that bought only one product.

Other findings of the study:
- 90 percent of customers that bought three to four products from a supplier were likely to be still doing business with the supplier in five years.
- Only 45 percent of customers that bought two products were likely to stay with the supplier over this five-year period.
- 20 percent of customers buying only one product were likely to stay loyal over the five-year period.

HOW TO OVERCOME COMMON REASONS FOR FAILURE

Organizations like PHH that have implemented successful customer care initiatives will tell you that their road to success was fraught with difficulties. And, not surprisingly, many will likely tell you that they did not, in fact, get it right the first time. Those that did had certain things in common. Here are four of the reasons for their success:
- The Need to choose the Right Team with the Right Perspective
- Look at the Customer Care Process and Its Linkages
- The Need to Get Senior Management on Board Early
- Communicate at the Right Time and with the Right Frequency

The Need to Choose the Right Team with the Right Perspective

The importance of teamwork to the success of a customer care initiative cannot be overemphasized. Successful organizations spend considerable time selecting team members and, like the Square D case study provided in Chapter 1, will often include the customer as part of the team.

When initiatives are less than successful, generally too little thought was given to customer involvement. In a similar vein, some organizations hold an antiquated perspective about customer involvement that can best be characterized by the expression "My way or the highway." Such organizations see the customer as the target rather than an integral part of the team process yet what better way to know and understand your customers than by involving them in your process?

There's also the error known as "No one on deck." Too often there is not someone in charge who has the power to act on the results of the initiative. This reflects short-sighted thinking of impressive magnitude—with this error, organizations end up with some invaluable information, but they lack the processes to use it to their advantage.

A most fatal error is underestimating the amount of time that needs to be dedicated to the development, launch and maintenance of the initiative. Less than successful initiatives do not give their teams enough dedicated support. The common view is that the teams can be put together as a part-time project, but nothing could be farther from the truth. As Square D has shown us (Chapter 1), both full and part-time involvement is required.

Teams do not just happen—they need nourishment and support. Both training and program development are integral components of the team-building process. And team members need to consider membership a mark of special regard and a route to promotion.

Look at the Customer Care Process and Its Linkages

Less than successful initiatives operate from a "home alone" perspective. In other words, unlike PHH and its recognition of its dependency on technology as an enabler, these organizations do

not tie their customer care initiatives into other internal improvement initiatives and therefore run the risk of coming up against
many cultural and technological roadblocks. Look at it as a set of
linkages, and you will only be as strong as your weakest link.

Take invoicing as an example. It is possible to streamline your
billing operation and standardize with minimal information. It may
however be more prudent to establish a more flexible billing system
that is more customer care focused, to establish greater clarity and
more customization. It may not be the most cost efficient billing
process, but it may differentiate you from the competition and thus
provide you with a strategic advantage. It's not surprising, therefore,
to find that less than successful initiatives are typically "disconnect-
ed"—the data generated and the systems developed are not linked
to internal processes or initiatives, leaving these initiatives sub-
optimized.

One final thought on positioning. Management needs to stop
calling strategic customer care a "program." In order to be success-

The Successful Initiative	The Less than Successful Initiative
• Dedicates a lot of time to the composition of the team and understands the importance of involving the customer as individual with decision-making authority.	• Approaches team member selection haphazardly and does not see the value of including the customer as a member of the team.
• Ensures that the individual charge has the power and thecommitment to act on the results.	• Usually does not place anyone in charge of the initiative, and if it does, it does not give that person decision-making authority.
• Is committed to dedicating the full amount of time needed to successfully develop and launch the initiative.	• Considers the initiative to be a part-time project.
• Gives its team appropriate support and resources.	• Does not consider the initiative of enough importance to dedicate adequate support.
• Ties in teamwork with performance, so that team members regard their membership as a mark of special regard and a route to promotion and other rewards.	• Does not include a performance dimension to team membership.in part-time project.

Table 7.1: Successful Versus Less than Successful Initiatives

ful, the commitment to customer care must permeate the entire organization. Customer care thinking techniques, vocabulary and systems must be instilled into every employee's day-to-day work. The bottom line? To be successful, strategic customer asset management must be much more than simply a program—it is, rather, a new way of thinking.

The Challenges of Establishing a Successful Customer Care Initiative

A Conference Board study[1] examined customer satisfaction and value initiatives in 113 companies in the United States and Europe. The research showed that organizations with successful programs that focus on customer satisfaction and value achieved expanded market share and increased customer retention. The key to the organizations' success was their ability to collect and creatively use customer input, sometimes refered to as Voice of the Customer (VOC) data.

However, the study also found that a successful initiative did not come without its challenges. Among them:

- Reorganizing to enable front-line decision making—a shift from the traditional power source
- Re-engineering the points of customer contact—sales and marketing, customer relations, order fulfillment and distribution.
- Raising employee awareness of customers as assets as well as enhancing employees' understanding of customer needs.

The Need to Get Senior Management on Board Early

Attempts to improve customer care too often operate with an ivory tower mentality. Some members of senior management do indeed put in an appearance at the start-up and at some of the rah-rah development meetings, but they are not fully involved. They don't truly walk-the-talk, and the initiatives lose momentum because of a lack of visible support.

The most successful initiatives—go back to PHH and Square D—are those where senior managers are committed to the entire process from the very start. They are actively involved in the teams, the training and the celebrations and they champion the cause to

---

[1] *Conference Board Report No. 1167, 1996.*

other members of senior management who are not as closely involved. Having senior management in an advocate's position can often make or break the success of the initiative.

There will always be some individuals who see the customer care initiative as their personal excuse to establish "fiefdoms." Senior management must ensure that this is not allowed. There will also be those who hold more powerful positions in the company but who don't want to get with the program. The success of a customer care initiative depends on the organization's ability to get everyone behind the initiative. Management therefore needs to control and motivate everyone and bring them all on board.

Communicate at the Right Times and with the Right Frequency

Less than successful initiatives tend to keep various departments in the dark about the project's activities. Either deliberately or without thinking, the team plays hide and seek and does not establish a clear plan for communicating results. Contrast this to the strategy developed by successful initiatives that view communication as the lifeblood of the organization, helping employees overcome their fears and resistance to change. One common communications tool is the creation of a vision statement specifically for the initiative. But be careful. Remember that a vision statement must be short, to the point and linked to visible actions and must possess a strong emotional component that everyone can support.

One final thing to keep in mind when crafting your customer care initiative. As Machiavelli once wrote:

It must be remembered that there is nothing more difficult to plan, more doubtful to succeed nor more dangerous to manage than the creation of a new system. For the initiator has the enmity of all who would profit by the preservation of the old institution and merely lukewarm defenders in those who would gain by the new one.

Your new customer care initiative does effectively create a new system, and its success depends on the commitment of everyone within your organization, no matter their position or title.

Benchmarks of Excellence

The following checklist highlights seven benchmarks of excellence that you can use as a guide to help you form your customer care initiative:

- Customer satisfaction is paramount.
- Top management takes an active leadership role.
- All individuals within my organization understand our customer care principles.
- Our organizational culture supports customer care principles.
- Everyone in all levels of our organization is involved in providing customer care.
- We gather corporate performance data using innovative approaches.
- Our organization actively seeks to partner with its suppliers.

A FORK IN THE ROAD AHEAD—WHICH PATH WILL YOU CHOOSE?

You have two options before you. Option one, take the suggestions and best practices described in chapters 1 to 6, and implement those that you are most comfortable with. Option two, follow a step-by-step process that links these best practices into a logical and dependent process, a closed loop that will lead to continuous improvement. There are many examples of organizations that have taken option one and failed. Option two requires more discipline and focus, but it *will* lead to success.

Organizations, and the people within them, need a process to know where to start, the steps that follow and the tools needed to enable you to move along the route map. Customers also need to know how they will be treated, and where they can be involved. After all, if it is not designed with them in mind, it is not customer focused. Accordingly, a defined process, a set of mandatory activities, is necessary in order for your organization to move along the customer care route map.

As mentioned earlier in this chapter, the goal in this and succeeding chapters is to provide you with a *proven* way to achieve Stage III customer care. It is *proven* because it has been developed based on practical research into the best practices of organizations that have succeeded in making it to Stage III customer care, where they continue to adapt and develop new best practices to meet the changing needs of today's business environment.

It is successful because it recognizes that while the process, the route map, will show you the path to success, there are enablers, or tools with which you must become proficient, to ensure that you reach this destination. What are these tools? How have best practice organizations positioned them in their process orientation?

Consider the following, and remember our previous case studies:

- Selective customer segmentation (Not all customers are the same. Your strategic customers require differentiated care.)

- Knowledge management (You must be willing to create and share knowledge. You must learn to mine it for advantage.)

- Strategic account management (Differentiated care starts with the right team and the right focus. There must be a leader and the proper team dynamics.)

- Customer involvement (Customers must be active participants in the process. You must do this *with* them, not *to* them.)

- Corporate culture (The organization as a whole must be committed and involved. You cannot afford weak links and subversive elements.)

Let's take each of these points and explore some additional best practice examples.

Selective Customer Segmentation

The Stage III organization understands the principle that some customers are more valuable than others. The challenge lies not only in identifying these customers, but also in determining the level of differentiated service that must be provided. The following examples show you how some best practice organizations have handled this tricky issue.

BAXTER HEALTHCARE
FLEXIBLE SERVICE FOR STRATEGIC CUSTOMERS

Baxter Healthcare Corporation, a distributor of health-related products to major health care institutions, recognizing that its customers have many suppliers from whom they could buy, developed a means of creating value and incentives for those customers that were willing to direct more of their business to Baxter than the competition. Rebates alone were not the answer, as they could be easily copied.

Baxter began its initiative by dividing its customers into two categories:

- **Strategic**—those that had committed themselves to contracts for building a broad, long-term relationship with Baxter
- **Transactional**—those that did business with Baxter on an order-by-order basis

Baxter then focused its services on helping its strategic customers to improve their medical services and financial performance. Even optional services offered to strategic customers reflected this priority: every service was carefully designed to provide value or savings that far exceeded its cost to the customer. Baxter let customers buy optional services wholly or in part with "bonus dollars." The more the customer concentrated its purchases with Baxter, the more bonus dollars it earned and the more optional services it could purchase. Not only did this allow its strategic customers to tailor Baxter's services to their particular needs, it also reinforced the message that they did not have to pay for services they did not want or need. Baxter created a customer dependency that it could not deliver to its entire customer base. The packaging of this offer required intimate knowledge of the customer and an incentive program that was difficult to copy. It created customer dependency with a select group of customers and created a win-win proposition, increased sales for Baxter, cost savings for its strategic customers.

AMERICAN EXPRESS
TECHNOLOGY-ASSISTED NICHE MARKETING

New generations of faster, more powerful computers allow American Express to zero in on ever smaller niches of the population, aiming ultimately for the smallest consumer segment of all: the individual. It has invested in a massive parallel processor that allows it to vastly expand the profile of every customer. The company can now store every transaction on one single database. Seventy workstations at the American Express Decision Sciences center in Phoenix race through mountains of data on millions of AmEx card members—the stores in which they shop, the places to which they travel, the restaurants at which they eat and even the economic conditions and weather in the areas in which they live. Every month, American Express uses this purchase information to create and update customer profiles, to identify likes and dislikes, and most importantly, predict the likelihood of the customer purchasing similar or related items. Using that information, they then send out precisely aimed offers uniquely geared to each recipient. These offers go out in millions of customized monthly bills that are essentially individualized newsletters sent to its growing number of customers around the world.

Knowledge Management

What is knowledge management? It's the important art of transforming information and intellectual assets into information bits of enduring value. Done properly, knowledge management allows you to harness the intellectual capital of your organization (marrying the knowledge of your workforce across the organization, with information available on your customer, the market and the competition) and bring it to your customers. Take a look at how these organizations have developed best practices perfecting the art of knowledge management.

BRITISH AIRWAYS (BA)
SELECTIVITY

British Airways' strategy is to identify and attract only those customers who will value its services and then retain them for as long as possible. Knowledge management was the key to its ability to execute this strategy.

Using its database marketing system, BA continuously studies its market to identify the segments that offer the possibility of the highest profit margins. It then shares this knowledge throughout the organization in the form of lifestyle profiles. By creating detailed lifestyle profiles of its selected customers, BA is then able to market to them and to entice them to buy more tickets and more services. In effect, it sells its strategic customers a "brand" of service that fits their profile, a profile built on knowledge management. BA sees one of its key competencies as its ability to learn ways of better designing and improving services that high-profit producing customers will value on a long-term basis.

It knows that 35 percent of its customers account for more than 60 percent of sales and possibly a significantly greater percentage of its profits. It also recognizes that these customers are willing to pay for differentiated service. Then, by isolating those customers, or having them identify themselves through special ticket counters, lounges and special sections of the airplane, BA can then follow through on its promise and provide a differentiated experience.

BRYLANE
CUSTOMIZATION

Knowledge management also allows an organization the ability to use its databases to identify patterns of behavior that exist among large groups of customers. With high-speed computers that can crunch huge amounts of data, a company can search out characteristics common to its good customers and use that knowledge to build tailored marketing.

Brylane, an American catalog company that specializes in clothes for large people, provides a good example of this type of database use. The company has 21 million customers on its database and each one has 75 different attributes linked to it.

Using the information generated, the firm customizes its catalogs for each particular customer segment—for example, pink dresses on the cover for one group, and blue trousers for another; free credit for the frequent buyers and express delivery for the impatient. While the catalog itself basically has the same selection overall, the catalogs are organized to meet the needs of key customer segments, putting those factors that are most likely to entice a particular group to buy, closer to the front of the catalog.

Brylane also has another database of 20 million people who have not yet bought from it. The company mines this database of prospects regularly for those most likely to succumb to an alluring "introductory offer."

Strategic Account Management

How do you align your best resources to your best customers? How do you create the best team to service the multidimensional needs of these customers? How do you ensure that there is cross-functional representation on this team, and that the customer has access to the well-informed people at the right time. The answer is strategic account management led by a single senior individual who has the best interests of the customer in mind.

It is also important to recognize that consistent customer service is a prerequisite for successful and lasting customer relationships.

SIEMENS
CORPORATE ACCOUNT MANAGEMENT

Siemens, a global electrical engineering and electronics manufacturer serving customers in over 190 countries, recognized the need to have the right resources assigned to its most strategic customers. Around the world it assigns an account manager to every strategic customer that does business with several Siemens groups. The objective, as indicated above, is to ensure that the customer has a single point of contact with the best interests of the customer in mind.

This strategic account manager serves as a central contact person, taking care of the special needs and coordinating the activities of a multidisciplinary team representing the different company groups. Corporate project account managers look after globally active companies in order to ensure that these large customers receive suitable solutions from Siemens in all corners of the world. Recognizing that regional differences must also be considered, Siemens has also intensified its "regional customer management," for both its high value global and non-global accounts. Its goal is to provide its customers with the best possible solutions to their complex problems. This means that for all related Siemens services in the region in question, the customer only has to turn to one contact person, the strategic account manager at Siemens who will coordinate all the activities.

Customer Involvement

What's the optimum basis for customer satisfaction? A constructive partnership. As discussed earlier, customers want to be involved in those activities that affect them. Developing a plan of action without their concurrence and involvement has a high probability of failure. Let's examine how these organizations involved the customer and obtained mutual benefit.

SIEMENS
CONSTRUCTIVE PARTNERSHIP

In order to streamline processes and promote cooperation, Siemens developed a simple fitness program. It had as one of its cornerstones a customer-oriented mindset. From the start of each project, Siemens works together with the customer to develop a solution that will meet its needs exactly. This form of cooperation often involves close collaboration for a period of some weeks between the customer's experts and Siemens' own specialists. At other times, Siemens' designers may work with the customer on site.

Setting up your own desk in a customer's office may seem out of the ordinary for most people, but for the mobile teams at Siemens' Electromechanical Components Group (EC), co-engineering has become part of day-to-day work. This kind of teamwork with its customers in the automotive industry has proved highly successful, improving communication, radically reducing the number of errors, cutting product development times and producing results tailored exactly to customers' wishes.

XEROX CANADA
ACTIVE CUSTOMER SUPPORT

With its commitment to its customers, and customer research, Xerox Canada could easily be called the "Document Company That Takes Care of Its Customers." Take, for example, its laser printing and document creation division. The group provides hardware and software support for a diverse and sophisticated group of printing systems. But, within this division, service and customer involvement through voice of the customer research has taken on a special meaning—it's both a smart business strategy and something every Xerox customer deserves.

Through its extensive customer satisfaction research—a core tenet of the organization —the division identified the necessary changes needed in order to address customers' needs. Providing direct input is something that the customer willingly provides, because they know that it will lead to enhanced levels of service. Based on these customer surveys and internal company evaluations, two key issues emerged that required resolution in order to improve customer service performance: 1) the need for an active logging system that would alert them to critical or urgent customer service requirements and 2) a need to allow users to access their service portfolio through electronic entry points such as e-mail and the Web. Armed with these requirements, the company re-engineered its approach to call center based customer support and installed an advanced customer support software solution.

The result was an active logging system that alerts the company to critical or urgent customer service requirements and an automated system interfaced with existing legacy systems that will eventually allow users to access their service portfolio through new electronic points such as e-mail and the Web.

Corporate Culture

A sensitive and competent management style, a flat hierarchy and clearly defined development opportunities are essential to the motivation of both management and workers. However, it is the training process that drives a large portion of corporate culture. How you train your people tells them a lot about the organization for which they work. Consider these best practice examples of corporate culture.

ALLIEDSIGNAL
TRAINING AND COMMITMENT

AlliedSignal, an advanced technology and manufacturing company, supplies a wide range of customers with aerospace and automotive products, chemicals, fibers, plastics and advanced materials. As part of its goal to be a premier company, the organization established a cross-functional team to put together a process that would efficiently resolve customer shopping and pricing discrepancies. The team, called the ASAS Reconciliation Quality Team, has as its specific objective the satisfaction of both internal and external customers. The entire team went through four days of leadership training in which they learned to collect the information needed to process customer claims (with respect to return parts and related loss time and damages) and process those claims in a timely manner. One of the goals was to identify the causes of claims and establish a basis for claim avoidance.

AlliedSignal also has a Sales Policy Reconciliation Team that identifies areas needing improvement, most particularly in sales. The team examines the processing of customer credits and adjustments to customers' direct accounts. Potential benefits from this team are cost savings, reduction in process cycle time (the time it takes to process and pay the claim), process efficiency, customer education, and improved employee morale.

NISSAN
INFINITI UNIVERSITY

When Nissan Motor Corporation decided to enter the competitive US luxury car market, it targeted customer service as its main priority. The problem was, however, that the company, and the industry in general, was not known to excel in this area. To show its commitment to succeed, Nissan's Infiniti division established a goal to create a best-in-class training facility and curriculum, learning from the best practices of others.

The division decided to use benchmarking, a process of searching for best practices and the enablers that allowed these organizations to achieve best practices status. It realized that it had to look outside its industry for help and studied the service sector giants that it admired—Walt Disney, McDonald's, Nordstrom and Ritz-Carlton among others—by taking an in-depth look at their employee training programs. Mercedes-Benz, the only car company in the study, was included because of its outstanding reputation and attention to after-sales service.

The company then institutionalized its own training program and established Infiniti University in Scottsdale, Arizona. The curriculum was based on the best practices it discovered during its benchmarking initiative.

- Walt Disney—Non-scripted empowerment (how to allow the front-line the freedom to make the customer experience exceptional)
- McDonald's—Consistency and power of teamwork (how to build and use teamwork to ensure that the power of the team was maximized, the whole being greater than the sum of its parts)
- Nordstrom—Rewarding excellence in customer satisfaction (an internal reward system and how to align the organization for mutual success)
- Mercedes-Benz—After-sales service (how after-sales service can affect customer satisfaction)
- Ritz-Carlton—Signatory customer service (how to establish standards and measure performance against these standards)

Today Infiniti is one of the top organizations in its field because of a strong product, teamwork and a dedication to continuously improve, through training.

LESSONS LEARNED

It's important for an organization to have a process orientation. Even as important is a focus on critical success factors; chosing the right team and empowering them with the right perspective; looking at the customer care process and its linkages; getting senior management on board early; communicating at the right time with the right frequency.

Without a process that has been developed specifically with your company's needs and goals in mind, achieving Stage III (or for that matter Stage II) customer care can be very difficult. And once you've developed your process, you also need to implement it. As you can see, organizations that develop successful initiatives keep an eye on both their process orientation and the key enablers they need to use in their implementation process.

Most likely you have pinpointed a number of enablers undertaken by PHH, the organization that we described at the beginning of this chapter, and Square D, the organization identified in Chapter 1. These include customer profiling, segmentation, VOC research, strategic account management, knowledge management and training to name only a few. You could effectively implement many of these principles and practices in your organization as part of your drive toward establishing a better customer care process.

But remember that restructuring your customer care processes requires a strict commitment to the principles outlined for this chapter and the route map that we will continue to focus on throughout the balance of the book. Success will not come easily. The trick is to capture your experience and capitalize on the lessons learned from successes and mistakes—both your own and others'.

CHAPTER EIGHT

Bringing the Process to Life

THE IMPORTANCE OF ALIGNMENT

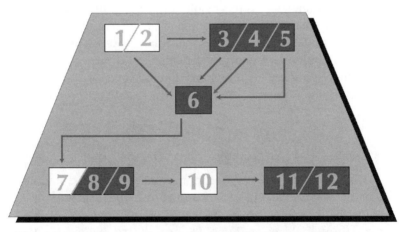

Figure 8.1: Strategic Customer Care Process—Aligning People and Process Steps

USING THE ROUTE MAP: ALIGNING PEOPLE AND PROCESS STEPS

Once you've committed yourself to embark on the process that orients you toward improved customer care (Stage II or Stage III), management and staff must get in alignment. And that alignment must be assessed and either reinforced or recalibrated at various steps throughout the process (Steps 1, 2, 7 and 10).

In this chapter, we will start with the first two steps in our process. We will lead with the importance of management alignment (Step 1) and the role that leaders must play in this critical area. Then, we will discuss the need to assess organization-wide readiness for change (Step 2). Further into the process, strategic account teams must be established (Step 7) and these teams must be aligned, not only to management's direction, but particularly to customer needs (Step 10). The role and importance of training will be discussed in this context.

As in the previous chapter, let's start with a case study of an organization that has achieved success and the role that alignment played. The company is Xerox Business Services, winner of the 1997 Malcolm Baldrige Award, an annual award given by the US Commerce Department since 1988, recognizing US companies that excel in quality achievement.

For years, Xerox has led the charge when it comes to best practices in training. However, the key to its success does not lie in training alone; rather, success has resulted from aligning management, staff and the customer, using training as one of a number of important enablers. The case example that follows, Xerox Business Services (XBS), points out many of the steps in our process, although we will highlight only the four steps that are covered in the balance of this chapter.

XEROX BUSINESS SERVICES
ALIGNMENT FOR SUCCESS

This division of Xerox Corporation has a business philosophy that focuses on customers and continuous learning for all of its 14,000 employees. For XBS, the first step in the alignment arose through its realization of the impact that aligned employees can have on customer satisfaction and the bottom line. In Part I, we discussed the importance of employee satisfaction and its linkage to customer satisfaction and increased profitability. XBS offers further proof. Customer satisfaction has increased as the business has grown—from a 63 percent favorable rating in 1993 to about 80 percent at the end of 1996—significantly higher than the average for a peer group of companies.

But recognition of this principle alone is not enough; it must be reinforced through action and senior management commitment. When compensation and recognition systems are aligned with division objectives, all XBS employees have a direct stake in the success of the business.

Management Alignment (Step 1)

For XBS, the first step in the alignment process occurs with management. To that end, for virtually every business goal, customer requirement and improvement target, there is an XBS process, measurement, and expected result. The senior leadership team achieves this clarity of organizational focus through an activity that is called "managing for results"—an integrated planning and management process that cascades action plans into measurable objectives for each manager, supervisor and front-line associate. Think of the impact that you can make and consider why you do not have this in place. The entire process, the company says, is designed to align goals from the customer's line of sight to the empowered employee and throughout the entire organization.

The major deliverables of the process are five-year and three-year strategic plans and a one-year operating plan. Thus the process encompasses the past, present and future. To encourage organizational learning, for example, the senior leadership team diagnoses the past year's business results and reassesses business practices. These reviews generate the "vital few"—similar to what we described earlier as recalibration— priorities for process and operational improvements.

XBS also develops strategic initiatives based on its understanding of the division's strengths and weaknesses as well as its reading of opportunities and threats, the traditional SWOT (strengths, weaknesses, opportunities and threats) analysis. This analysis draws on the division's extensive competitive intelligence, "voice of the customer" and "voice of the market" information systems. Other inputs include benchmarking data and storyboarding scenarios, which help the division to home in on future customer requirements, anticipate potential risks and challenges, and quantify the resources and action plans necessary to accomplish strategic goals. (More on this in the next chapter.)

Strategic planning generates a "strategy contract," priorities for investment and business partnership plans. These are distilled into a human resources plan, an investment plan and operational plans for each organizational unit, customer account and employee—now that's alignment!

Readiness for Change: Using Information Create Empowered Employees (Step 2)

Empowered employees are at the heart of XBS's customer-focused culture. This is created by understanding employees and their readiness for change. There are many tools that can be used and we will talk about these shortly. In XBS's case this is done through monthly and quarterly reviews, when the effectiveness of work processes is assessed against performance measures. Jobs, work processes and work environments are designed by individuals and work groups to help ensure that they can satisfy the unique requirements of their customers.

Employee commitment and empowerment is woven into the fabric of the company. In brief, XBS offers several innovative assistance options to employees and their families. For example, Life-Cycle Assistance gives employees a $10,000 account, which can be used to fund special needs, including adoption, elder care and first home purchase.

Alignment with Customer Needs: The Role of Teams and Training (Steps 7 and 10)

The division invests more than $10 million annually for training, and it is continually searching for innovative ways to learn. Examples are mini-camps—designed to help employees contemplate and prepare for future changes in the way they work and in how XBS addresses evolving customer requirements. Each employee's personal learning plan is regularly reviewed by assigned "coaches."

Customer satisfaction is the division's number-one priority, and XBS has made knowing the current and future requirements of existing and prospective customers its business. To provide ongoing input to the customer teams, it uses a three-pronged customer satisfaction measurement system to systematically track XBS and competitors' performance in this critical area and to furnish regular feedback to organizational units and account teams. An open, networked architecture provides XBS teams with rapid access to customer data.

Four categories of customer requirements—service quality, sales support, performance of on-site XBS personnel, and billing and administrative support—are subdivided into detailed performance attributes that are measured in semiannual surveys and monthly reviews with customers and then used for planning purposes by the customer teams.

Through XBS's 10-step selling process, a structured tool in which all teams must be trained, on-site services are customized to meet the unique needs of each account. Dedicated account teams develop "standards of performance" according to customer service priorities. These standards, which XBS pledges to meet through its "total satisfaction guarantee," are formalized in operations handbooks developed specifically for each customer.

Results

XBS's commitment to total quality is organization-wide and has generated multiple dividends. On the strength of this approach, XBS—headquartered in Rochester, NY—has grown into a $2 billion business in less than five years. Revenues and profits have increased by more than 30 percent annually, and XBS's share of the US document-outsourcing market has grown to 40 percent, nearly three times the share of its nearest competitor.

The Importance of Alignment

Let me quote from a book written well over two and a half thousand years ago. In his classic book, *The Art of War*, the famous Chinese general Sun Tzu wrote about some profound theories on leadership and alignment, theories that still have application in today's complicated world. According to Sun Tzu, "If you know the enemy and know yourself, you need not fear the result of a hundred battles. If you know yourself but not the enemy, for every victory gained you will also suffer a defeat. If you know neither the enemy nor yourself, you will succumb in every battle."

The message is that you must understand what your strengths and weaknesses are, as well as where your opportunities and threats may be, from a customer's perspective. You must also understand how the customer's perspective aligns with yours and where it does not. Where are the gaps? How can you take advantage of your strengths? How can you best shore up your weaknesses for the battle lying ahead? The steps that follow should help you accomplish this.

STEP 1: MANAGEMENT ALIGNMENT AND MOBILIZATION

This step enables you to gain the buy-in, understanding and consent of your management team. It is a critical first step in which alignment between senior management and the balance of the organization must be achieved. If alignment is not accomplished, the customer care process will be less than optimal.

The Leadership Dimension

What is leadership and why is this so important? Because without the active involvement of your leadership, your customer care initiative has no true champion and you will be out of alignment—it will simply be hanging out there without any anchors. When my colleagues and I review organizations and customer care trends, we inevitably find that for many organizations leadership presents one of the most serious challenges they face today.

Why is leadership so elusive? Because it is hard to define, difficult to discover and almost impossible to create. A review of the organizations that have initiated and achieved success in their customer care processes display a number of common traits among their leaders. For the successful organization, properly aligned leadership will:

- Do the right things the right way.
- Be aligned with its willing followers.
- Influence behavior.
- Be anchored in reality.

Leaders Do the Right Things the Right Way

Is your leadership using the right tools to ensure success? Think about the tools used by XBS (training, incentives, rewards and process). Basically, leaders can do two kinds of things: the "right" things and the "wrong" things. How do you tell which is which?

"Right" things are tasks that serve the customer well and meet their needs appropriately, while "wrong" things create problems and do not help your customers at all. Examples of wrong things include rework, mistake correction and inspection. None of these activities add value for your customer.

Let's take this even further. There are also two basic ways you can do your job: the "right" way, by accomplishing your objectives, and the "wrong" way, which means erroneous actions or actions based on faulty decisions. The goal is obviously to do the right things the right way. Aligned leadership helps you to meet this goal.

Leaders Are Aligned with Their Willing Followers

Does your leader know if his or her troops will follow? By definition, a leader has followers. To be a leader, you must align yourself with others and gain everyone's support—staff, peers and supervisors. You might have a powerful vision, a planned course of action and know exactly what you want to do—but if people don't follow you, you're just an "ideas" person.

The following anecdote underscores what strong leadership can accomplish. In 1993, Craig Weatherup, president of Pepsico, created a crisis. During a three-day meeting with his top 11 managers, Weatherup bluntly explained that while most executives would be satisfied with 10 percent annual growth in earnings, he was not. From now on it was 15 percent or bust. "There's a freight train out there," he said to the startled group, "and it's called 15 percent earnings. We're standing on the track, and we'd better figure out something or it will run us right over."

To emphasize his point he handed each manager a model train featuring an engine with 15 percent painted on its side. On the accompanying toy tracks, facing the oncoming train, were 11 tiny, frightened figures.

It didn't take long for Weatherup's managers to catch his drift. Over the next two years he and his team, working from headquarters in Somers, New York, restructured the organization, redesigned how it did its work and redefined jobs. The change included breaking the division into 107 customer-focused units and dramatically revising processes like beverage delivery and special sales promotions, moves that ended up saving Pepsi-Cola tens of millions of dollars. The division, says Weatherup, will make its 15 percent earnings growth target by the end of this year, three years after he declared the crisis. Profits for the first quarter of 1993 rose 22 percent and employees are changing the organization with gusto.

But remember, leadership means more than the leader alone. It's the relationship or interaction that occurs when the leader and the followers connect. Once leaders have followers, they must work hard to enhance and maintain relationships with them. A true leader's influence arises not from his or her position in the hierarchy but rather as a result of followers being willing to interact with the leader. You cannot demand a certain type of behavior; you can only influence it.

Leaders Are Anchored in Reality

Leaders manage on fact not passion. Do you know the facts, and are they giving you the true picture? Leaders and followers process information from their own subjective, internal frames of reference. Aligned leaders anchor themselves in fact, not perception. Everyone sees the world in a particular way—the same is true of leaders. The question is, is their perception aligned with the employee base, and if not, how do you present the facts in such a way that the gap can be closed, if not eliminated?

Why are these alignment issues so important? They relate to the need of all leaders to know their followers and understand their needs and concerns. Without this knowledge and understanding, a leader cannot hope to be successful. In the following section, we will examine how to get to know your employees—your followers and internal customers—and understand their issues using a tool, called a "change readiness assessment," described more fully under the Step 2 description later in this chapter.

Best Practices in Alignment and Teamwork

The following case study provides a demonstration of how best practice organizations have dealt with implementing change, establishing alignment and exemplary training. Consider how this approach might have a major impact on your organization's development of a customer care initiative.

QANTAS
ALIGNMENT AND THE PEOPLE FACTOR

With so much lip service given to the concept of customer care, how can organizations really make a difference? For Qantas, Australia's major airline, alignment proved to be the answers. Over the past four years, one of the highest priorities within the organization has been to focus on developing an energetic, vigorous, customer-driven organization.

In order to succeed in its goal, the organization identified a number of areas that can drive commitment and a passion for service. Chief among these areas were leadership and the support of its chief executive. According to Karyn Baylis, general manager, customer service and marketing services, there are a number of other factors as well:

- The implementation of a successful improvement program not only ensures competitive standards in the organization, it also represents the ideal vehicle to create the dynamic culture and spirit required for outstanding performance.
- If management's behavior is consistent with stated intentions, it will build credibility, but if it is inconsistent, it will destroy it. Desirable behavior and expectations of leaders/managers must be specified and communicated widely in order to influence behavior.
- What you do for your people will have a profound effect on the success of the initiative. It's therefore important to consider how employees are treated as individuals on a day-to-day basis and how they are involved in opportunities that allow them input on changing the way things are done so they can participate in bringing about change. Also important is the training made available and the opportunities for self-advancement, and the attitude of management at all levels of dealing with people can make or break the initiative.

Senior management took the lead. It caught the attention of its people by convincing them of beneficial results both on a personal level and also throughout the organization. Then came the reinforcement. A great deal depends on how things are done, as behavior is the most powerful form of communication. It's do as I do, not just as I say. To that end, senior management became active participants in the process and ensured that they, in fact, walked-the-talk.

Without a doubt, Qantas relies a great deal on its people. After all, as is the case with almost any organization, they are the tangible point of contact with customers. But, if your employees and the organization's leadership are not aligned, success will be elusive.

Project Management: An Underrated Tool to Support Alignment

Most organizations don't often consider project management a tool for alignment. Consider the following principles of project management as it relates to customer care—goal directed project managment (GDPM)—developed as part of a global Pricewaterhouse-Coopers approach to project management. (If you're interested in further exploration of GDPM refer to the recommended reading list at the end of the book.)

1. Customer care initiatives do not exist for their own sake. Organizations initiate them in response to a business need and conduct them in pursuit of business objectives. All decisions about the initiative should be made by reference to these objectives.
2. The customer care project needs a sponsor or owner—the person or group of people who perceives the need or desires the objective (more on this later in the chapter).
3. It's vital that you clarify, communicate and agree on the objectives at the outset. You need to prioritize these objectives, so that sensible decisions can be made if conflicts arise.
4. In every project, both technical and the human change must be managed simultaneously. If you fail to consider the human factors, the technical change will usually be ineffective and the project will fail to meet its business objectives.
5. Project management is an integrating process, concerned with using skills and aptitudes from people with widely differing backgrounds, in order to maximize contributions to change.
6. It is the critical task of the project manager to structure the relationships between the sponsor and the customer, contractors and suppliers, and all other interested parties, so that everyone knows precisely their roles and responsibilities. The project manager must recognize the conflicts that may arise between different parties and resolve them in an orderly way.
7. Project management needs to be flexible and pragmatic. The

degree of structure, the level of detail and the formality of the methods used should be only those most appropriate to the project and the circumstances.

8. Systems do not manage projects, project managers do by making decisions and initiating action.

9. Project managers must be proactive, anticipating events and planning to avoid problems before they arise. History can be useful to help the project manager manage the future.

10. Each project is unique. We can never plan and predict exactly how a project will turn out, and this introduces risks. The project manager must identify the risks, assess them and avoid them or take action to manage them in order to minimize the uncertainty.

TIP

The Strategic Customer Care Charter

Every time you initiate a strategic customer care initiative, you must consider a number of organizational and functional factors. This is known as the project charter. If you give these factors appropriate consideration, you will greatly enhance your chances of success.

The Project Charter is described more fully in Appendix B.

STEP 2: READINESS ASSESSMENT—IS EVERYONE READY FOR CHANGE?

With this step, the readiness for change of management and the organization is assessed. This serves a dual role, first for pinpointing potential constraints and relevant issues that must be addressed proactively, and second, to assist in selecting the composition of the strategic account management teams (Step 7) that are needed to support the customer action plan (Step 8).

A readiness assessment should not be confused with an employee survey, which looks at how things were and how things are today. However, a change readiness assessment will:

• Determine whether your organization is ready for change.

• Identify areas for action before you roll out your customer care process.

• Identify issues, constraints and requirements.

The internal change readiness assessment encompasses two components. One focuses on senior management and a second on the organization as a whole. Together the two parts of your internal readiness assessment allow you to take the pulse of your internal customers.

Management Readiness

One very common criticism of senior management is that it has allowed itself to drift away from the customer. Senior managers will often deny this, pointing to their visits with major customers and to trade shows, their awareness of sales and their understanding of leading trends.

The fact is, though, that senior management must ask the right—usually "tough"—questions, and when they do, they must be willing to listen to the answers. Many managers will tell you they follow this principle, but often a "management readiness assessment" proves to be a real wake-up call.

The Management Assessment Questionnaire

In order to get input, you need a well-designed framework for receiving comments. The questionnaire must be positioned as a tool to assist the organization in learning about its current perceptions about the customer and those factors that might impede progress (i.e., how strong is the management base and will the front-line react positively to change). So let's look at how it should be built.

In designing the management assessment questionnaire you need to consider a number of factors, including:

- **Context**. You must establish the context of the exercise before you ask your senior management to complete your assessment questionnaire. Why is it being circulated? What key terms and issues is the survey designed to address? Often, definitions of terms used in the questionnaire can be very helpful in establishing the proper context.
- **Current internal perceptions**. Your assessment needs to address senior management's current perceptions. It must identify not only how the respondent perceives current performance, but also how he or she feels other members of senior management, middle management and front-line staff perceive the current

state of alignment. You need to know where the gaps are in order to work to close them.

- **Current customer perceptions.** You also need to understand the perception senior management has of the level of alignment the organization has with its customers' needs. You will ask the customer similar questions (we will discuss this more in the next chapter). By taking a look at the perceptions of both management and your external customers, you can identify significant gaps in perspectives and take corrective action.

- **Customers' future needs.** Again, you need to assess how closely aligned senior management is to issues addressed in your external VOC survey. You gain the most value from your change readiness assessment when it can identify key gaps and issues. Turn the warning light on if you find senior management to be misaligned on issues addressing the customers' future needs.

A Sample Questionnaire

Here's a questionnaire that provides sample wording for each of the key components of the management assessment questionnaire. While you will most likely need to tailor the wording to suit the particular circumstances of your organization, this sample will provide you with some idea on how to go about creating an effective change readiness assessment tool that contains all the necessary elements.

Context

Purpose of this questionnaire:

This brief questionnaire is designed to help us understand how we perceive our current level of service. It is also designed to help us think about the opportunities and challenges that lie before us.

Instructions:

It is important to obtain your views, perceptions, critical concerns and expectations on where the organization is today, and what we must look like in the future. Remember that there are no right or wrong answers to these questions.

Now please answer the following questions.

Current internal perceptions

- *How would you compare your organization's customer service rating ten years ago to the rating that you would get today? On a scale of 1 to 10—where 1 means "declined significantly" and 10 means "improved significantly"—how would your customers rate you?*

- *Some say that a direct link exists between improving employee motivation and improving customer satisfaction. On a scale of 1 to 10—where 1 means "not believable" and 10 means "very believable"—how believable do you rank that statement when applied to our organization?*
- *To what extent would you say employees are currently motivated to improve customer satisfaction?*
- *Some say that there is a direct link between improved customer satisfaction and improved profitability. On a scale of 1 to 10— where one means "not believable" and 10 means "very believable"—how believable do you rank that statement when applied to our organization?*
- *For the same statement, on the same scale, how believable would you say staff other than senior management would rank that statement when applied to our organization?*

Current customer perceptions
- *From your perspective, would an increased focus on improving customer profitability lead to an increase or decrease in our organization's global profitability?*
- *Do you think our customers currently believe that we are actively trying to increase their profitability?*
- *On a scale of 1 to 5 (with 1 being weak and 5 being strong)—how would your customers rate you on the following? (Insert key items from your external VOC questionnaire performance wheel—for example, customer focus, product and service focus, fiscal/financial focus, operations/logistics focus)?*
- *On a scale of 1 to 5 (1 being weaker and 5 being stronger)—how would your customers rate you on these same factors against best practices companies with which they deal that are our direct competitors and other suppliers?*
- *On a scale of 1 to 5 (1 being lowest priority and 5 being highest priority)—how would our customers prioritize, in order of importance, the issues outlined above?*

Customer future needs
- *How is your customer's business changing and developing overall?*
- *Profitability is:*

1	2	3
Increasing	Stable	Decreasing

- *Internal efficiency is:*

1	2	3
Increasing	Stable	Decreasing

- *The top three issues facing my customers are:*
  1.
  2.
  3.

Organizational Readiness

Now that we have management's input, let's take a look at organizational readiness. The organizational readiness questionnaire follows somewhat the same model as the management readiness questionnaire. With this questionnaire you will gain a perspective on how your organization as a whole, your employees, perceive both management and customer alignment. But the assessment must do more than that. It must also look at issues that can inhibit change, thereby playing a major role in identifying key implementation issues that must be addressed even before your plans have been developed. Remember, when you implement your customer care initiative, there will be change throughout your organization.

In addition to questions related to senior management alignment and your alignment to customer needs, the organizational readiness assessment must address questions related to:

- The customer care vision (How far is the organization prepared to develop its customer care process—Stage II or Stage III?)
- Leadership (Will the organization willingly follow current leadership on the path to improved customer care?)
- Commitment (To be successful, senior management, middle management and the front line must be in alignment and committed—will they be?)
- Organization for change (Does the organization believe that they are organized for action and will be able to execute against a plan?)

In Appendix C are some sample questions from organizational readiness assessment questionnaires used in other client situations.

This represents only a small sampling of the questions that can be asked—the average questionnaire usually poses approximately 100 questions. If more than that are used, the questionnaire starts to become a burden to complete. The answers to these questions are then sorted by the respondent's function or position in the organization, by organizational unit, by region and by profit center, to name a few categories. Note that the questions in your assessment survey should have some common questions to those asked in the senior management assessment so that a proper gap analysis can be made.

STEP 7: MANAGEMENT CALL TO ACTION—USING YOUR RESULTS TO BUILD YOUR TEAM

Within this step, your task is to determine the composition of the strategic account management teams, one for each strategic (Tier IV or V) customer. You will use input from the previous gap analysis stage, with particular attention to customer needs, as identified in Step 5. It is important that you identify and select members who will be best able to manage the development and implementation of a customer care strategy and define roles and responsibilities for those that will interface with and support these teams.

By the time you get to this stage, you will have also completed Steps 3 to 6 (to be discussed in the next chapter). You have had the benefit of not only assessing management and organization-wide readiness but also had an opportunity to obtain input from the customer. Even as important, you have been able to analyze this information and identify where gaps exist between internal perception and customer reality.

This analysis should help to identify the magnitude of the task to evolve to either Stage II or Stage III customer care and the type of care and attention that will be required for each of your strategic customers; that is, what the makeup and composition of each strategic customer team must be. And by identifying the gaps in perception that exist between your organization and those of your customers, you can more clearly define the role to be played by your leaders.

We mentioned recalibration at the beginning of this chapter — it often occurs at this step, but if you consider it at Step 1, you will have less need for it here.

Team Membership: The Importance of Roles and Responsibilities

What role must senior management play? Who is responsible for the customer? Who will lead the activity? Will there be an account/customer team and what role will each member of the team play? These are all important questions that must be addressed, and the sooner the better, as they have a significant effect on alignment. The process can fail if it is not clear who is expected to make what contributions and who is responsible for which priorities. There are seven primary roles that must be played, as follows:

- The president/sponsor (quite possibly the CEO or owner)
- The steering committee
- The champion/coach
- The project leader
- The facilitators
- The strategic account management team
- The strategic account manager

The President/Sponsor

More than anyone else in the organization, the president or general manager is the individual who sets your organization's vision, the standards of behavior and the methods for achieving customer care goals. All other staff members look to the sponsor for leadership and support. And they set their behavior and workplace priorities in accordance with those modeled by him or her. It's therefore essential that the sponsor strongly support the initiative implementation, showing true commitment to the entire process in both words and deeds.

The Steering Committee

The steering committee goes by many other names, but essentially it's a group of senior individuals from both management and lower ranks who are in a position to influence functional and organization behavior. As senior members of the organizational elite, they have a vested interest in the ultimate result of the process. In addition to the president/sponsor, members of the steering committee will typically include the organization's vice presidents, other members of the senior management team and representatives of the employees.

These individuals are responsible to the sponsor for the successful implementation of the customer care initiative. Together they develop the customer care strategic plan and participate in steering committee activities geared to motivate their peers and subordinates throughout the development and implementation process. They also support and internalize the customer care initiative, demonstrating visible leadership and enhancing the customer care vision. Lastly, they are responsible for the selection of the additional roles of champion/coach, project leader, facilitators, strategic account management team and the strategic account manager.

The Champion/Coach

The champion guides the process. He or she is a member of the steering committee and guides and supports the customer care process at the senior level. The champion also facilitates communication across all functional lines within the organization (finance, production and sales and marketing, to name a few). He or she is expected to demonstrate a very high level of visible leadership and be actively involved in planning and organizational development. This individual is also responsible for guiding and ensuring the successful implementation of the customer care initiative within a single division or multiple divisions of the organization.

The Project Leader

The project leader makes things happen. Chosen by the steering committee, this individual represents the only line employee involved in a full-time basis in the planning and development stage of the process. Therefore, the responsibility for communicating and interpreting the process to other staff members often falls to the project leader. He or she will usually be selected from among middle management. Reporting to the champion, the project leader's task is to build a strong facilitator network and provide daily coaching and guidance through the customer care process. He or she works to maintain a high level of motivation in all participants and shares ideas and successes with members of the steering committee and department managers throughout the organization.

The Facilitators

Facilitators lead the training process and are most often individuals who have been selected based on their ability to train, motivate and work with other members of the organization. After training employees in the customer care process, facilitators ensure that each member develops sufficient skills and the understanding to participate in and succeed with the customer care teams. They therefore assume the role of internal consultants working with the account teams as advisors on the customer care concept, philosophy and problem-solving skills. By working to encourage and motivate employees and help account teams to focus on specific improvement issues, facilitators serve as central assets to the process.

The Strategic Account Management (SAM) Team

Each strategic customer will have its own strategic account management team and each team will most likely have different membership. Not only that, the composition of the team is dependent on the gap analysis (discussed earlier) and the customer's unique needs.

Your SAM team plays a very important role in the development and implementation of your customer care initiative, because the process your team develops is the very one by which you expect to achieve Stage II or Stage III customer care. Therefore you need to spend considerable time and attention in selecting and aligning your account management team. One of the best ways of defining the team makeup is for the steering committee to assemble for a full day session to review customer information and the gap analysis. This will help to put the issues in context and identify the functions that have to be represented on each team and the best individuals to be invited to be members of the SAM team.

Your team will be the heart and soul of your customer care process. In order to deliver strategic customer care, you need a strong account management team that will manage the development and implementation of your customer strategy and be responsible for proactively managing the customer relationship.

Your account management team will manage the development and implementation of a holistic customer strategy that:

- Identifies your customers' needs and expectations.
- Ensures that your delivery of service is responsive to your customers' requirements and expectations.
- Strengthens and broadens your relationship with key decision-makers in your customers' organizations.

- Ensures that your products and services add value and are of world class quality.
- Ensures the timely delivery of products and services that are appropriately innovative.
- Ensures consistency in the quality and nature of the service provided to your customers irrespective of geography.
- Organizes resources into an integrated and cohesive approach.

The Strategic Account Manager

Chosen by the steering committee, the leader of the team, the strategic account manager, is crucial to the success of your customer care initiative. As team leader, he or she provides a focal point for the company's team in delivering service to the customer. The account manager needs authority and the responsibility to match that authority. Therefore, you must ensure that you give your account manager the mandate to manage the overall customer relationship and to lead the customer team.

The strategic account manager role includes responsibility for the following:

- **Understanding the customer's needs and expectations**. Knowing the customer involves not only understanding its business and industry but also its organization, people and way of doing business. In addition to relevant experience, an account manager must be a good business person, with good leadership skills and a holistic view of your organization's environment. The account manager must also be able to develop a strong relationship with the customer and understand key strategic issues.
- **Developing a solid customer service strategy**. With the help of the account team, the account manager must develop a customer service strategy that is focused on and relevant to the customer.
- **Mobilizing the best people, skills, technologies and products to service the customer's needs**. The issues that arise in an account team require the account manager's personal involvement and sensitivity to balance the interests of each team member in relation to the overall service response to the customer. With the increasing pace of change, the strategic account manager needs to be sensitive to the need to consider changes to the account

team, including changes to his or her own role, as part of an ongoing process of revitalizing the customer relationship.

- **Establishing a communications network between the account management team and the customer**. This includes a schedule of visits to customers. Again, the strategic account manager must play an active role in the customer relationship and demonstrate a solid understanding of the important strategic issues.
- **Making coordination arrangements**. The account manager must also coordinate and monitor the nature, value and timeliness of all services provided to the customer.
- **Achieving customer satisfaction and retention and improving service penetration**. In a way the strategic account manager needs to be seen as the customer's business advisor who also happens to be a supplier, which requires that he or she understands the customer's business issues in a broad, yet meaningful way.
- **Maintaining long-term profitability**. The account manager must look to maintaining the long-term profitability of both the organization and the customer.

In order to be effective, the account manager must be given complete authority that extends to all action plans undertaken for the customer. In light of the significance of this position, sufficient time and attention must be given to the appointment process for a strategic account manager. Management must ensure that he or she can be all things to all people—the customer, the strategic account team and the organization.

The Principles of Team Selection

The strength of customer relationships depends primarily on your organization's ability to help resolve the business issues that your customers consider most pressing. Therefore, you must give the customer access to a multidisciplinary capability, usually through the active participation of all functions of management. Doing so will give you a legitimate contact with a much broader range of customer executives and enable you to provide more broadly based products and services. Full involvement also ensures that product and services offered to customers are the best in class. Prime customers rightly expect world class service and need to be treated as world class players.

If you cannot offer the appropriate expertise in response to a customer's needs and expectations, you risk losing them. You therefore need to give your customer easy access to people with a thorough understanding of their industry. In building your team, you must ensure that team members ultimately represent all relevant disciplines that may have an impact on the critical issues facing your customers—for example, marketing, information technology, R&D, human resources, legal and manufacturing. Within each discipline, at least one team member should be building his or her own links with the customer.

In addition to a multidisciplinary team membership, other factors merit consideration when building your team:

- The customer's organization structure and needs
- The customer's geographical spread
- A flexible team structure. If the customer needs to deal directly with a particular person or department, perhaps for matters of expediency or comfort, your structure must be flexible enough to permit it, yet formal enough to ensure that all customer contact information is shared
- A strategic account manager who stays on top of all interactions with the customer, even in cases where the customer chooses not to go through him or her
- A team that reflects the customer's desired approach
- Team members who can communicate and work well together

It is not unusual for Stage III organizations to let the customer help structure the account team. After all, the purpose of the team is to establish strong customer relationships and serve as the customer's "touch" point. Ask your customers about the type of team structure that would let you respond to their needs across the board. For example, if easy access to your resource base is important to your customers, ensure that the communication channels stay open and accessible.

You must also ensure that you keep abreast of customers' structural changes as they take place. For example, if a customer begins to manage its operations on a market rather than regional basis, you must be willing to change with them. This can be a blow to some of your regions that will no longer be able to provide services to that customer, but your first duty is to respect your customer's wishes.

STEP 10: TEAM TRAINING

Proper training is essential to effect the changes necessary to address your customer issues and the management of change internally. While training will occur throughout the customer care process, this must be completed by this point to ensure that a cohesive, knowledgeable team is prepared to implement the customer care action plan.

When is the best time to deal with team training? There is no clear best practice answer to this question. Some proponents, among them Xerox Business Services (XBS) described in the opening of this chapter, might suggest that training is an ongoing exercise, while others suggest that it should occur immediately after the team is formed. Still others contend that the training is best done— and this is consistent with the approach taken in the example of Square D in Chapter 1—only after the customer care plan has been agreed to by the customer. The reason for that is at that time, the true team makeup and priorities will be finalized and the training needs in the area of product knowledge, communication, planning and team dynamics clearly defined.

Some Best Practice Examples

SOUTHWEST AIRLINES
LESSONS IN LEADERSHIP

Southwest Airlines has often been described as one of the leaders in customer satisfaction, an organization that is admired and emulated because of its financial success. From its modest beginnings in 1971 as a low fare no-frills airline, it has turned its commitment to the customer into a 25-year profit string. Sales in 1997 were $3.8 billion, a 12 percent increase over the previous year.

Southwest has earned its reputation as a leader in customer satisfaction through plenty of hard work and a commitment to training—not only for its front-line employees but also for employees in management roles. Among the courses taught at its University for People is one targeting the different management levels of the organization. While certain elements of the course may differ slightly depending on the functional departments involved, many of the objectives remain the same.

Three of the central elements of the course curriculum are:
- Listening. In a unique exercise, the facilitator presents a discussion topic to a group of students and then notes which ones comment and how frequently. The facilitator is instructed not to talk unless asked a question. At the end of the exercise, he or she shows the group a diagram illustrating how frequently, or rarely, each individual provided input during the class. The lesson to be learned is that if you are too busy talking, you're probably too busy to listen, and that can be fatal.
- Staying in touch. Described humorously as "Get-HOOYO"—get the heck out of your office—this course teaches skills related to the importance of interacting with the front line and getting to know the people: who they are and what their values are.
- Handling change without compromising values. This course deals with ethics and how they should be uncompromising. While the company may grow in the number of planes or cities serviced, what must not change is the individual's integrity, ethics and personal mission.

Southwest also encourages employees to see the organization through the eyes of others by requiring them to spend time in the field working in various departments and learning how the company operates. For example, people in the marketing department may spend a day loading baggage onto planes, taking reservations or helping out as a customer service rep. The purpose is not only to provide them with a broad view of the organization, what every employee does and how it affects profitability but also to demonstrate that everyone must work together, because everyone plays a role in the success of the organization.

How has all this training affected the organization's financial results, relative to its competitors? Southwest was ranked first in customer service among major US carriers in a 1997 *Money* magazine survey. Clearly, Southwest is aligned for success.

SIGNATURE GROUP

In 1995, Signature Group, one of North America's largest outsourced telemarketing organizations, increased its customer service training program from 10 to 34 hours per associate. Part of that time is spent at a core service program entitled "Achieving

Extraordinary Customer Relations." The course teaches Signature associates the skills and strategies required for a visible improvement in internal and external customer service. As well, it provides a common language and understanding of service quality and the necessary skills to respond to various customer situations. The validated adult learning methods ensure that participants master the skills and put them to use. Follow-up training takes place for participants 90 days after the initial training.

The company also offers additional courses like "Coaching Extraordinary Customer Relations" and "Keeping the Skills Alive" for managers and supervisors. In addition to these courses, the entire customer service management team, from operations and systems to data entry and claims, also participates in "The Leadership Challenge." This program lays out the foundation for management to cultivate a work environment that ensures high quality and open, honest communication. The curriculum consists of titles such as:
- The Basic Principles for a Collaborative Workplace
- Personal Strategies for Navigating Change
- Coaching: Bringing Out the Best in Others
- Dealing with Emotional Behavior
- Giving Recognition
- Managing Your Priorities
- Helping Your Team Reach Consensus
- Giving and Receiving Constructive Feedback
- Reaching Team Consensus

New-hire customer service associates are required to complete 10 competencies during a 13-day initial training program. The course consists of six components:
- Signature culture and expectations
- Product and benefit information
- Call processing
- Technical systems
- Quality process
- Extraordinary customer relations

Signature associates who are in training are given daily quizzes and tests that they must pass with a minimum mark of 90 percent. Participants practice phraseology, what to say and how to say it, with role plays that are tape recorded for feedback purposes. As well, videos are used to dramatize customer sensitivity and problem resolution.

New hires as well as other associates are also required to complete customer relations training. Signature developed this series of six modules to provide performance guidelines and models for exceptional service and one-call resolution. The course consists of:

- Customer excellence (to highlight the importance of customer care and the role that each customer service representative plays in the overall success of the company)
- Seeing things from the customer's point of view (to reinforce the important of understanding the customers perspective when probing for clarification or responding to customer requests)
- Customer sensitivity (to help CSR's create a bond with the customer and their need)
- Listening skills (to ensure that the voice of the customer is accurately heard)
- Dealing with problems (to address the issues of conflict and conflict resolution)
- Telephone techniques (which stresses basic telephone skills and an understanding of how what you say, and how you say it have an impact on customer care)

The Need to Communicate: Tools and Techniques to Support the Process

While some might not categorize communication as pure training, it is one of the most important tools to ensure that the training is reinforced, and it is essential for those organizations that wish to maintain a team structure to support the customer care process. Design your team structure to encourage communication between all team members. When it comes to communications, make sure that you do not apply any hard and rigid rules of hierarchy within the team. Though the account manager is the head of the team and has ultimate responsibility for it, encourage other team members to communicate with everyone else regardless of their function, department or seniority. Rank plays no role in team communication.

Because it is critical to the success of your team, you must also make the communication process an explicit part of your service to your customers because it is critical to the success of your team.

Communication truly does affect the bottom line, both in your customer relationships and also in the relationships among team members. And it most certainly has an immense effect on team spirit. If the team goes down, everyone goes down together. You must therefore make sure that everyone on the team understands they have a responsibility to communicate and that communications will always be a top priority.

Here are some guidelines that should help you align your communication process to the needs of your team, your customer and your organization as a whole.

Communication Is between People

Without a doubt, there is no substitute for frequently and regularly communicating relevant information and feedback. With so many options for communication available today, there are no excuses for a lack of communication. Here are five of the most frequently used methods of communication:

- **Face-to-face contact**. You can never go wrong with face-to-face contact. Of course you can keep in touch by fax, e-mail and memo, but these methods will not be effective if you don't see either team members or customers regularly. Successful teams communicate frequently and in a variety of ways, with an emphasis on face-to-face communication (occasionally through videoconferencing) and the active participation of all members. Communicating in person is best, by telephone is simply OK and by fax or e-mail is much less effective. Some teams try to substitute the telephone for face-to-face contact. While it may not always be convenient to travel long distances for just a short, personal meeting, remember to keep things balanced. It's always easier to postpone awkward decisions on the telephone; with a face-to-face meeting, you will be more likely to resolve issues on the spot.

- **Newsletters**. A newsletter will keep the team updated on news about the customer and the team. Send one out regularly every few months. It can be more lasting than a brief telephone conversation and may serve to be a reference document in the future.

- **Regular meetings**. When your team starts meeting regularly, you'll often find that what appeared to be major barriers between team members will simply disappear. Team meetings allow the team to share ideas, identify needs and pinpoint opportunities, but all this can't happen without the involvement of everyone in the team; therefore, a bit of structure and discipline will be required. Meetings also reinforce team commitment to action plans and help generate momentum. Specifically, meetings will push the team to focus its efforts, open up a dialogue with the customer and in some cases customers should be invited to the meeting and share ideas not only between team members but also between different teams.

At a minimum you should schedule a team planning meeting at least once a year to focus on continuous improvement.

- **Workshops**. Bringing the account team together in a workshop forum provides a basis for sharing, understanding and identifying fundamental issues and for producing an initial strategy complete with action plans. Workshops also provide an excellent way to get started, allowing team members to get to meet one another. When you start holding workshops, bring together the whole team to ensure that you understand all the perspectives of the various members.

  You may also want to consider bringing in the customer—perhaps not to the very first workshop but to subsequent ones, as appropriate. Invite your customer to give a presentation at the workshop and use the opportunity to identify and focus on the issues most important to his or her organization. As a result, your action plans will become more relevant and you will have a made a greater impact on the customer's overall perception of your organization.

- **Positive Conflict**. That's right, conflict can be positive! Remember that the absence of conflict is just as apt to be a breeding ground for apathy as it is for harmony. In all organizations, conflicts arise among employees charged to provide the best products and services worldwide. This is only natural.

THOMAS & BETTS

Thomas & Betts, a worldwide electrical organization, welcomes healthy and positive conflict. The company encourages employees at all levels to question thoughts, ideas and alternatives in order to arrive at a more complete understanding of the options, generate a richer range of alternatives and enhance the likelihood that the final solution will improve shareholder value and differentiate Thomas & Betts from its competitors. Positive conflict can enable authentic communication, serves as a release for pent-up emotion, anxiety and stress, and helps individuals to grow and develop.

Technology and Communication

Although personal communication is best, it is not always possible in our fast-paced, hectic world. If it is not possible then consider voice mail, e-mail or videoconferencing if necessary—whatever it takes to ensure all team members are updated on developments. What follows are some other related ideas.

- **Conference calls.** Hold monthly conference calls that involve the entire team. It will help you formalize your communications and will supplement regular ad hoc calls. Set the dates six months in advance and stick to them rigorously. This strategy will help enforce accountability, make team members more open, concentrate more focus on the customer and give your team an identity.

- **Voice mail and e-mail.** As mediums of communication, voice mail and e-mail are enormously underused. Both of them are forms of communication that can be very successful within the team environment, and here's an example of their effective use: Because your strategic account manager must know more about what's going on from the customer's perspective than anyone else on the team, he or she should, on a weekly basis, make a point of keeping everyone up-to-date by broadcasting a message to the team via voice mail or e-mail.

- **Databases.** Consider setting up a dedicated discussion database on each customer. It can be kept confidential for your account team only and allow everyone to pass on any information or intelligence gained in customer meetings quickly and easily. Once established, the team will be able to report to strategic account managers on all issues, opportunities, leads, meetings and customer feedback. After all, if you have a problem in one area that affects the customer, it needs to be understood by people in other areas. Remember, you have no excuses for not circulating information—positive or negative.

Putting Communication into Perspective

A joint study conducted by the Quality and Productivity Management Association (QPMA) and *Industry Week* magazine puts the issue of communication into perspective. The study found several factors that are crucial to communications success. However, it found that organizations' proficiency in these areas is disturbingly weak. A particularly important red flag involves communication between teams and departments about what each is doing and how it might affect others.

The following are among the many meaningful recommendations of the study:

- Encourage active participation in continuous improvement activities by establishing a formal process for suggesting improvements.
- Openly share information about your organization's performance with people at all levels.
- Use newsletters, bulletin boards (electronic or otherwise) and staff meetings to share success stories and give recognition.
- Identify a few primary measures that demonstrate how well your organization is meeting its strategic customer care objectives and communicate progress frequently in newsletters or on bulletin boards.
- Hold town hall or employee update meetings on a regular basis.
- Produce a video at least once a year that openly reviews your organization's situation and future goals.

Change and Stress Management

When designing or implementing any training initiative, it must be recognized that most organizations today are faced with the challenge of scarce resources, which requires the implementation of sweeping changes if an organization is to survive. But, while it's easy to talk about change, it's much more difficult to achieve it—especially when it involves altering people's perceptions of themselves, their roles and even their beliefs. Talk about a tough sell.

Organizations that have already gone through some form of major change have recognized the importance of training but have also learned a few lessons about change and the management of change-related stress as it relates to training.

- **Expect resistance.** If your organization fails to adopt the new disciplines and attitudes necessary to spark transformation, resistance to the changes will occur. No amount of training or technological enhancements can deflect this resistance, although it may temporarily defer it.
- **It's an evolutionary process.** There is nothing instant about change. All organizations dream about a quick and easy implementation of a successful new quality process but the operative word here is "dream." Your people must first understand the process before they can begin to incorporate it into their way of life.
- **Change must be managed.** The change process occurs on three levels within every organization: cultural, organizational and personal. Changes affect different people differently. Although change is stressful, it's also a normal and natural process. The alternative to change is worse: a state of constancy that is at best inflexible, monotonous and stifling.
- **Leadership behavior is critical.** While always important, good leadership behavior becomes crucial during the change process. Remember, leadership behavior inspires others.
- **Stress is predictable and purposeful.** What may seem very incremental and trivial to individuals at one level may be viewed as a major disruption to those at another. Combat stress through an open sharing of the information necessary to make informed decisions and effectively establish recognition for those who support the change process.

Stage III organizations recognize the importance of both the internal and the external customer and how these two groups must be interlinked in order to effect sweeping change within the organization. But more than that, these companies understand that there must be a central cause that brings the organization together. Let's take a look at how Florida Power & Light went about managing change and stress.

FLORIDA POWER & LIGHT: CONTINUOUS IMPROVEMENT IS THE ANSWER

Florida Power & Light Co. (FP&L) began its quest for continuous improvement in quality and customer care—which they see as synonymous—in 1982. At that time, it created an initiative to generate both internal and external customer satisfaction through total quality.

One of the cornerstones of this initiative was the establishment of improvement teams designed to work together to identify ways to solve problems and make improvements. FP&L uses two types of teams—functional teams composed of volunteers who typically work together, choose which problems to address and meet regularly to address problems; and task teams, which are assigned to address specific problems.

When FP&L first introduced this initiative, it implemented the following programs to gain employee support for its change initiatives: training; an employee recognition program; and active communications with union representatives. FP&L's training program evolved from one modeled after Japanese programs to the current one that offers 13 training courses for three different employee levels—facilitators, leaders and team members.

FP&L's program also includes a Vendor Quality Improvement Program (VQIP), which gives recognition to suppliers who join the utility company in embracing the principles of continuous improvement and customer satisfaction. FP&L's Research, Economics and Forecasting Department identifies customer groups and their requirements. Based on the findings, the company translates requirements into prioritized, controllable elements, followed by improvement actions.

What lessons has FP&L learned from its journey?
- Customer satisfaction forms the nucleus of any successful improvement process.
- Employees must be equipped with the proper tools to do a good job.
- Customer needs must be continually assessed.
- Senior management must be totally immersed in the quality process.
- Large companies should consider implementing improvement processes one division at a time rather than attempting the whole company at once.
- The best time to undertake an improvement process is during a crisis because this gets everyone motivated.
- While improvement methods can be borrowed from others, each company must develop the customer care improvement program that best fits its needs.

SEARS
USING PERFORMANCE INDICATORS AS A
DRIVER OF CHANGE

Sears self-engineered turnaround from big losses to big profits resulted from more than a change in marketing strategy. In order to make its successful transition to a best practices company, Sears also had to change both its logic and corporate culture.

CEO Arthur Martinez lead the charge toward change, but he did not do so alone.[1] He worked with a group of more than 100 top-level Sears executives who together developed a business model for the company that tracked success in a number of areas—from management behavior and employee attitudes to customer satisfaction and financial performance. This employee-customer-profit model, as it was called, provided a tool that every individual in the company could use for self-assessment and self-improvement. The principle underlying the model is that a chain of cause and effect runs from employee behavior to customer behavior to profits and that behavior depends primarily on attitude.

By means of an ongoing process of data collection, analysis, modeling and experimentation, Sears developed and continues to refine its total performance indicators (TPI), a set of measures that shows how well it is doing with its customers, employees and investors, the three critical links to success. TPI is more than a measurement system. Sears manages the company on the basis of these indicators, with remarkably positive results. The key is its ability to manage the factors driving employee and customer satisfaction to the benefit of all three stakeholders.

In addition, the company aligned management around the model and its measures. Equally important, sales associates and staff feel a sense of company ownership. The logic behind this model is quite straightforward: unless employees grasp the purpose of the system, understand the economics of their company and industry, and have a clear picture of how their work fits into the employee-customer-profit model, they will never succeed in making the whole thing work.

[1] Rucci, Kirn and Quin, "The Employee-Customer-Profit Chain at Sears" *Harvard Business Review*, Jan.-Feb. 1998. 82-97

The results of its initiative are impressive. In 1997, independent surveys showed that national retail customer satisfaction, which had fallen for several consecutive years, had risen by almost 4 percent in the course of that year. The TPIs had also risen by a corresponding 4 percent. These percentages translated into more than $200 million in additional revenues in 1997 for the company.

LESSONS LEARNED

As we reflect upon the chapter we have just completed, there are a number of lessons learned that are worth repeating.

Alignment is often uncomfortable and difficult. People, in particular the leaders, must manage that alignment so it does not defeat their positive purposes. Alignment must be created at every level of the organization.

Management must lead and be totally involved. Managers can't delegate involvement. They must be visible, vocal and totally involved. Once they lose this role, the process will cease to exist.

Emphasize people and improvement in people. A customer care process views people as resources. It emphasizes identifying their expectations and then meeting or exceeding them. This internal priority reflects itself outward to the external customer and improves the organization as a whole.

A team, not just individual performance, must drive the customer care process forward. Once a strategic account management team is developed, it enables the organization to focus on the achievement of its goals. The team must be responsible for the development of the action plan which must form an integral part of a long range plan that will carry the organization forward into the future.

The process relies on training and experience. Customer care is a discipline. Like any discipline, it is mastered only through the accumulation of knowledge and diligent practice. As the organization's improvement process grows, each individual's understanding will grow through direct hands-on involvement.

Each customer must be treated as unique. While the customer care process provides a conceptual framework on which to build the organization's improvement process, the plan developed for each customer by each account team must be uniquely designed to meet the customer's needs. Each plan is unique, because each customer is unique.

The customer care process encourages the evolution of change. The customer care process is an evolutionary one. Change occurs at a pace with which both the customer and the organization can be comfortable. How they react to the change depends a great deal on the environment in which they work.

CHAPTER NINE

How to Support the Process

THE TOOLS AND PRACTICES NEEDED FOR INFORMATION GATHERING

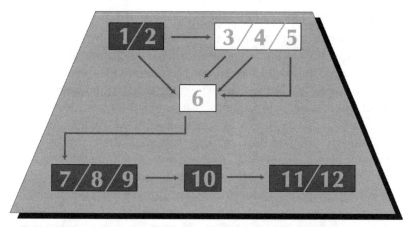

Figure 9.1: Strategic Customer Care Process—Focus on Information Gathering and Analysis

USING THE ROUTE MAP: ACQUIRING NEW SKILLS AND EMBRACING NEW TECHNOLOGY

As shown in the diagram above, the steps related to information gathering are:

- Step 3—Customer Segmentation (see also Chapter 3). Can we identify our strategic customers, and those that we want to move to that tier (Stage III), or should we define our key customer groupings more broadly, by customer need, revenues or geography (Stage II)?

- Step 4—Customer Profiling (Chapter 2). How much data must we collect on each customer? Will we accumulate information by market sector or by product grouping (Stage II), or will we drive for more detailed information on strategic customers (Stage III)? And what infrastructure will we need to support this data collection or data mining need?

- Step 5—Voice of the Customer (see also Chapter 4). Are we prepared to proactively seek out customer needs through personal one-to-one interviews with multiple contact points within the organization (Stage III) or will a representative sample be sufficient to develop action plans (Stage II)?

- Step 6—Gap Analysis. Will we do this on a customer-by-customer basis and then define the composition of the strategic account management team (Stage III) or is an account team structure not necessary (Stage II)?

Organizations set to evolve to either Stage II or Stage III customer care must address these questions and then acquire the appropriate skill sets and technology to prepare for the move to its required stage of customer care. The route map in this chapter takes you through these critical steps of the evolutionary process and addresses the technology and skill sets required. We'll explore the tools needed for success and examine some best practices for strategic customer care (SCC) that can push you and your organization into the forefront of the twenty-first century.

You will find that numerous books, articles and speeches have been written on each of these topics. I've included some of these in a recommended reading list. But before we start in to describe the content of the steps, let's revisit why there is such a strong need to gather information on the customer, understand their needs and address the gaps that have to be filled in order that we may progress to Stage II or III customer care.

Why bother collecting information, segmenting and listening to the voice of the customer? You need to know which customers to keep, which customers to fire and which to target for a stronger relationship that will eventually translate to loyalty.

REVISITING THE IMPORTANCE OF CUSTOMER LOYALTY AND RETENTION

For years organizations have been concentrating so hard on trying to provide excellence in customer satisfaction, they may have been missing the point of strategic customer care and creating inefficiency and adding unnecessary costs. Study after study has shown that it costs a minimum of five times more to obtain a new customer than to keep an existing one. Customer loyalty is a more important determinant of profit than market share. Reichheld and Sasser[1] estimate that a 5 percent increase in customer loyalty can produce profit increases from 25 percent to 85 percent. And if more proof is needed, consider Banc One, which achieved a return on assets more than double that of its competitors, through a concentration on customer retention, depth of relationship (the number of services used by each customer and the level of customer satisfaction). Here's why these measures and a concentration of effort in these areas are so important.

Driving Success through Customer Loyalty

What's the secret to business success? If you said customer loyalty, you're right. But satisfaction and loyalty are not synonymous. Consider this: between 15 and 40 percent of all customers who say they are satisfied actually defect from a company each year. Customer satisfaction in general has a poor correlation with bottom-line improvement. Customer loyalty, on the other hand, as measured by retention rates, is very strongly correlated with overall profitability.

Successful companies no longer focus simply on customer satisfaction. Instead, the strategies are to target customer loyalty, zero customer defection and lifelong customer retention in order to achieve breakthrough profits. Loyalty-based customer management is not just an intuitively good thing to practice; it also has quantifiable links to increased profitability and long-term revenue growth.

Let's look at the customer satisfaction facts once again. Satisfied customers will tell an average of five other people about their positive experiences with a company's product or services. The average dissatisfied customer will tell nine other people about a negative experience with a company's product or service; 13 percent of all dissatisfied customers will broadcast their unhappiness with a company's product or service to 20 others; and a whopping 98

---

[1] Frederick F. Reichheld and W. Earl Sasser Jr., "Zero Defections: Quality Comes to Services," *Harvard Business Review*, Sept.-Oct. 1990.

percent of all dissatisfied customers never complain to the organization—they simply switch to a competitor.

Customer defection exacts monumental costs reflected not just in today's sales loss but the losses resulting from a potential lifetime of purchases by the defecting customer. Combine this with the fact that these customers broadcast their disenchantment with the company and may turn other potential customers away, and the term "monumental" barely describes the losses that might be experienced. Since long-term customers generate much higher profits than customers that have been with you for only one or two years (see Chapter 1), the costs of long-term customer defection denotes an even greater profit loss.

A strong correlation exists between customer loyalty measured by retention rates and corporate profitability. Look at the facts.

The Return on Investment in Customer Loyalty

Parameter	Customer Focused Companies	Average Company	Gap
Return on equity	17.0%	11.0%	6.0%
Profit on sales	9.2%	5.0%	4.2%
Market share growth	6.0%	2.0%	4.0%
Cost reduction	10–15.0%	2–3.0%	7–13.0%

Source: K. Bhote, *Quality for Profit*, Strategic Directions Publishers, 1995.

Table 9.1: The Value of Customer Loyalty

To minimize customer defection and enhance customer loyalty, companies should concentrate on communication, organizational accountability and segmentation.

We've already discussed segmentation in detail (Chapter 3), and we will talk more about this shortly, so let's look at some suggestions on how your organization can best focus its efforts on communication and organizational accountability.

Communication

The importance of quality internal communications cannot be overstressed. Effective communication with employees results in their awareness and can affect their behavior positively. What should your communications goal be? Simply put, to share information throughout your organization with clarity and consistency. Internal communication should be both comprehensive and regular. And don't forget about feedback. Feedback mechanisms that collect customer information and communicate it to individuals who can best take action are an important part of the communications process.

What about external communications? Perhaps the primary focus of any customer care initiative is to communicate the initiative to your customers. After all, these initiatives serve to show your customers how far you're willing to go to make them happy. Furthermore, many customers will regard such initiatives as the sign of a progressive supplier with whom they will want to form valuable partnerships that go beyond the average customer relationship. You should also have a policy of openness with your strategic core customers. Your books on your technologies, your corporate strategies and in a manner similar to that practiced by Square D, our best practice example in Chapter 1, your cost data should be open to your core customers, who should also be willing to do the same. The policy of openness and trust builds unquestioning loyalty and paves the way for the type of strategic partnership the Stage III organization strives to achieve.

Organizational Accountability—From Senior Management to the Front Line

What about accountability? By holding yourself accountable to your customers, you strengthen the loyalty bond between you. If you're not sure how to work toward total organizational accountability to your customers, consider the following suggestions:

- You'll gain employee acceptance if senior management models the behavior you're looking for. This means that management must take strong action to correct any elements of customer satisfaction missing from your organization's service.

- Don't just share your information. Successful companies realize on their investment in their customer satisfaction program when they use the data collected to implement change. When you uncover a problem, follow up with the customer in order to ensure that your resolution has worked to their satisfaction.

- Give your customer contact employees the power to make their own decisions when dealing with customers—especially irate ones— even if it costs the company to do so.

- Ensure that your employees understand that they are links in the chain of customer service and that the chain is only as strong as its weakest link.

- Encourage your employees and reward them for their ideas. Not only do such initiatives serve to raise employee morale, but implementing ideas from employees who touch the customer will enhance your customer care process and build customer loyalty.

- Reward your employees for providing excellent customer care and recognize them as achievers. It can be as simple as saying "thanks."

Best Practices in Customer Loyalty

Let's briefly look at how one best practices organization honed its ability to strengthen customer loyalty. Take a look at the following loyalty idea. Why not take a chance? After all, what have you got to lose? And consider what you stand to gain.

GE PLASTICS
TRAINING THE CUSTOMER

GE Plastics, headquartered in Pittsfield, MA, sells its plastic commodity product and then dispatches teams of trained staff to the customer's factories to teach them how to use less of its product. As part of its productivity program, GE Plastics also sends industry specific teams to help its strategic customers develop new products and process technologies, design new manufacturing processes and keep costs low. In addition, they send follow-up teams to resolve questions—for example, production of too much scrap or inventory problems.

In 1995 alone, the program saved customers more than $68 million, while GE plastics experienced an 11 percent increase in revenues.

As you can see from the examples, you can and should approach your customer loyalty programs with a generous dose of ingenuity and innovation. Customer loyalty heads the list of must-haves for any organization wishing to survive and succeed. So take your pick, adapt and hone a little here and there, and implement your own customer loyalty program.

Now let's turn our attention to the steps in the information gathering process.

STEP 3: CUSTOMER SEGMENTATION

Customer segmentation allows you to concentrate on the select few— your strategic customers. These are the customers for whom you can add value and with whom you can increase profitability (both yours and theirs). It is therefore essential that you use the right criteria and develop the appropriate models for this segmentation exercise. Remember, not all customers are the same, and not all customers contribute equal value to the organization.

Putting Your Knowledge to Work through Profitability Modeling

In Chapter 3, we devoted a considerable amount of time to the definition of customer segmentation. In our discussion of Stage III customer segmentation, we defined a number of criteria that could be used, including:
- willingness to become a partner
- trend of increased revenues generated for your organization
- your current share of customer's business
- potential for this customer to represent a significant share of your organization's business
- significance of your company's product or service to the customer's business
- customer's degree of innovation orientation
- current gross profit achieved from this customer
- potential to cross-sell additional products and services

- current gross profit achieved from this customer
- customer's gross profit potential

Let's spend a little more time on these last two points as they are the most difficult to obtain for most organizations. Customers must be measured on a number of dimensions, including their current profit contribution to the organization and their potential to provide increased profitability in the future. If some products contribute more profit to your organization than others, and some customers have the potential to buy more of these, it stands to reason that these customers should be encouraged. The challenge is how to identify this scenario and how to use information currently in your database to create a model that can estimate profit contribution and profit potential. In a word, how do you create a customer profitability model?

A customer profitability model is generally a unique development exercise—there is no one size fits all. But before you set off on the development road there are a number of lessons to be learned. Organizations within the financial services, telecommunications and utilities sectors have undertaken the most significant amount of work in this area. Those that have been most successful in meeting this particular challenge have essentially developed the ability to tailor and fine-tune their strategies specifically to their most profitable customers (typically the Tier IV and V customers).

But these companies all overcame some significant hurdles in order to reach their current level of success. Consider the following examples of the lessons learned by these best practice organizations:

Relevant Information to the Right People

John Quick, corporate vice president, quality management for Baxter International, puts this principle into perspective:

> *While I see an explosion in the use of IT in the next few years, we must watch for information overload. New technologies will be needed to handle the larger volume of information, distill it into useable knowledge and distribute it across organizations on a real-time availability basis.*

Remember that measuring customer profitability should not be an end unto itself, but rather a means to manage your most profitable customer relationships. All relevant information needs to be delivered to the functions—for example, marketing, planning and budgeting—and points of contact (sales and call centers) that use this information to retain and extend customer relationships. What's needed to put this principle into practice? Good planning and a passion for information sharing.

Compromise and Collaboration Are Essential

To assess and use customer profitability, many of your organization's players must work together and be committed to the concept. It is essential to ensure that your senior managers articulate a customer-centric vision that forces compromise and collaboration among the many different actions your company undertakes.

Monte Alkier, manager, quality and human resources, of the technical services division of Caterpillar, puts this spin on the tale: "We've found tremendous value in encouraging the sharing of best practices, and as quality professionals, we ensure that we maximize this sharing."

Don't Get Mired in Detail, Adopt a Pragmatic Approach

Avoid getting caught up in searching for the single best method—with the many available, you can never ensure that you have the single best method. Instead, be pragmatic and allow for a multidimensional view of profitability in terms of product mix, channel usage and market segments. This allows the initiative to move forward with its business objectives and at the same time enables the adaptability required for the continuous fine-tuning of your process.

One Size Will Not Fit All

Many organizations try in vain to develop a single integrated application that will meet the needs of all users in need of customer profitability information. As Ron Kubinski, manager of commercialization services at 3M, commented, "One size doesn't always fit all—we've learned this from benchmarking. We try now not to make small nonaligned fixes to complex systems."

> *The Challenges*
>
> According to Gartner Research, one of the world's most promi-
> nent information technology consulting and research organiza-
> tions, more than two-thirds of attempts to improve customer
> profitability will be hindered by an inadequate information infra-
> structure, cultural resistance and inertia and the lack of a cus-
> tomer-centric vision. By failing to address these challenges, it's
> very likely that the cost of your customer profitability initiative
> will escalate and your implementation cycle lengthen. In short,
> your chances of failure will increase. The route to success is the
> identification of pitfalls early on in the game, senior manage-
> ment's buy-in to overcome these identified pitfalls and, finally, a
> commitment to a customer-centric vision.

STEP 4: CUSTOMER PROFILING

*With this step, you will assemble information that will help you under-
stand the characteristics of your strategic customers. There is much information that must be collected, analyzed and shared, and technology will
play an important role in this process. Stage III organizations require
more depth and detail than Stage II organizations.*

In Chapter 2, the concept of customer profiling was first introduced, and we discussed what should be collected within the profile and for which customers it was critical. Once you have this
information, it must be analyzed to assist you in developing action
plans to obtain a greater share of your customers' business. What
follows are some examples of what some best practices organizations have actually accomplished.

Setting the Infrastructure through Data/Knowledge Management

MERRILL LYNCH

Merrill Lynch Credit Corporation (MLCC) is a wholly owned
subsidiary of Merrill Lynch & Company. It offers real estate and
securities-based consumer credit products—including personal credit, home, investment and commercial real-estate financing—to primarily affluent individuals. In 1997 it won the

Malcolm Baldridge Quality Award (referenced earlier in Chapter 8.)

The fact that it won the award is insignificant compared to what it accomplished to merit recognition as a best practices organizations. Today, it is powered by intimate knowledge of its customers' needs and a systematic, data-driven approach to performance excellence.

The company relies heavily on a continuous flow of information and a business planning process (BPP) that encompasses both long- and short-term plans. Similar in concept to Step 6 which will be discussed later in this chapter, company strengths and weaknesses as well as opportunities and threats are identified. Monthly and quarterly information about MLCC's performance in eight core and 10 support processes needed to generate and complete a transaction are factored into this plan, as are customer characteristics and market data.

As part of the BPP, every July senior managers translate the strategic imperatives into the company's critical few objectives (we'll talk more about this in Chapter 10, Step 8), critical performance measures for those CFOs, and specific targets for the next one and three years. For example, a CFO might be given the goal to increase process productivity with an aim of increasing shareholder value as measured by the number of days to approve applications, with specific, ambitious and measurable goals. In turn, these CFOs provide the basis for determining partner performance management plans. By involving all of the firm's partners in providing information for the business planning process, and in regular refinements and progress reviews, MLCC ensures that its plans are fact-based and linked to individual goals and objectives.

The client data come from an array of sources, ranging from surveys of clients and financial consultants in the field to written or telephone feedback, internal audits, syndicated research, and benchmarking studies (Step 5). Satisfaction levels of competitors' clients also are used in analyzing client needs. Customer complaints are analyzed in depth, reviewed monthly, and reported back to MLCC regions to identify any sudden changes and to share lessons learned. Negative trends and recurring problems trigger process improvement teams (Step 8) to develop countermeasures and to prevent recurrences. Clients receive acknowledgment of any complaint within two business days, and resolution is arrived at in no more than five business days (Step 11).

MLCC's impressive results show how the information-gathering process, if assembled and analyzed properly, can feed other customer care process steps. It also shows how MLCC's focus on quality management and performance excellence was a wise investment. The company's net income rose 100 percent from 1994 to 1996, exceeding the industry's average, and return on equity increased approximately 74 percent and its return on assets about 36 percent in that same time period.

HUGGIES

Diaper manufacturer Huggies has spent more than $10 million on a database marketing system that collects the names of over 75 percent of expectant mothers in the United States. The names are obtained from doctors, hospitals and childbirth trainers. During their pregnancies, the mothers-to-be receive personalized magazines and letters with ideas and advice on infant care. When the baby arrives, Huggies delivers to the potential customer a coded coupon that enables it to track which mothers have tried the product.

Armed with the information generated by its database technology (based on the mothers' lapse time to redeem the coupons and the number of coupons used, the company can then correlate this information with other research which identifies predisposition to remain a loyal customer and/or actions to influence this), Huggies can determine which mothers will continue to buy its products in the future. Not only is the company selling diapers, it's also creating relationships with mothers that can be utilized across other products over the long term. Knowing who these customers are, their likes and buying frequencies, is invaluable information for targeting other products marketed by Huggies' parent company, Kimberly-Clark.

The Care and Feeding of Critical Information through the Customer Call/Contact Center

Much has been written about the call center, sometimes referred to as the contact center or the customer care center. In fact, we have already written about it to some extent in Chapter 6, where we examined how organizations can use it to provide a proactive sales and service.

Consider the following bit of background on the North American call/contact center industry.

The Industry in Canada

The call center industry in Canada continues to expand at a rapid pace. Impressive telecommunications technology, a highly educated bilingual (and even trilingual) work force, high standards of living and attractive exchange rates provide some reasons why Canada has become a world leader in the establishment of call centers.

A recent study of the North American customer contact center market, conducted by PricewaterhouseCoopers in 1998 for the Ontario government, suggests that by the end of 1997 there were approximately 6,500 call/contact centers in Canada employing over 330,000 staff, with almost half of these operations located in Ontario.

Even though call/contact centers have become big business in Canada, total investment continues to lag behind that of the United States, Europe and even Asia. Because of this, Canada appears to have tremendous opportunities for future growth.

In 1990 and in 1994, PricewaterhouseCoopers completed comprehensive studies of the call center industry in Canada on behalf of Stentor Canadian Network Management. The results of the 1994 study concluded that 86 percent of all call centers were established in order to improve their companies' customer service, up from 74 percent in 1990. Ninety-two percent of the call centers surveyed also expected their operation to continue indefinitely.

While the study noted a 59 percent increase in the number of outbound calls, there was a 134 percent increase in the number of inbound calls, consistent with the greater focus on customer service. As a main application, the use of call centers to handle inquiries and complaints increased from 9 to 32 percent between 1990 and 1994.

This study also concluded that 49 percent of call centers expect their operations to expand by the year 2000, with 70 percent projecting increases in staff, systems upgrades and in employee training.

Attracted by well-educated employees, sophisticated techno-logical infrastructure, recreational amenities, a more congenial pace of life and lower housing costs, organizations with established call centers have rejuvenated the economies of many midsize Canadian cities. They have also been successful in attracting other companies that provide call center support services such as systems integration, personnel training and venture capital.

The Industry in the United States

A recent report by Datamonitor[2] showed that with a compound annual growth rate (CAGR) of 6.5 percent, the call center industry represents one of the fastest growing markets in the United States. Our 1998 PricewaterhouseCoopers research study underscores this and estimates that:

- New entrants as well as incumbents that are starting up or expanding marketing departments focused on winning customers. These organizations rely heavily on call centers to achieve their objective.
- Technology and telecom industries will increase their use of call centers with a CAGR of nearly 12 percent.
- Remote shopping, consumer products and financial services that together make up over 60 percent of the market will continue to see moderate but sustained growth.

As in Canada, organizations in the United States increasingly use their call centers primarily for inbound customer service/customer care type functions, with the average call ratio of inbound to outbound calls being 8 to 1. Other activities handled by call centers accounting for the change in nomenclature to contact center include the help desk, sales order taking, payments and sales. Call centers almost universally use ACD (automatic call distributor-software used to queue and route calls) and call management statistics technology, with CTI (computer telephony integration—software used to integrate telephone with the legacy systems), speech recognition and Internet integration technologies cited as most probable future investments.

---

[2] US Call Centers, *DataMonitor*, 1997.

The increased use of call centers signals a significant investment in both people and technology. This successful combination targets more interaction and intimacy with the customer, while at the same time achieving more productivity internally and an increased ability in delivering increased customer care to those warranting it.

Leading Trends in Call Center

To be effective, you must be cognizant of leading trends and practices in this field as it is the cornerstone of customer care. Some of the trends affecting the customer contact center environments of tomorrow are: 1) personalized electronic service delivery, 2) more outsourcing, 3) integration, and 4) training.

1. **Personalized electronic service delivery**. Stage III organizations in particular will show an increased need for on-line, interactive and real-time support. Through the use of sophisticated on-line tools that enable individuals to evaluate and solve problems quickly, contact center representatives will be able to take inquiries and process each one to determine its priority as well as quickly direct the query to the appropriate representative.

Some Gallup Results

A 1998 Gallup survey asked 555 CEOs of mid- to large-size businesses to forecast competitive practices that will lead to success in the future. Information technology was cited by 74 percent as having the biggest impact on their companies' ability to respond faster to customer needs. Forty percent said that they have already begun exploring IT and its use within the call center environment as a means of communicating with their customers, and 36 percent reported that IT had already boosted their customer responsiveness and loyalty.

---

2. **More outsourcing**. Conventional wisdom suggests that as the size of an organization and its customer base increase, so must the number and locations of its help desk environments. On one level, this logic is correct—after all, all organizations want to remain close to their customers. However, advances in technology no longer make this type of decentralization necessary. There are significant advantages to centralizing operations,

among them the ability to efficiently use technology and reduce the number of employees. Added to that, the outsourcing industry is well advanced both from a technology as well as a training and customer care perspective. As this is their core competency, in many cases they can provide a level of service that is superior to that which can be obtained by the originating organizations themselves and at a significantly lower cost.

3. **Integration**. In areas they are not outsourcing, companies are always looking at how to better manage the services they provide. One of the most important trends is integration—working with marketing and other areas within the organization to combine customer information and to work with common database marketing systems. Telephone systems are often integrated as well, with a centralized phone number for all call centers and systems that quickly routes callers to the most appropriate service provider.

The secret to integration lies in the technology itself. Best practices call centers use computer telephony integration (CTI), automatic call distributors (ACD) and client server technology. These allow the center to use agents more effectively by switching them between a variety of tasks as well as between inbound and outbound calls during overflow periods.

Best practices organizations also offer integrated voice response (IVR), allowing callers to conduct transactions and search for information electronically without assistance from call center support staff. And, not surprisingly, a number of organizations are offering services through the Internet. Services currently provided on the Internet include technical support, product or price inquiries and order processing.

Another important integration trend is an increased use of standardized operating platforms, standardized technology, which results in cost savings in both technological support and agent training.

Best practices companies view database marketing as a knowledge generator, leading to improved customer loyalty and retention. As our discussion suggested earlier, the trend toward integration of information on common database marketing systems has yielded impressive results for participating companies.

Among the benefits reported:
- Improved customer segmentation (31 percent of respondents)
- More attentive, specialized customer service (23 percent)
- Increased customer retention (26 percent)
- Enhanced target marketing (37 percent)
- Increased cross-selling opportunities (24 percent)

Do Businesses Value the Net?

In PricewaterhouseCoopers' 1997 IDEAS survey, respondents differed greatly in their assessment of how they saw the value of the Internet. Forty-seven percent felt that having a Web site was "important," while 39 percent saw it as "not important"—an interesting illustration of the need to evaluate new technologies carefully and to implement them only if they make sense and offer value in your particular situation.

---

4. **Training**. It's been said before, but it's worth repeating: Technology and people must go hand in hand. You need to see faster, smarter service technologies as tools to equip your organization with faster, smarter customer service representatives (CSRs). But that won't happen without the right training. Respondents to the IDEAS survey that reported on the outstanding abilities of their CSRs were those that equipped their front-line representatives with top-notch client service skills, strong product knowledge and up-to-date technology training. The tools most commonly used by best practices companies to assist CSRs include:
   - Standard benchmark models, used to evaluate the strengths and weaknesses of each call center
   - Silent monitoring (the ability of a third party, usually the quality control or training group, to listen in on the conversation without knowledge of the customer and agent) and incentive programs to reward excellent customer service
   - Performance support systems (PSSs—databases, electronic policy and procedure manuals and even video clips that are linked to the agents' desktop to provide support for nonroutine questions) often combine a number of expert technologies that provide advice to CSRs.
     Best practices organizations also take a strategic approach to workforce management, differentiating service levels by customer segment and providing flexible staffing based on the requirements of each call center.

STEP 6: GAP ANALYSIS

*This step allows you to identify where gaps exist, both internally and exter-
nally, between your senior management, middle management, front-line
support staff and your customers. Remember that many areas of potential
disconnection can exist. This step helps to facilitate this identification and
cause pause before proceeding with customer action plans.*

Using Performance Measurement to Assist in Gap Analysis

*The three most important things that you need to measure in a busi-
ness are customer satisfaction, employee satisfaction and cash flow.
If you are growing customer satisfaction, your global market share is
sure to grow. Employee satisfaction gets you productivity, quality,
pride and creativity. Cash flow is the pulse, the vital sign of life in a
company.*
—Jack Welch, Chairman and CEO of General Electric
(Fortune, 1/93)

Do you know where you stand in terms of your organization's performance? It is absolutely critical to know where you are today in the
heart and mind of the customer and be in a position to address it.
During the steps of the strategic customer care process information
is being obtained from a variety of sources (Steps 2, 3, 4 and 5) and
then must be compared, synthesized and a gap analysis formed.

One additional factor—performance measurement—must also
be introduced, and its importance is underscored through the
examples that follow. It can be a critical driver of change within
your organization. Too often, organizations limit gap analysis to
customer satisfaction measurement alone. In truth, multiple measures must be considered. In the Merrill Lynch case earlier in this
chapter, the company obtained client data from an array of sources
which include surveys of clients, written or telephone feedback,
internal audits, syndicated research, benchmarking studies and
surveys of satisfaction levels of competitors' clients.

Even more important, Stage III organizations use performance
measurement to drive process improvement in a never ending
struggle for continuous improvement. Consider the way Prudential
Insurance and FedEx went about this.

PRUDENTIAL

Prudential Insurance Company defines its mission as helping its customers achieve financial security and well-being by providing them with information, advice and products that best meet their needs. To accomplish this, the organization has taken a progressive approach to identifying customer needs through internal performance measurement.

At Prudential, customer focus is a business method that determines how an internal process affects customer decisions and shapes customer perceptions. Customer focus gives customers increased weight in Prudential's decision making by reminding decision makers that the customer is ultimately the person who drives the business.

Establishing customer-focused transaction standards played a critical role in moving the operational areas of Prudential toward an externally focused perspective. Managers use a multistep method to let their customers drive this process. In fact this process has many linkages to our twelve-step process:

1. Prioritizing processes based on customer satisfaction, frequency of occurrence and overall impact on the formation of company perceptions (Steps 6 and 8).

2. Identifying customer satisfaction drivers for each key process (Step 5).

3. Analyzing performance gaps in order to understand how Prudential performs relative to customer expectations and industry benchmarks (again, Step 6).

4. Identifying cycle-time (the time taken from start to end of the process) and cost contributors for each process, using an activity-based cost (ABC) analysis. By being able to break down the process into a set of discreet activities, the organization is aware of the costs to service the customer and in turn customer profitability for each product and service purchased (Step 3).

5. Completing a cost-benefit analysis to determine how much incremental revenue would be gained by improving service levels, thus allowing an investment dollar target range to be set for improvements (Step 8).

Prudential's commitment to building a business based on customer needs and expectations requires focused attention on developing and tracking measures that reflect customer needs and perceptions, so that the company can obtain the necessary information to guide its business decisions. As they begin working with their business partners on each new project, members of the customer focus group ask a standard set of questions:

- What business processes influence customer perceptions of the company?
- How do customer needs, expectations and perception translate into retention, referral and defection?
- How do those behaviors affect revenue?
- How do sales agents and other employees influence customer opinions, and what must we do to support them so they can meet or exceed customer expectations?
- How do essential activities affect the cost of providing service, and how do process changes impact the bottom line?

Prudential has applied customer focus beyond its life insurance division to other business units, including investments, mutual funds, annuities, retirement services, property and casualty insurance and group medical insurance. Not only does this provide a valuable model for balancing customer feedback and company objectives, it also demonstrates the importance of an unrelenting customer focus across the key points of customer contact.

FEDEX
MEASURING CUSTOMER SATISFACTION

Over the years, FedEx has developed a number of measurement systems and goals to help keep it on the service track. These include measurement of customer satisfaction levels through its service quality indicators (SQI), employee satisfaction through its survey feedback action program and competitive impact through outside studies. The goal is quite simply, 100 percent customer satisfaction, 100 percent of the time, regardless of customer segment served. That is the core service level to which it must deliver, not strive toward, although there may be enhanced services offered for its strategic customers. By establishing a core level of service, it's always clear to every employee how well the company's doing in achieving its long- and short-term objectives.

SQI Category	Point Value
Wrong day late	5
Right day late	1
International	1
Invoice adjustments	1
Missing paperwork	1
Traces	3*
Damaged packages	10
Complaints reopened	3*
Lost Packages	10
Late Pick-ups	3*

*The Customer Service Department has an effect on or is affected by these issues.

Table 9.2: FedEx's Service Quality Indicators

At the heart of FedEx's measurement system is SQI. The SQI lists the 12 most frequent customer complaints and assigns a relative weighting to each one depending on the corresponding level of customer frustration. The greater the weight, the greater the impact on the customer. The company then assigns each category, (*see* above), a given point value (which may be changed over time) and which the company tracks on a weekly basis. By looking at the scores, relative to its stringent standards, the company can quickly identify where its gaps are and which processes warrant attention. Note the high weighting associated by lost or damaged packages, which obviously causes the highest level of frustration for the customer.

The multifaceted SQI does not limit the concept of customer satisfaction to simply on-time delivery. Even when the company meets the "bottom line" of a service commitment—professional rendering of the service on time and within pricing expectations—the customer may still be disappointed for any number of other service-related reasons. The SQI therefore allows the company to identify and measure its own critical points, implement the necessary information management tools to manage and track actual service performance and customer satisfaction for each point, and work to eliminate root causes of service failures through ongoing quality improvement processes.

Discourage Employees from Playing the System

Have you ever thought about linking your performance measures to your employee compensation plans? Ideally, your monetary incentives should reach across all levels of your organization. Structure your incentive programs so that all employees in an organizational unit receive compensation if the unit meets its customer satisfaction goals. You can also reward exemplary service on the part of individual employees on an ad hoc basis.

There's a danger, though, with linking customer satisfaction measures to financial rewards. Some people will play the system—they'll plead with customers to fill in the survey the "right" way. How do you ensure that your performance surveys are not being subject to employee doctoring? Best-in-class companies regularly audit their rewards system to ensure that employees aren't spending their time, resources and energy trying to figure out a way to manipulate their customer ratings instead of concentrating on filling the gaps. Remember, as long as you can ensure that you use your customer satisfaction to help your people understand how they are doing and what improvements to work on, your system will be less likely to become corrupt.

LESSONS LEARNED

In this chapter we discussed a number of tools to help you in your evolutionary journey to Stage III customer care. As with all best practices, these tools and skills are used to their best advantage when you tailor them to the individual circumstances of your organization. As you get ready for our next chapter on action planning, consider the lessons we can learn from Merrill Lynch and other best practices examples covered in this chapter.

The data that help in the segmentation and gap analysis will come from not just one but a variety of sources (internal, external VOC, competitive, customer profiling data and more). Data gathering and its management cannot be viewed as a one-time effort to be assembled once and then ignored; it is soon outdated. Effective management of customer relationships requires an integrated approach to gathering and using customer information and delivering the appropriate action warranted by a gap analysis.

Knowledge management—the art of transforming information and intellectual assets into enduring value for your customers and your people—is all about accessing the intellectual capital of the organization and bringing it to your customers. New products, new services, new organizational capabilities and quicker response and time-to-market result not only from an ability to manage knowledge but also from an understanding of how to effectively use that knowledge.

Information gathering is an art and a science. The challenge is to determine the right amount of information to be gathered, for the right customers and then translating it to action plans that can enhance the customer relationship.

CHAPTER TEN

Action Planning

BUILDING THE PLAN WITH TOOLS
AND PRACTICES IN PLACE

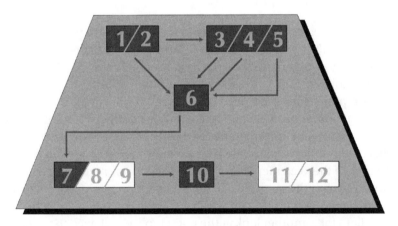

Figure 10.1: Strategic Customer Care Process—Action Planning and Recalibration

USING THE ROUTE MAP: TIME FOR ACTION

With this chapter we're nearing the end of the evolutionary journey that forms the basis of this book. By this point on the route map to Stage III customer care, we've walked through the process definition, critical steps and enablers.

In the previous chapter, we also discussed a number of important tools and skills that can help you as you progress in your evolution toward strategic customer care.

Now we put these tools and skills to work. First we will build the strategic action plan (Step 8—Strategic Action Planning). Following that we will discuss the need for customer alignment (Step 9). We will then skip a step (Step 10—Training) as this has already been covered in Chapter 8 and move to implementation development and mobilization (Step 11). We close with the step that starts the route map all over again, Step 12—Performance Monitoring and Adjustment. Without knowing where you are relative to where you plan to be, you will never succeed in achieving strategic customer care.

STEP 8: BUILDING YOUR STRATEGIC ACTION PLAN

In this step, you plan and document specific action items that are most important to the customer and establish ways in which to address these items with profitability enhancement in mind. This is the heart and soul of the customer care process.

Before you can begin building your strategic action plan, you need to ensure that you have all the information you need and all the necessary components to start the action plan process. What needs to be done before you can start working on building a strategic action plan? First, you need your research information: data from your customer profile, your voice of the customer (VOC) measurements and your internal change readiness assessments. You also need your team in place, with an account manager to head it. Once you have these elements in place, your account manager can begin working with the team to take the information you've collected and shape and mold it into your strategic action plan.

Let's take another look at the main tools you'll need to get to this point.

1. **The customer profile**. This important data collection provides us with information on:

   • The size of the customer's wallet

   • The customer's potential

   • Your share of the customer's wallet

• The competitive map

• Your current relationship and target zone

2. **Voice of the customer (VOC) survey.** This research tool provides critical action items that will meet customer needs and assesses customer perceptions of your strengths and weaknesses relative to your competition.

Now your strategic account manager and strategic account management team can begin developing the plan.

Two additional considerations must be taken into the development process. First, the components of this plan should be presented to the customer for validation. Second, the complete plan will now form part of the client profile, to be accessed and referenced by any member of the account team and any others who touch the customer.

Before you start to work through the series of activities that will give rise to your new action plan, let's consider some important concepts and terms as they relate to the customer profile and VOC.

The Size of the Customer's Wallet

Before you can develop that plan, however, you need to understand each customer's total expenditures on products and services—the customer's wallet. With this knowledge you can allocate your resources effectively.

• **Sizing the wallet.** How much money has been spent? By whom? On what? With which vendor? Break down the customer's expenditure by buying center, line of business (LOB) and customer need.

• **What drives expenditure?** You'll also need to identify the factors driving the customer's expenditures, such as market issues (expected market growth, competitive entrants, new product entrants), and the influence of buying centers (what role does each play in selecting strategic partners) and will these factors continue to operate with the same level of intensity in the future?

• **Understanding wallet structure.** This includes an exploration of how concentrated the expenditure is and how stable is the expenditure.

- **Forecasting wallet growth**. Determining how much growth a customer's wallet will undergo can have a significant impact on your strategic plans for that customer. Ask yourself the following questions: Where is the wallet likely to grow? By LOB? At a particular buying center? And how much will it grow?

- **Your share of the wallet**. You also need to evaluate your revenue in terms of your share of the customer's total wallet. You must address these questions.

  –What is your share by product/line of business and buying center?
  –Which LOBs account for the bulk of the customer's wallet?
  –Do you maintain a presence in the largest parts of the wallet?
  –What is the relative profitability of different parts of the wallet, and are you in the most profitable sections?
  –What is your share by area of potential?
  –Are you in the fastest growing parts of the customer wallet?
  –Are the largest parts of the wallet also growing the fastest?
  –Where can you gain market share?
  –Are you positioned appropriately against the key elements of the wallet?

Competitive Analysis

The competitive analysis also focuses on the customer's wallet, because the competitive structure of the customer's wallet both shapes your profitability and constrains your options. Before you can hope to expand your share of the customer's wallet, it's important that you understand whom you'll be competing against. It's critical for you to identify:

- Who are your competitors by LOB and buying center?
- Do you face different competitors in each LOB and buying center?
- Is your competition concentrated or fragmented?
- How are they positioned? Who is gaining share and who is vulnerable?
- Where are your competitors' home bases?
- Who seems to be building new home bases?
- Are you targeting those competitors who seem vulnerable?
- How important is this account to your competitor?
- What is the customer's view of your organization?

- Does the customer see you as a niche provider or a major provider of products and services in several areas
- Does this perception match your revenues generated from the customer and your share of wallet?

New Product and Cross-Sell Opportunities

Your customer's changing wallet and the competitive structure of this wallet provides you with an opportunity to cross-sell and market new products/services. You need to make some strategic decisions to determine where you should focus your marketing efforts and why. Who are your competitors? Why will you win? To do that you must know the most attractive parts of the wallet to target.

Other issues that should be addressed include the cross-sell opportunity. Ask your team if you will be able to cross-sell services into the buying centers in which you have strong relationships and a good track record. Can you anticipate how your competitor will respond?

There may also be new product opportunities. What new products/services can you offer that the customer has not previously bought from your organization? Do you think it is appropriate for this customer? Have you positioned the LOB?

Wallet Expansion

If your customer's wallet doesn't show signs of growing or if there is a great deal of competition over it, your account manager must focus on areas of emerging importance to the customer where the competition is not strong. This essentially creates a new wallet or expands the current one. You have created a new wallet when customers identify new strategic issues and problems that need to be addressed. Account managers should participate in the dialogue that prompts the customer to move ahead on a new course of action. As you're developing your account plan, ask your team which issues or buying centers present your organization with the potential to create a new wallet.

Seeds for the Future

Because it may take several years before your customers are ready to buy a new product or service, your account manager therefore must plant "seeds" to educate them. In some cases this may be a long-term wallet expansion strategy. If so, you need to begin ongoing dialogue with the customer about the long-term challenges of its business. In team discussions, you should be addressing the central uncertainties, the problems this customer will face and ways in which you can help solve these problems.

With your seeds, you plant in the customer's mind the view that this is your issue—you identify it, you help the customer develop and define it and you remind them of this from time to time. You own the issue. In order to succeed with your seedlings, you must get your customer to associate your organization with being a part of the solution—that you're an expert in solving the problem.

A successful strategic plan will also depend on your account manager understanding how customers evaluate the products and services they buy. With this understanding, your account manager can become more efficient in marketing and positioning. For you to enhance your positioning with the customer, you must understand:

- What expertise and capability the customer values in each of your lines
- How your customer evaluates its different providers
- Your customer's view of service expectations
- Your customer's assumptions on price and value

And finally, before you can develop your action plan, you must understand how your customer views your capability in that particular product/service. How the customer sees your strengths and weaknesses relative to your competition in each LOB is critical. If you do not know this, it will be difficult to develop a strategy to build on your strengths and protect against your weaknesses in relation to the customer's buying criteria, which is why you must build this fundamental issue into your VOC questionnaire.

Developing Your Action Plan

You are now ready to embark upon the planning process. The purpose of action planning is to synthesize the information, analysis and understanding that you completed earlier, and to allocate your resources to realize your clearly articulated and defined objectives. To accomplish this, you must complete the following five activities:

1. **Understand Your Current Positioning**

2. **Develop the Competitive Map**

3. Evaluate Your Current Relationship Tier and Your Target Tier

4. Develop Alternative Strategies

5. Identify Constraints

Activity 1–Understand Your Current Positioning

In this step you determine the attractiveness and potential of your customer's total spending on services and where you want to go. To make an accurate determination, complete the following three charts.

Activity 1A: Sizing the Wallet. Determine the total amount of customer spending, how much the customer actually has budgeted to spend for the products and services you have the potential to provide and identify the spending by customer buying center (CBC) and line of business (LOB). Then ask yourself the following questions:

    Given the size, structure and composition of the wallet:

- Do you have an appropriate level of resources relative to the size of the wallet?
- Do you have a competitive position that forms the major part of the wallet?

Activity 1A : Sizing the Wallet							
	Customer Buying Center (CBC)						
Line Of Business (LOB)	A	B	C	D	E	F	G
Product Group A							
Product Group B							
Product Group C							
Product Group D							

Table 10.1: Sizing the Wallet

Activity 1B: Understanding Customer Potential. You must understand how the customer's wallet will change over the next two to three years. For each of the cells—the intersection points where LOB and CBC intersect—ask your team to identify:
- Where is the wallet growing and declining? How will the wallet change over the next two to three years?
- Do you have a competitive offering that is well positioned against the wallet parts that are experiencing growth?

Activity 1B: Understanding Customer Potential							
	Customer Buying Center						
Line Of Business (LOB)	A	B	C	D	E	F	G
Product Group A							
Product Group B							
Product Group C							
Product Group D							

Table 10.2: Understanding Customer Potential

Activity 1C: Determining Your Share of the Customer's Wallet. This next step gives you a representation of your current positioning within each of the cells. For each cell, figure out your share of the customer wallet as it exists today. At the conclusion of this step, you must know:
- Your share of the total wallet
- How many home bases do you own in the customer's organization today? Remember, a home base is one in which you hold a dominant share position, generally the result of a good relationship with the customer and strong competitive positioning.

Activity 1C: Determining Your Share of the Customer's Wallet							
Line Of Business (LOB)	Customer Buying Center						
	A	B	C	D	E	F	G
Product Group A							
Product Group B							
Product Group C							
Product Group D							

Table 10.3: Share of Customer Wallet

Activity 2–Develop the Competitive Map

In this step you must consider whether the competitive landscape can be changed, and whether you have an opportunity to benefit from any such changes. Using the template created earlier, you need to determine the leading supplier in each major cell or part of the wallet and identify what constraints, if any, the competitive map imposes on your account plan. Remember also to question the profitability dynamics. Ask yourself:

- Is this a profitable relationship?
- What can be done to maintain or improve the profitability of this relationship?
- Should we invest in further coverage to expand our share? Will it be profitable?
- Are you positioned in the right parts of the wallet?
- Are you positioned on the right issues?
- What is the appropriate target tier for this relationship given the analysis of the wallet, the competitive map and the customer's potential?

Activity 2: Develop the Competitive Map—Who Is the Leading Provider in Each Cell?							
	Customer Buying Center						
Line Of Business (LOB)	A	B	C	D	E	F	G
Product Group A							
Product Group B							
Product Group C							
Product Group D							

Table 10.4: Creating the Competitive Map

Activity 3–Evaluate Your Current Tier and Your Target Tier

You need to make a decision as to whether you can improve your customer relationship zone and whether this target tier will be profitable. In order to do this, you must first evaluate your current relationship tier. Here's a review of the five tiers (which we examined in depth in Chapter 3), ranging from Tier I, Competitive Supplier, the lowest relationship, to Tier V, Strategic Partner, the most integrated.

Transactional/Competitive Supplier. At this stage, sometimes described as "no home base" positioning, you are a me-too supplier and the customer's primary concern is obtaining the best price and delivery. You'll find that the customer, while satisfied with your product and service, is willing to shift its loyalty at a moment's notice.

Niche. As a niche supplier, you most likely have one home base but no opportunities to cross-sell your products or services. You'll likely improve your positioning only with a new product or service but even this will be a difficult task. There is no depth to your relationship with the customer.

Diversified. The customer sees you as a value-added supplier, but you're not yet a strategic partner. You find that the customer values your judgment and that the potential exists to move beyond your single home base positioning.

Major provider. At this stage you are moving up the spectrum of valued supplier. You most likely have at least two home bases, and the potential for further cross-sell exists

Strategic Partner. At this stage, you share risks with the customer, with whom you're both horizontally and vertically integrated. The customer places a high degree of dependence on you, and the products and services you offer your customer are perfectly aligned with your customer's needs. The buying centers within the organization see value in the relationship.

What tier is your customer relationship in, and why? Given the nature of your customer's wallet, the competitive map and the fit of the relationship with your strengths, are you in the appropriate tier? Using the chart below, identify your current relationship tier today (position the arrow on the appropriate tier) and a target tier (represented by the star), in which you could realistically be within the next 12 months.

1 Competitive Supplier	2 Niche	3 Diversified	4 Major Provider	5 Strategic Partner
•No secure revenue	•One "home base" and no cross-sell	•Present in several parts of the wallet •Only one "home base" •Presence but no share presentation	•2 "home bases" •Solid, secure revenue •Opportunistic cross-sell	•Multiple "home bases" (more than 4) •Vertical and horizontal integration •Risk transfer and high leverage

Figure 10.2: Current and Future Positioning

Activity 4–Develop Alternative Strategies

You can use five broad strategies to move a customer to a higher tier:

1. **Gain share**. This strategy will require you to gain share within a component of the wallet in order to establish a home base. There may be more than one home base that you wish to pursue, but you must be realistic.

2. **Offer new products and cross-sell**. When you have secured at least one home base, the account team can expand into new areas usually within that same base. With this strategy you must address which new products/services you wish to sell and prioritize.

3. **Identify and penetrate new buying centers**. One buying center will not be sufficient for your strategic accounts. You may therefore wish to identify new buying centers in the organizations of your strategic customers for the services for which you have already established a track record. Your goal is to identify your strategies for penetrating them.

4. **Implement margin strategies**. Your positioning within a customer improves when you create a value-added relationship, which usually translates into higher margins and improved customer retention. With this strategy you must plan how best to create a value-added relationship.

5. **Develop new ideas and expand your wallet.** As a strategy, wallet expansion can improve customer retention, as it increases your customer's dependency on you. From your customer's perspective, it has been introduced to a new opportunity by a strategic partner who is looking out for its best interests. Wouldn't you like to deal with a company like that too?

In the chart that follows, identify which of these strategies, individually or in combination, you wish to follow for each of your customers. Again, be careful not to take on too much. It's far better to show progress by getting on base rather than always trying to hit that grand slam home run.

Activity 4: Develop Alternative Strategies
Gain Share • •
Product/Service Strategies • •
New Buying Centers • •
Margin Strategies • •
Wallet Expansion • •

Table 10.6: A Strategy Template

Activity 5–Identify Constraints

In many cases, constraints prevent the capture of attractive wallets. The most common constraints include:

- **LOB/product capability.** A lack of competitiveness or product superiority in your LOBs means that your opportunities for winning an increased share of wallet are reduced.
- **Customer perception.** The customer may perceive your organization as a specialized, narrow provider, which places constraints on the ability of your account manager to cross-sell.
- **Competitive position.** The competition may have a stranglehold on certain components of the wallet.
- **Service quality problems.** Negative experiences that your customer has had with your organization in the past could be a major obstacle to success.

   How do you identify the constraints that may be preventing you from securing an attractive wallet? Your VOC interview should contribute significantly to the information you will need to determine whether constraints exist. Fashion the probes in the VOC to determine the customer's best suppliers and why your organization has achieved below satisfactory ratings on the performance wheel. Once you know what they are, make sure that those differentiators become part of your action plan to this customer.

In the chart below, list all the relevant constraints that will affect the execution of your strategies.

Activity 5: Identify Constraints
LOB/Product Capability • •
Customer Perception • •
Competitive Position • •
Customer Satisfaction Issues • •
Other • •

Table 10.7: A Template for Identifying Constraints

STEP 9: CUSTOMER ALIGNMENT

Aligning your customers lets you gain both customer input and customer support of your draft strategic action plan. This is critical to the Stage III customer care process as it signals a one-to-one alignment between the strategic customer and the organization.

Obtaining Customer Feedback/Input

The foundation of all your relationship development activity rests on your ability to obtain customer satisfaction with the implementation of your action plan. Therefore, it's important that you examine your customer feedback process prior to building your account plan. While this will be addressed in more detail later in this chapter, here are some of the criteria that will assist you as you build your action plan.

Does your organization have a regular or systematic process to collect customer feedback on its performance? This feedback will become the foundation of your customer profile. Accordingly, you must be able to identify who at your customer's organization participates in this feedback process and how actively that participation occurs.

The feedback you collect will only be as good as the use to which you put it. You must evaluate your customer feedback and satisfy yourself as to the reliability of the information. Do not challenge customer perceptions—in the eyes of customers, their perception is reality. Instead, ask your team what they believe must be done to improve the customer's perception and to what extent a problem or risk exists.

Not only must you seek out customer input, you must verify it. Therefore, before implementing the action plan, it's essential to validate your customer feedback. Discuss the feedback with the customer and ensure that you fully understand the context and specifics of your customer's perceptions.

Account Teams Must Solicit Agreement

Establishing standards and measures is not an end in itself. Once you have defined the standards, account teams should solicit agreement with these performance measures with the customer and also internally.

Internal performance measures concerned with the quality of products and service delivery will clearly be of interest to the customer. Remember that your customer's input into the process will raise further expectations of future involvement. To meet these expectations, you should establish a clear account team response policy that covers several activities. Here's an example:

- **Define responsibility**—for receiving, processing and resolving issues raised by the customer.
- **Spell out authority**—to resolve problems and identify available resources.
- **Set up procedures**—to ensure that those who need to know are kept informed.

- **Set time standards**—for a quick response.
- **Establish follow-up procedures**—to ensure that complaints and inquiries are brought to a successful conclusion.

Although the account team has primary responsibility for the relationship with the customer, the team's role also includes an element of stewardship. They manage the relationship on the organization's behalf. Management, therefore, must keep an interest in and remain responsible for the team's performance. Normally, management will be involved at the point when service is being reviewed. However, it is usually appropriate to gain input from management regarding the design of performance measures as well.

The Role of the Strategic Account Manager

A strategic account manager must ensure that the team is managing customer relationships successfully. However, it would be a mistake to think of the role of the strategic account manager as a monitoring one only. He or she must add value to the account team. To this end, you may find it helpful to assess performance on an ongoing basis. Ask the account manager to use a one-page self-assessment form to focus on the essential issues. Even if the results are not reported to anyone, the form can still serve as a "stabilizer" that ensures the manager is responding to developments as he or she needs to.

Competitors' Activities

An analysis of an account team/client relationship would be incomplete without an assessment of the activities of your competitors. Teams can gain invaluable guidance on a customer's service expectations when they have an understanding of the factors underlying competitors' successes. More importantly, with this knowledge teams can also better understand how these expectations have been met. An analysis of competitive activity can also provide valuable information on the customer's perception of the role played by the account team.

Access to Relationship Information

Effective management and administration of a strategic account requires access to and management of information on the relationship. An effective review of the relationship requires, at a minimum, internal data on:

- Total revenues and profit
- Products and services sold
- Revenues by product line and service
- Service team contacts

You should therefore establish internal information systems that can provide up-to-date information. This means making someone responsible for updating the information and interpreting it. You risk embarrassment otherwise. For example, you would be rather red faced if you were unable to answer a customer's question about the total volume of products and services that have been delivered.

Accountability

The strategic account manager should be accountable for the team's performance in managing each customer relationship. Judge success against certain criteria for which performance measures should be established in the service strategy. These criteria could include the following:

- An assessment of the state of customer relations and the level of satisfaction, based on direct customer solicitation
- The customer's perception of the quality of products and service provided and the value added
- The customer's recognition and use of the organization as a major source of products and services
- The breadth, depth, diversity and profitability of products and services provided

Independent Review

An annual review of customer satisfaction for each client should also be carried out by the management team against the criteria set out above. This review should assess the state of the relationship, progress, achievements and opportunities. Lessons learned and experience gained should then be communicated throughout the company. While strategic account managers have overall responsibility for the customer relationship, a review manager should be assigned who will have responsibility for reviewing the success of the service strategy.

The review manager should aim to add value to the operations of a service team through the review process. In most instances, the review will be conducted on a face-to-face basis with the strategic account manager and, where appropriate, with the service team rather than through a remote review of documentation.

The review manager might complete the service review by:

- Participating in the strategy development process, for example, by attending a workshop or other customer satisfaction team meeting or by reviewing the output (for example, the service strategy document).
- Participating in the service review meeting or by reviewing the outputs from such a meeting.
- Convening a specific review meeting with the management team and possibly also with the account team.

    The review manager may choose to involve others in the review process—specialists or industry group leaders, for example—but the responsibility for conducting the review remains with the review manager.

STEP 11: DEVELOPING AN IMPLEMENTATION PLAN

This step enables you to effectively design the implementation strategies and activities that you have previously identified and agreed with your strategic customers. It is important to recognize that some of these activities may not be provided by the organization, and that is where outsourcing and strategic alliances play a role.

The Elements of the Plan

The account manager and account team must now focus the implementation effort on three central points:

1. **Critical few objectives**. Every account plan should contain critical few objectives (CFOs)—the "must win" imperatives on the account. Establish your CFOs with input from your VOC and concentrate the team on the most important tasks with the highest probability of success.

2. **Who, what and when milestones**. A timetable outlining the specific actions the account team will take allows the account manager to monitor progress and track marketing activity.

3. **Target economics**. While the primary purpose of the account plan is not to develop account budgets, you'll find this invaluable in formulating financial and nonfinancial goals and benchmarks.

Developing an Implementation Plan		
Critical Few Objectives	Responsibility	Critical Milestones
1.		
2.		
3.		
4.		

Table 10.8: A Framework for Implementation Planning

In developing your implementation plan around your critical few objectives (CFOs), consider the following:

- Target the decision makers carefully and the issues against which you want to position yourself. The larger the matrix of relationships, the more challenging the task of positioning your firm.
- Analyze the buyers' criteria for buying, their framework for thinking about the issues and the organizational context shaping their decisions.
- Define product/services emphasizing the right connection with your customer's problems/objectives and the connections between the services you offer.
- Differentiate vis-a-vis competitors including sharp differences in the action plan you offer, your approach to the problem and the capabilities of your organization.
- Enhance service value by positioning services against high intensity customer problems and more senior decision makers.
- Build a track record using past successes and building a reputation for superior product/services.

    Use the following template:

Setting Goals		
	Year 1	Year 2
Revenue (by buying center and/or LOB)		
Gross margin (by buying center and/or LOB)		
Number of home bases		
Target zone		

Table 10.9: A Framework for Tracking Goals

You may wish to add additional goals into the following template. Just make sure that they can be quantified and measured.

Now that you've created your action plan, obtain input from the customer and monitor it to ensure that you are on track and committed. Read on.

Your Implementation Plan and Outsourcing

Why is outsourcing so important to your evolution to Stage III of the customer care process? To answer that question, let's first understand what activities are candidates for outsourcing, and through the results of the IDEAS 97 survey results, what activities are most frequently outsourced.

Not all activities are candidates for outsourcing. It is essential to retain key activities that are not provided in the marketplace at the same level of expertise and cost benefit that you can provide. Unique activities and those processes that are not easily separated from the organization are not generally candidates for outsourcing. Activities that are often outsourced are those that are readily available in the marketplace and which can be delivered more efficiently and effectively by someone else. IDEAS 97 gives us some of the answers. According to the study, some of the most common functions currently being outsourced include:

- Pension administration
- Customer care functions
- Equipment and building maintenance
- Staff training

The answer to using outsourcing is selectivity. Organizations that have outsourced selectively—a full 35 percent of IDEAS respondents—report the following benefits:
- Decreased operating costs (33 percent)
- Improved operations (23 percent)
- Reduced capital costs (23 percent)
- Increased flexibility (26 percent)
- Improved customer service (32 percent)

Companies who selectively outsource their noncore functions (those which do not offer a strategic advantage in the marketplace) stand a good chance of enhancing their ability to service their customers while at the same time reducing the costs of operations. With these kinds of figures, it's easy to see why Stage III organizations embrace the concept of outsourcing so eagerly.

Will You Need a Strategic Alliance?

In addition to outsourcing, there's something else that goes hand in hand with outsourcing and sets Stage III organizations above the crowd—the willingness to use strategic alliances and partnership to create value for its customers.

In today's rapidly and constantly changing business environment, we all know that being good enough just isn't. Not only do we need new processes simply to stay competitive in the new economy, but we must also refine our more traditional mindset about the customer relationship. The fact is, an organization will likely be unable to compete if it tries to be all things to all people or tries to house all its offered competencies within one organization. Do you really think you can afford to be state-of-the-art—or even proficient—in all things?

Some organizations have chosen to identify the activities and processes that are core to their competitive advantage and outsource all noncore competencies. Some have taken an even bolder step—one modeled after a Japanese business model of the fifties called *keiretsu.*

About Keiretsu

Before World War II, large family-controlled corporate groups called *zaibatsu* characterized Japanese business. Major *zaibatsu* included Mitsubishi, Mitsui and Sumitomo and controlled a majority of Japan's large industrial, financial and service firms. The occupation forces broke up most of these *zaibatsu* after the war.

During the period of economic recovery in the 1950s, 1960s and 1970s, many firms that were formerly components of the defunct *zaibatsu* formed relationships based on their common traditions and business relationships. Known as *keiretsu*, these federations were formed for a variety of reasons, including the thwarting of foreign takeover of Japanese companies. The *keiretsu* accomplished this through share interlocking, in which *keiretsu* participants held equity shares in each other's companies. Banding together stabilized the value of the participant companies. A significant number of shares were held by parties that valued the shares based on their own financial requirements and those of the company being held rather than on the basis of a public equity market. This served as a stabilizing factor in the determination of the value of the companies.

Keiretsu in the Twenty-First Century: The Virtual Company

Stage III organizations have taken the concept of *keiretsu* and translated it into twenty-first century principles. Namely, these organizations identify with its main underlying concept: band together and add value to the customer relationship while at the same time making the customer more dependent on your organization.

You've likely heard of the virtual company. In effect, virtual companies arose from an application of the principle underlying *keiretsu*. Successful companies in the new millennium will be composed of business components that can be mixed, matched, reused and outsourced as needed to meet the company's business objectives and ultimately, the customers' needs.

In effect, the virtual company is simply a series of business partnerships developed by a company to help it meet its objectives. Whereas the traditional *keiretsu* was often a partnership based on cronyism, the twenty-first century version embraced by Stage III organizations will be based on business expediency and information sharing.

DELL COMPUTERS AND *KEIRETSU*

In 1996 Michael Dell and his company gave shareholders a 198 percent return on their investment. The results flowed in part from Dell's practice of a form of *keiretsu* as well as from a focus on the customer. Dell used a simple business model that wouldn't have been successful if it had not continually considered the customers' needs and its own desire for increased profitability flow. The business model's prime principles included:

- Dealing directly with sophisticated, high volume customers
- Building product on demand
- Eliminating resellers
- Focusing on quality, reduced inventory and increased cash flow

How are these principles relevant to *keiretsu*? Consider the following. Dell Computer has been very selective in its appointment of senior executives at the board level, its selection of strategic suppliers and its focus on high-value customers. Also, rather than supply customers with identical, mass-produced models, Dell Computer transformed the telephone staff from order-takers into custom builders and designers. To his credit, Michael Dell focused on the things that allowed the company to add value.

THE DELL BUSINESS MODEL
Balanced Priorities

Figure 10.3: The Dell Business Model

Today, when a customer calls to place an order, a salesperson takes the requirements and then configures a custom-built system from a wide range of custom components—from suppliers whose core competencies lie in building quality products. The end product is a uniquely tailored computer system designed to meet each customer's specific needs. The Dell concept created a near-perfect union of low-cost, low-overhead direct marketing with high-margin, high-profit custom sales.

Dell's business model is shown below. This model, combined with an uncommon approach to keep people focused on Dell's business objectives, lies at the root of Dell Computer's success.

Dell believes that the way the organization communicates within the company is as important as the incentives that it offers its people. The company spends a lot of time talking about its strategy, explaining to its employees how it works and why. It tells its people about the things that it has done and explains to them what the competitors are doing. And it explains how the model works against competitors' practices. It has segmented its business very clearly and it understands the economics in each segment. By targeting the richest areas of the market, it avoids the customers who are not as lucrative for the company.

STEP 12: PERFORMANCE MONITORING AND ADJUSTMENT

This step is both the end and beginning of the journey to strategic customer care. It is a necessary tool for conducting ongoing, repetitive evaluation of the existing state of affairs and the tracking of performance against goals. Remember, customer expectations are progressive.

Monitoring Your Performance against the Action Plan

In Chapter 9, we discussed performance measurement as a driver of change for Steps 5 and 6 (voice of the customer intervention and gap analysis). Now we will discuss performance monitoring, in the context of the action plan you developed in Steps 9 and 11.

Within each of the action plans you have developed, you must identify service standards—both qualitative and quantitative. In order to ensure that you achieve the desired results outlined in your plans, you must also monitor your plans and ensure that proper reaction mechanisms are put in place to adjust them should conditions change in the market environment or the plan prove ineffective.

The following sections address the issues of 1) Setting Service Standards and 2) Quantitative and Qualitative Measurements.

Setting Service Standards

It's an underlying principle of strategic account management that account teams must manage their customer relationships in a way that achieves the objectives set out in your action plan. In other words, you must meet—or exceed—the customer's expectations. Accordingly, account teams need access to information that allows them to measure their success against this dual objective.

This is where service standards come in. In a nutshell, service standards let you deliver service in line with predetermined and agreed-upon expectations.

Standards Based on Objectives

Individual customers need individual attention. Remember we rejected the old one-size-fits-all theory. General standards are simply not enough. The action plan must therefore identify specific service standards that can be applied to each customer. The standards should be designed so that when your teams apply them, they will meet the relationship objectives that you defined in the action plan.

Service standards provide important guideposts to help you meet your objectives that are defined in terms of the issues that matter to the customer. But you must also address the following challenges head-on at the very start of the implementation process:

- Standards won't be applied unless everyone in the team knows what they are, what they mean and why they're there.
- The team needs to agree on the standards that count.
- You should publish the standards so that team members can continually refer to them.
- Identify the standards you need to separate out the "nice to haves" from the "need to haves" and then prioritize and select a few that can be applied.

Use the VOC interview as a tool to assist you in this selection process by defining the features of service your customers perceive as most valuable. Then establish service standards to make sure that you deliver.

You use standards because you want to deliver a quality of product and service that you have defined with reference to the benefit the customer receives. It is, therefore, essential to ensure that your customer agrees with the standards.

An account team's overall relationship with a customer depends on a variety of individual and personal interrelationships. When you establish service standards for the overall relationship, base the

Service Feature	Service Standard
Effective Account Management	• Same-day acknowledgment of all telephone contacts • Letter responses (reply within three days) • Technical inquiries, solutions or progress report (reply within two days) • Feedback process -Annual review of relationship -Response to feedback within one week
Delivering value for money	• Quarterly summaries of product and service benefits (reports to explain value added) • Feedback process (explicitly request comments)
Demonstrating a knowledge of the business	• All reports to assess operational impact of recommendations • All account team members to attend the customer's induction course • Required attendance at quarterly team meetings • Feedback process (to explicitly request comments on team understanding)

Table 10.10: Service Standards

expectations on those of your key customer contacts. You may need to adapt your standards to suit the needs of other contacts your team members may have.

Involve your customer in the strategy meeting. Once they're in agreement with your standards, you have a clear direction for the year ahead. Realistically that is the maximum length of time that action plan will cover. At the end of each year you must recalibrate and again set short-term objectives. Following that, you can then scope your work so that when you review your performance—with the customer, of course—you understand the criteria against which you will be assessed.

Quantitative and Qualitative Measurements

Want to be effective in monitoring performance? Then restrict your measurements to a vital few standards that can truly make a difference in your customer relationship. Keep your standards to one page; then publish them and give them to each account team member. If the standards have been developed in conjunction with your customers, give them a copy. It will give your team incentive to deliver when they know that the customer also has a copy of the standards.

Quantitative Measures: Past Performance

Quantitative measures provide hard evidence of a service team's success but are usually generated some time after the delivery of products and services. Such measures are, however, invaluable for gauging the past success of team performance. For example, financial measures can be used only to assess the quality of past relationships—they result from good relationships in previous periods. They do, however, give you a solid reference point. Further, even if you can't be precise, you can still use these measures to help you set targets and goals. Although it's always difficult to make future commitments, remember that they do not need to be firm commitments. You should consider them to be moving targets, whose purpose is to provide you with a focus.

Qualitative Measures: The Current State of the Relationship

Qualitative success measures are of greater value to an account team as they can complement the quantitative measures by explaining the numbers. This is particularly true of customer responses to VOC questionnaires. With qualitative measures your team receives information on the current state of the relationship.

Objective	Success Measures
Enhancing perception of product/service	Positive response to the VOC survey
Quality	Improved performance in: • Delivery of value for money • Service team understanding of the business • Service team cohesion
Strengthening trust	No surprises to the team on: • Business issues • Major developments
Increasing product penetration	Product line extensions known and valued
Enhancing perception of our capability	Internal contact and referrals

Table 10.11: Qualitative Measures

In developing measures, remember to target objectives rather than activities. Measures must relate to the objective of an action and not the action itself. If you aim to spend time helping the customer increase profitability, your measure should be the extent to which you've helped your customer increase profitability and not how much time you've spent on the activity.

BRITISH AIRWAYS: USING CUSTOMER COMPLAINTS TO IMPROVE CUSTOMER RELATIONS

British Airways' customer relations department used both qualitative and quantitative measures to become "the customer's champion" through a focused research initiative. It studied why customers defect. Intrigued, the company did more research and ultimately decided to develop a plan to encourage all customers to stay with the airline.

To champion the customer, BA's new management instituted a number of changes within its customer relations department. They now:

- Use customer feedback more effectively to improve service.
- Prevent future problems through teamwork with other departments.
- Apologize to the customer for the problem he or she has experienced.
- Reply to the customer on the same day if possible and no later than within 72 hours.
- Assure the customer that the problem is being fixed.
- Contact the customer by phone to follow up.

BA's results? The retention rate among those who complain to the customer relations department has more than doubled to 80 percent. In addition, the business saved—plus increased loyalty and new business referrals—relative to the department's total costs has increased by 200 percent.

LESSONS LEARNED

Are we there yet? Only you are the judge. We've come to the end of the process now and with it, the final stops on the route map to Stage III customer care.

We have learned that the action plan must focus on key opportunity areas. This can only occur if a detailed customer wallet analysis is completed and the input received in the VOC intervention (Step 5, Chapter 4) is acknowledged. You must review your plans with the customer, before the plan is finalized. By so doing you have made a commitment to the customer that you will take action with them and hopefully a bond between your organization and theirs will be established.

Training, while important for all steps in the process, is critical at this stage. No one individual will execute against the plan, rather it will be a team effort. And that team requires training in how to act as one, the need to share, team dynamics as well as product and customer care knowledge.

Implementation planning must focus on the short term. As you start off in the strategic customer care process, be sure to not bite off more than you can chew. Work on items that are important to the customer and which can be implemented quickly. Success breeds success. You will never be able to establish a trust relationship, if you do not honor your commitments.

Set goals and measure against them. You will need both qualitative and quantitative goals to guide you. That is the only way that you will be able to gauge if you are on course or if you need to take corrective action.

The steps that have been outlined in this part of the book play a very important role in the success of your evolutionary process. But remember, as with all elements of this process, nothing is ever static—and the process steps must stay in tune with the changes taking place almost daily in our business environment today.

CHAPTER ELEVEN

Destination: Success

You've prepared for the journey. Your foundation is fortified, and you have your route map in hand. Now it's time for the journey itself. Your destination is hopefully, Stage III strategic customer care. Let's take one last look at the skills you've acquired, the pillars and the step-by-step process—the route map—we've developed to help you achieve Stage III customer care.

PART I: BUILDING THE FOUNDATION

In Part I of this book, we examined the fundamental practices and skills that organizations must build upon in order to complete the evolutionary process toward Stage III customer care. Each chapter discussed one of the five pillars, the skills and knowledge that you will need to acquire in order to start the process.

These five pillars are customer/information profiling; segmentation; customer research; technology investment; and customer management.

1. **Customer/Information Profiling (Chapter 2)**—As you evolve through the three Stages, the detail needed to support the customer care process must also change. At Stage III, you are fully evolved. But in order to accomplish this, you must understand in

which supplier category you are today and to which category you wish to evolve. The five tiers are:

Tier I: The Transactional/Competitive Supplier. In this category, you are a "me-too" supplier. Merely one of many who can meet your customer's needs, your customer is mainly concerned with obtaining the best price and delivery.

Tier II: The Niche Supplier. If you are a niche supplier, you most likely have one strong home base within your customer's organization but no opportunities to cross-sell your products or services.

Tier III: The Diversified Supplier. If you find yourself in this category, you're on the right track. Your customer sees you as a value-added supplier although not yet a strategic partner.

Tier IV: Major Provider. Although your relationship with your customer cannot be described as a strategic partnership, you are well on your way. Your customer sees you as a valued supplier and respects your input.

Tier V: Strategic Partner. This is the pinnacle of customer/supplier relationships. You share the risk with your customer. Your customer depends on you to a high degree as a true business partner.

2. **Segmentation (Chapter 3)**—Once you've acquired that basic database of invaluable customer information, which we discussed in Chapter 2, you can begin practicing segmentation. But as you evolve to Stage III customer care, there are certain principles that you must accept. You must recognize customers as assets, each unique and having different values, some more important than others. It is therefore necessary to focus your efforts on your most profitable customers and a resulting lesser focus on the less strategic customers. You need to focus your efforts on those customers that, on in-depth analysis, displayed the greatest potential if not currently the greatest profitability. After all, all customers not being equal, some simply may not be worth the time and effort required to maintain them.

3. **Customer Research (Chapter 4)**—As stated above, not all customers are the same, and thus the techniques used to gain the voice of the customer must reflect their relative importance. Also as you evolve to the next stage, there are many benefits to be gained. This research will allow you to get closer to your

customers, and give you input upon which to base your strategy and your actions. The results will allow you to develop a service strategy rather than merely relying on a gut reaction. In addition, it will allow you to meet the expectations of an increasing number of customers who have VOC initiatives of their own and, moreover, who consider the employment of VOC measurement a mark of a progressive organization.

Effective VOC programs produce information previously unknown, no matter how much your service team thought of itself as in touch with the customer. VOC data provides a baseline against which to gauge future improvement, providing you with an invaluable ability to measure that improvement.

4. **Technology Investment (Chapter 5)**—What you want is not just the best technology but the right technology for your stage in the evolutionary process. Whether or not your organization should invest in any particular new technology will depend on a number of factors, such as your stage of evolution; the effect of the technology in driving or enabling change in your organization; what is available to your customers from your competitors; your customers' needs; and your goals and strategies.

   As you progress through to Stage III, so must your technology and your skills in using it. In making technological investments, organizations must stay true to the distinct goals of the stage they're in. For those in Stage I, technology must be able to assist you in acquiring new customers. For Stage II organizations, technology must be used to enhance customer satisfaction and drive loyalty. Stage III organizations must use all of the above and more. If you do not know what stage you are in and make the appropriate technology investments, you will court failure.

5. **Customer Management (Chapter 6)**—Despite the fact that each stage of the customer care evolution has a different set of goals and needs, you must focus on customer management regardless of which stage your organization is in. And as you progress through the stages, your treatment of your customer base must change. Organizations that have evolved to Stage III customer care successfully implement a strategic approach to customer management. They recognize that, in order to manage strategic accounts, they must appreciate why we need a common

approach to strategic account management, and understand the role of the account manager and the composition of the strategic account team. It is of the utmost importance to recognize the customers' strategic needs, both today and in the future—*(What is happening on this account?)* and to develop a strategic plan that balances your organization's capabilities with your customer's needs *(What do we—customer and provider as a team—want out of this account?)*. Finally, it is essential to develop an implementation plan that keeps the process on track *(How will we achieve what we want?)*.

In summary, Part I outlined the three different stages in the customer care evolutionary process, and the five pillars of the foundation. It also drew your attention to the focus and goals unique to each stage and provided examples of best practices of organizations at each of the three stages.

PART II: USING THE ROUTE MAP

In Part II, we concentrated on the 12 steps that organizations must follow in order to complete their evolution to Stage III customer care. To succeed in Stage III, you need to change your focus. You can no longer be all things to all people and must concentrate instead on adding value to your most important customer relationships. Armed with the skills you acquired in Part I, and the evolutionary route map set out in Part II, you will be able to develop initiatives unique to the special circumstances of your company and your strategic customers. There are 12 steps in the route map that leads to Stage III customer care.

1. **Management Alignment and Mobilization (Chapter 8)**
You've learned that gaining buy-in, understanding and consent from management for your customer care initiative will be integral to success. In particular, our key learnings have included:

- **The importance of alignment at every level of the organization.** Alignment is often uncomfortable and difficult. People, in particular the leaders, must manage that alignment so it does not defeat their positive purposes.
- **Why management must not only lead but also be totally involved.** Managers can't delegate involvement. They must be visible, vocal and totally involved. Once they lose this role, the process will cease to exist.

- **The need for internal staff growth.** A customer care process views people as resources. It emphasizes identifying their expectations and then meeting or exceeding them. This internal priority reflects itself outward to the external customer and improves the organization as a whole.
- **Why it requires team rather than individual performance to drive the customer care process forward.** Once a strategic account management team is developed, it enables the organization to focus on the achievement of its goals. The team must be responsible for the development of the action plan which must form an integral part of a long-range plan that will carry the organization forward into the future.

2. Change Readiness Assessment (Chapter 8)

You've learned that success will also depend on determining your organization's readiness for change. You know that you must identify potential constraints and develop proactive change management initiatives wherever necessary. In developing the change readiness assessment, you must consider senior management alignment and the organization's alignment to customer needs. You must consider these questions:

- The customer care vision (How far is the organization prepared to develop its customer care process—Stage II or Stage III?)
- Leadership (Will the organization willingly follow current leadership on the path to improved customer care?)
- Commitment (To be successful, senior management, middle management and the front line must be in alignment and committed—will they be?)
- Organization for change (Does the organization believe that they are organized for action and will be able to execute against a plan?)

3. Customer Segmentation (Chapter 9 and Chapter 3)

You've learned that segmentation will help you concentrate your marketing and sales effort on your crown jewel customers—those *for* whom and *from* whom you can add value and increase profitability. And you've learned that Stage III organizations use more than revenue to segment their customer base. Accordingly, you now know that you can segment customers using a combination of factors, including:

- The revenue trend within each customer account

- Your current share of the customer's business
- The customer's share of your business
- The significance of your company's product or service to the customer's total business
- Current gross profit achieved
- The customer's gross profit potential
- Your potential to cross-sell additional products and services
- The customer's willingness to partner

4. Customer Profiling (Chapter 9 and Chapter 2)

You've learned to assemble information that will help you set your strategy. Key components of your customer profiles should now include:

- Corporate history
- A general description of the customer's business
- Their major products and services
- The markets served by the customers
- The customer's spend or potential
- The size of the customer's wallet
- Competitive mapping (who holds the strongest competitive threat, by product and service segment)
- Relationship targeting (where your relationships exist within the customer's organization and how they must be improved)
- Constraints and impediments (what actions need to be taken to improve positioning within the customer organization)

5. VOC Research (Chapter 9 and Chapter 4)

You've learned that "voice of the customer" research is a key step along your path to Stage III customer care. You know that you must identify, from the customer's perspective, the areas where you can improve your customer service.

6. Gap Analysis (Chapter 9)

You've learned that you must identify where gaps exist—between the customer care perceptions of your internal and external customers, senior management, middle management and your front-line support. Disconnects can be deadly.

7. Strategic Account Team Mobilization (Chapter 8)

You've learned how to identify and select members for customer specific cross-functional teams that will manage the development and implementation of a customer care strategy. To be successful, there are many roles and responsibilities that must be assumed and many questions that must be addressed. What role must senior management play? Who is responsible for the customer? Who will lead the activity? Will there be an account/customer team and what role will each member of the team play? These are all important questions that must be addressed, and the sooner the better as they have a significant effect on alignment. The process can fail if it is not clear who is expected to make what contributions and who is responsible for which priorities. Here are seven key roles that must be played:

- The president/sponsor (possibly the CEO or owner)
- The steering committee
- The champion/coach
- The project leader
- The facilitators
- The strategic account management team
- The strategic account manager

8. Strategic Action Planning (Chapter 10)

You've learned how to plan and document specific action items that are important to the customer and to determine how you must address these issues with profitability enhancement in mind. Using information you've gathered from your change readiness assessments and from your customer profiles and VOC interviews, you can now follow the six steps of strategic action planning:

- Size the wallet
- Develop the competitive map
- Evaluate your current relationship zone and your target zone
- Develop alternative strategies
- Identify constraints
- Develop your implementation plan

9. Customer Alignment (Chapter 10)

You've learned that your plan will have limited effect if your customer is not involved in the process. Accordingly, you know you must seek customer input and buy-in for the strategic action plan.

10. Team Training (Chapter 8)

You've learned that you cannot assume the account team has the skills necessary to manage change and address a customer's issues. You know that you must formulate a commitment to team training that will equip your team with the skills they need to develop and implement your customer care initiatives.

11. Implementation Mobilization (Chapter10)

You've learned the importance of taking action and effectively implementing the strategies and tactics outlined in your strategic action plan.

12. Performance Monitoring and Adjustment (Chapter 10)

You've learned that you must conduct ongoing evaluation of your plan. You must set service standards for each customer, evaluate both qualitative and quantitative measures, and understand the roles played by the various key players involved in the team process.

Now for what could be the most important lesson of all: Which is the most important of the 12 steps outlined above? Some organizations may be tempted to think that the most important one is the segmentation exercise (Step3), because it serves as a wake-up call: "Are some of my customers really more important than others? Am I really willing to give differentiated service to the customers that are more valuable?"

Other organizations may think the most important step is presenting your strategic action plan to your customer. Or perhaps it's the establishment of a strategic account team or the appointment of a strategic account manager. After all, how can you implement the plan if you haven't got a team?

But I can't help remembering a conversation I had with the CEO of an organization that had achieved year-over-year improvements in customer service ratings, financial performance and new product innovation. His words had a profound effect on me and on my assessment of the most important part of the process of strategic customer care. When I asked him the secret of his success, he pointed out that most of his "rules of customer care" could be found in a number of published books, books that explained methodologies and procedures that were available to his competitors as well. So, how did he explain his own success given the poor performance of his competitors?

His answer consisted of one word: Alignment.

The only difference between his company and his competitors were his people—people who were aligned, motivated, trained and rewarded, all with a clear focus on what was important to the customer.

You have the skills. You have the route map. You have the secret to success. Get on with it. And good luck

Syndicated Research on Customer Care

THE EVOLUTION OF IDEAS

IDEAS 97

The Evolution of Customer Care is the most recent in a series of seven syndicated annual studies undertaken by Stanley Brown, Leader of PricewaterhouseCoopers' Centre of Excellence in Customer Care. Since its inception in 1990, these studies have been designed to address topical areas and leading trends in customer care. IDEAS 97 uncovered the three stages in the evolution of customer care described in this book.

Previous studies include:

IDEAS 91

The Status of Innovation and Service Excellence in Canada identifies a direct link between innovation and service excellence. It also highlights the importance of establishing an internal service culture—best typified by the golden rule "Do unto your internal customers as you would have them do unto your external customers."

IDEAS 92

A North American Perspective on Quality Service Practices was designed to identify customer service needs and the current service practices of organizations in a broad range of industry segments.

IDEAS 93

Developed during the zenith of the quality service movement, *A New Quality Paradigm* concludes that the organizations most likely to maintain successful quality initiatives are those that set meaningful and measurable goals and embrace the human side of quality as a vital component of the overall initiative.

IDEAS 94

Excellence Through Improved Customer Practices highlights the four common practices of successful customer service organizations: aligning senior management in the commitment to excellence, listening to the voice of the customer, focusing on customer-related processes, and supporting a culture of continuous improvement. This study formed the basis of a book published by John Wiley & Sons in 1995, *What Customers Value Most*.

IDEAS 95

The Role of Technology in Enhancing Customer Satisfaction was designed to assess how organizations use technology to meet the needs of their customers. The findings conclude that technology alone is not the key to success but rather an enabler of it.

IDEAS 96

Designed to discover the best customer service practices of North American companies, *Breakthrough Customer Service* identifies three key trends: consolidating and in some cases outsourcing certain operations; integrating customer care functions to minimize points of customer contact and maximize resources; and managing the workforce by equipping customer service representatives with superior customer service and technology skills. This study formed the basis of another book published by John Wiley & Sons in 1997, *Breakthrough Customer Service*.

The Project Charter

THE PROJECT CHARTER CONTENTS

Objectives

A definition of the objectives of the customer care initiative identified in a way that permits subsequent assessment of the success of the project.

Scope of Work

A definition of the work to be undertaken. This definition should be sufficiently detailed to clearly identify the boundaries of the work and where these meet the outside world. The scope of work statement is used as the basis for all subsequent planning activities.

Organization

A description of the organization of the project, normally given in chart form that indicates not only the links within the organization of the project, but also the links between this organization and operating units and support units such as the information department.

Roles and Responsibilities

A definition of the roles and responsibilities of each member of the project or strategic account management team.

Definition of Authority Levels

A definition of the authority delegated to the project manager and a similar definition of authority delegated to specified members of the project team, such as the strategic account manager or the strategic account management team. These delegations of authority statements effectively give decision-making power to the individuals concerned, and relate to commitments of costs, control of resources and definition of objectives.

Major Milestone Listing

A list of the key events or milestones. These relate to specific decision points within the project—for example, when internal communication must take place and at what point the customer must be involved in the process.

Risk and Assumptions Statement

An outline analysis of the known risks and a summary of the assumptions made during the generation of the plan. Where risk has been identified, the fall-back plans or an appropriate level of contingency should be present.

Work Breakdown Structures (WBS)

The work breakdown structure is a logical division of the scope of the project work into manageable portions. Depending on the size of the project this breakdown may be hierarchical, and it may be made up of a number of different levels. The WBS is normally depicted in a graphical format, with each item within the structure being allocated a unique reference number or code.

Activity Summaries

A definition of the critical data relating to the elements of the WBS. The data to be defined include:

- *Scope of the individual work element*

- *Inputs required to enable the work to be performed*

- *The outputs required*

- *A definition of assumptions and known risks*

- *The effort required to complete the work*

- *The resources required to perform the work*

The activity summaries may be supported by detailed estimating sheets justifying the time, cost and resource information given in the summary.

Cost Budget

A summary of the budgeted costs for each element of the customer care initiative as defined within the WBS and for the project as a whole. The budget should be supported by a cost schedule indicating the relationship between cost commitment or expenditure and time.

Schedule

A full definition of the duration and start and finish dates for each element in the WBS, normally given in a bar chart (Gantt diagram) format. The schedule should be supported by a project calendar showing the dates of all milestone events.

Sample Readiness Assessment

YOUR RESPONSE TO THE QUESTION					
Strongly Disagree	Disagree	Neither Agree nor Disagree	Agree	Strongly Agree	Unable to comment
1	2	3	4	5	6

The Change Vision

There is a clear and compelling need
for this change

1	2	3	4	5	6

It is clear what this change will mean

1	2	3	4	5	6

I have a clear and realistic view of how
much change will be required to move this
organization into the future

1	2	3	4	5	6

I am not well enough informed about
the direction of the organization

1	2	3	4	5	6

I believe that the Customer Care project
is taking the organization in the right direction

1	2	3	4	5	6

Change Leadership

Leaders communicate a common
understanding of this change
Leaders are creating a sense of urgency
to change in the operation
The senior managers in my operation
cannot implement changes successfully
My manager fully explains <u>why</u> changes
are being made

1	2	3	4	5	6
1	2	3	4	5	6
1	2	3	4	5	6
1	2	3	4	5	6

Commitment

People expect this change to succeed

Changes over the last year have taken
us in the right direction

I am clear about what I am accountable for

I have enough information about what
is going on in my operation

I am burnt out on "change"

1	2	3	4	5	6
1	2	3	4	5	6
1	2	3	4	5	6
1	2	3	4	5	6
1	2	3	4	5	6

Change Management

There is sufficient cross-functional
cooperation for this project to succeed
The range of current and planned initiatives appears to
lack cohesion

1	2	3	4	5	6
1	2	3	4	5	6

Organization for Change

Our culture is compatible with our future growth objectives	1	2	3	4	5	6
This operation spends too much time analyzing an issue or decision before we take action	1	2	3	4	5	6

If you believe that there are other issues that this questionnaire has not addressed, or if you have any further comments, please use the space below or a separate sheet if necessary.

The Customer Profile

THE CUSTOMER PROFILE

Customer Name

Strategic Account Manager:
Strategic Account Management (SAM) Team:

1)

2)

3)

4)

5)

6)

Current Customer Tier (See Chapter 3)

❏   Tier I

❏   Tier II

❏   Tier III

❏   Tier IV

❏   Tier V

Information Sources Used to Derive Profile	Sources
Internal Personnel	
Internal Documents	
Annual Report	
Other Customer Documents	
Customer Web Site	
The Internet	
Public Databases	
Trade Journals	
Competitors	
Analysts	
Research Groups	
Other Sources (List)	

I) Customer Review

Corporate Name:

Address:

Telephone: Fax: Web Site:

Type of Organization:

Multinational❑   National❑   Public❑   Private❑

Annual Revenue(US$):

Total # of Employees:

Major Divisions:

Operating Units:

Parent Company:

Corporate Mission Statement:

Board of Directors:

Name	Title	Company
1)		
2)		
3)		
4)		

II) *Introduction:*

General Description of the Customer's Business:

Major Products and Services:

Markets Served by Customer:

Major Customers of Customer:

Major Competitors of Customer:

III) *Financial Profile*

(Insert Financial statement, if available)

IV) Background Information

Brief History: (Innovations, Milestones, Myths, Legends, Mottos, Themes)

Critical Success Factors for Customer Industry/Market Sector:

Critical Success Factors for Customer Organization:

Organization Chart:

(Attach up-to-date organizational chart)

V) Customer Relationship

Divisions and business units maintaining relationships with the customer:

Key Contacts and primary needs:

<u>Contact Name</u>   <u>Primary Needs</u>

1)

2)

3)

4)

Strategic Importance of the Customer:

(Attach segmentation profile...reference Chapter 9)

Key sales and marketing activities to date (Buying History)

(Attach buying history for the last 2-3 years)

Known issues between the customer and your organization (e.g. unresolved complaints, upcoming concerns, major barriers to winning increased business):

(Attach previous documentation, results from past surveys, etc.)

(Attach customer VOC survey)

Future plans and growth expectations:

VI) Competitor—Customer Relationship

Competitors serving customer:

Supplier best practices:

(Attach best supplier slides from VOC—Chapter 9)

VII) Action Plans

Strategic action plans as agreed with customer:

(Attach strategic action plan—Chapter 10)

Implementation Plan

(Attach implementation plan showing timelines and resources)

Recommended Reading List

The following is a short listing of books related to key topics discussed in this book.

PROJECT MANAGEMENT

The AAA Handbook of Project Management, Paul C. Dinsmore (Editor); Amacom, 1993.

Breakthrough Technology Project Management, Bennet P. Lientz, Kathryn P. Rea; Academic Press, 1998.

Creating an Environment for Successful Projects: The Quest to Manage Project Management (Jossey-Bass Business & Management Series), Robert J. Graham, Randall L. Englund (Contributor); Jossey-Bass Publishers, 1997.

Customer-Driven Project Management: A New Paradigm in Total Quality Implementation, Bruce T. Barkley, James H. Saylor; McGraw Hill, 1994.

Dynamic Project Management: A Practical Guide for Managers and Engineers, Deborah S. Kezsbom, Donald L. Schilling (Contributor) and Katherine A. Edward (Contributor); John Wiley & Sons, 1989.

Effective Project Management: How to Plan, Manage, and Deliver Projects on Time and within Budget, Robert K. Wysocki, Robert Beck and David B. Crane (Contributor); John Wiley & Sons, 1995.

Field Guide to Project Management, David I. Cleland (Editor); John Wiley & Sons, 1997.

Goal Directed Project Management, Erling Anderson, Kristoffer Grude and Tor Haug; Kogan Page, 1998.

Information Systems Project Management: How to Deliver Function and Value in Information Technology Projects, Jolyon E. Hallows; Amacom, 1997.

The New Project Management: Tools for an Age of Rapid Change, Corporate Reengineering, and Other Business Realities (The Jossey-Bass Management), J. Davidson Frame; Jossey-Bass Publishers, 1994.

CUSTOMER LOYALTY

Beyond Customer Satisfaction to Customer Loyalty: The Key to Greater Profitability (Ama Management Briefing), Keki R. Bhote; Amacom, 1996.

Creating Customer Loyalty (Management Action Guides); Nichols Publishing Company, 1993.

Customer Loyalty: How to Earn It, How to Keep It, Jill Griffin; Lexington Books, 1996.

The Customer Loyalty Pyramid, Michael W. Lowenstein; Greenwood Publishing Group, 1997.

Customer Satisfaction Is Worthless, Customer Loyalty Is Priceless: How to Make Customers Love You, Keep Them Coming Back and Tell Everyone They Know, Jeffrey H. Gitomer; Bard Press, 1998.

The Loyalty Link: How Loyal Employees Create Loyal Customers, Dennis G. McCarthy; John Wiley & Sons, 1997.

The Quest for Loyalty: Creating Value through Partnerships (Harvard Business Review Book Series), Frederick F. Reichheld (Editor), Scott D. Cook; Harvard Business School Press, 1996.

Sales, Marketing, and Continuous Improvement: Six Best Practices to Achieve Revenue Growth and Increase Customer Loyalty, Daniel M. Stowell; Jossey-Bass Publishers, 1997.

The Service Profit Chain: How Leading Companies Link Profit and Growth to Loyalty, Satisfaction, and Value, James L. Heskett, W. Earl Sasser, Leonard A. Schlesinger, James L. Herskett and Earl W. Sasser; Free Press, 1997.

What Customers Value Most: How to Achieve Business Transformation by Focusing on Processes that Touch Your Customers, Stanley Brown; John Wiley & Sons Canada Ltd, 1999.

The Wizardry of Customer Value: An Action Guide to Measuring & Managing Loyalty, R. Eric Reidenbach, Gordon W. McClung; Rhumb Line, Inc., 1998.

KNOWLEDGE MANAGEMENT

Empires of the Mind: Lessons to Lead and Succeed in a Knowledge-Based World, Denis E. Waitley; Quill, 1996.

Harvard Business Review on Knowledge Management (Harvard Business Review Series), Harvard Business School; Harvard Business School Press, 1998.

If Only We Knew What We Know: The Transfer of Internal Knowledge and Best Practice, Carla O'Dell, Nilly Essaides, Nilly Ostro (Contributor) and C. Jackson, Jr. Grayson; Free Press, 1998.

The Infinite Resource: Creating and Leading the Knowledge Enterprise (Jossey-Bass Business and Management Series), William E. Halal (Editor), Raymond W. Smith (Editor); Jossey-Bass Publishers, 1998.

Information Ecology: Mastering the Information and Knowledge Environment, Thomas H. Davenport, Laurence Prusak (Contributor); Oxford University Press (Trade), 1997.

The Knowledge Game: The Revolution in Learning and Communication in the Workplace, Gordon Wills; Cassell Academic, 1998.

Knowledge Management and Organizational Design (Resources for the Knowledge-Based Economy), Paul S. Myers (Editor); Butterworth-Heinemann (Trade), 1996.

Knowledge Management Tools (Resources for the Knowledge-Based Economy), Rudy L. Ruggles (Editor); Butterworth-Heinemann (Trade), 1996.

Knowledge Organizations: What Every Manager Should Know, Jay Liebowitz, Thomas J. Beckman and Tom Beckman; Saint Lucie Press, 1998.

Knowledge-Driven Work: Unexpected Lessons from Japanese and United States Work Practices, Joel Cutcher-Gershenfeld (Editor),

Michio Nitta, Betty Barrett and Iwao Ishino; Oxford University Press, 1998.

The Knowledge-Enabled Organization: Moving from 'Training' to 'Learning' to Meet Business Goals, Daniel R. Tobin; Amacom, 1997.

Value-Based Knowledge Management: Creating the 21st Century Company, Rene Tissen, Frank Lekanne Deprez, Daniel Andriessen, Daniel Andriessen and Frank Lekanne Deprez; Addison-Wesley Pub. Co., 1998.

Working Knowledge: How Organizations Manage What They Know, Thomas H. Davenport, Laurence Prusak; Harvard Business School Press, 1997.

CALL/CONTACT CENTERS

Automating Your Support Center—A Practical Guide to Assessing Service Automation Tools, Monica David; Knowledge Networks, 1997.

Breakthrough Customer Service: Best Practices of Leaders in Customer Support, Stanley A. Brown; John Wiley & Sons, 1997.

The Call Center Handbook: The Complete Guide to Starting, Running and Improving Your Call Center, Keith Dawson; Miller Freeman Books, 1997.

Call Center Management on Fast Forward: Succeeding in Today's Dynamic Inbound Environment, Brad Cleveland, Julia Mayben; Call Center Press, 1998.

Customers: Arriving with a History and Leaving with an Experience: How to Build Your Sales, Service or Help Desk Call Center to Please Customers, Andrew Waite; Miller Freeman Books, 1996.

Online Customer Care: Applying Today's Technology to Achieve World-Class Customer Interaction, Michael Cusack; American Society for Quality, 1998.

PERFORMANCE MEASUREMENT

Baldrige Award Winning Quality: How to Interpret the Baldrige Criteria for Performance Excellence (7th Ed), Mark Graham Brown; Quality Resources, 1997.

Benchmarking: A Tool for Continuous Improvement (The Coopers &

Lybrand Performance Solutions), Kathleen H.J. Leibfried and Carol J. McNair; John Wiley & Sons, 1995.

Harvard Business Review on Measuring Corporate Performance (Harvard Business Review Series), Harvard Business School; Harvard Business School Press, 1998.

Keeping Score: Using the Right Metrics to Drive World-Class Performance, Mark Graham Brown; Quality Resources, 1996.

The Manager's Pocket Guide to Performance Management, Sharon G. Fisher; Human Resource Development Press, 1997.

Managing Bank Capital: Capital Allocation and Performance Measurement, Chris Matten; John Wiley & Sons, 1996.

Measuring Performance, Bob Frost; Measurement International, 1998.

Operational Performance Measurement: Increasing Total Productivity, W. J. Kaydos; Saint Lucie Press, 1998.

Performance Measurement for World Class Manufacturing: A Model for American Companies, Brian H. Maskell; Productivity Press Inc, 1994.

CHANGE MANAGEMENT

The Challenge of Organizational Change: How Companies Experience It and Leaders Guide It, Rosabeth Moss Kanter, Barry A. Stein and Todd D. Jick; Free Press, 1992.

The Change Management Handbook: A Road Map to Corporate Transformation, Lance A. Berger, Martin J. Sikora (Contributor) and Dorothy R. Berger (Contributor); Irwin Professional Pub., 1993.

Diagnosing and Changing Organizational Culture: Based on the Competing Values Framework (Addison-Wesley Series on Organization Development), Kim S. Cameron, Robert E. Quinn; Addison-Wesley Pub. Co., 1998.

Effective Enterprise and Change Management (Effective Management), Alan H. Anderson, Dennis Barker (Contributor); Blackwell Pub., 1996.

Harvard Business Review on Change (Harvard Business Review Series), Harvard Business School; Harvard Business School Press, 1998.

High Performance Leadership: Creating Value in a World of Change (Management Master Series. Set 4, Leadership), Leonard R. Sayles; Productivity Press, 1996.

Mastering Change Management: A Practical Guide for Turning Obstacles into Opportunities (Management Skills Series), Richard Y. Chang; Chang Assoc., 1994.

SALES FORCE EFFECTIVENESS

Building the High-Performance Sales Force, Joseph A. Petrone, Amacom, 1994.

Contemporary Sales Force Management, Tony Carter; Haworth Press, 1998.

Customer Centered Selling: Eight Steps to Success from the World's Best Sales Force, Robert L. Jolles, Rob Jolles; Simon & Schuster, 1998.

High-Impact Sales Force Automation: A Strategic Perspective, Glen S. Petersen; Saint Lucie Press, 1997.

Management of Sales Force, William J. Stanton, Rosann Spiro and Richard Buskirk; McGraw Hill, 1998.

Sales Force Automation Using Web Technologies, Navtej Khandpur, Jasmine Wevers and Kay Khanpur; John Wiley & Sons, 1997.

Sales Force Automation: Using the Latest Technology to Make Your Sales Force More Competitive, George W. Colombo, John Williams; McGraw-Hill, 1993.

Sales Force Management (Irwin Series in Marketing), Gilbert A., Jr Churchill, Neil M. Ford amd Orville C. Walker; Richard D. Irwin, 1997.

STRATEGIC ACCOUNT MANAGEMENT

Key Account Selling, Mack Hanan, Amacom, 1993.

Key Accounts Are Different: Sales Solutions for Key Account Managers, Ken Langdon; Pitman Pub. Ltd., 1996.

Manage Globally, Sell Locally: The Art of Strategic Account Management, A. Lee Blackstone; Irwin Professional Pub., 1994.

The New Strategic Selling: The Unique Sales System Proven Successful by the World's Best Companies, Stephen E. Heiman, Diane

Sanchez (Contributor), Tad Tuleja and Robert B. St. Miller; Warner Books, 1998.

Successful Large Account Management, Tad Tuleja, Robert Bruce Miller and Stephen E. Heiman (Contributor); Warner Books, 1992.

RELATIONSHIP MANAGEMENT

Customer Relationship Management: Making Hard Decisions with Soft Numbers, Jon Anton; Prentice Hall 1996.

Enterprise One to One: Tools for Competing in the Interactive Age, Don Peppers, Martha Rogers; Currency/Doubleday, 1997.

Managing Salespeople: A Relationship Approach, Wesley J. Johnston, Robert E. Hite; West/Wadsworth, 1997.

Marketing Channels: A Relationship Management Approach (The Irwin Series in Marketing), Lou E. Pelton, David Strutton and James R. Lumpkin; Richard D. Irwin, 1996.

Supercommunity Banking Strategies: Winning the War for the Customer Relationship, Anat Bird; Irwin Professional Pub., 1996.

Index